CANUCK CHICKS
CHICKS
and
MAPLE LEAF
MAMAS

McArthur & Company

CANUCK CHICKS

and

MAPLE LEAF MAMAS

Women of the Great White North

A Celebration of Canadian Women

ANN DOUGLAS

McArthur & Company

Toronto

First published in Canada in 2002 by
McArthur & Company
322 King Street West, Suite 402
Toronto, Ontario M5V 1J2

National Library of Canada Cataloguing in Publication

Douglas, Ann, 1963-
Canuck chicks and maple leaf mamas / Ann Douglas.

ISBN 1-55278-312-X

1. Women—Canada—History—Miscellanea. 2. Women—Canada—Miscellanea.
3. Popular culture—Canada—History. 4. Canada—History—Miscellanea. I. Title.

FC95.4.D678 2002   305.4'0971'09   C2002-903440-X
F1021.2.D678 2002

Design & Composition: *Mad Dog Design*
Cover: *Mad Dog Design*
Printed in Canada by *Webcom*

The publisher would like to acknowledge the financial support of the Government of Canada through the Book Publishing Industry Development Program (BPIDP) and the Canada Council for our publishing activities. The publisher further wishes to acknowledge the financial support of the Ontario Arts Council for our publishing program.

10 9 8 7 6 5 4 3 2 1

Contents

To Janet, Lorna, and Sandra, Sisters Extraordinaire:
Thank you for electing me Good Girl Club President for Life
and for understanding my need to hog both the Barbie camper
and Mom and Dad's attention.

Billions and billions of years ago, when I started researching this book, I had every intention of publicly acknowledging the help of each and every person who assisted me in my research. Many thousands of phone calls, faxes, and e-mails have since convinced me that I'd need a staff of 12 to pull that off. So rather than setting myself up for disaster by trying to thank everyone individually and accidentally leaving someone out, I've decided to offer a blanket thank you to everyone who helped me out with this book. Consider yourself duly hugged.

I would, however, end up getting kicked out of the Good Girl Club for good if I failed to acknowledge the contributions of the quartet of Canuck Chicks who made this book possible: my publisher Kim McArthur (one of the most enthusiastic and inspiring people on the planet as well as a Canuck Chick extraordinaire); my editor Pamela Erlichman (a damned good editor and truly saintly soul who never let on how crazy I was making her when I kept missing deadline . . . after deadline . . . after deadline); Linda Pellowe of Mad Dog Design who came up with the sizzling layout; and my research assistant Diane Wolf (a one-woman dynamo who moved heaven and earth and rattled people's chains from here to eternity to help me obtain all the necessary photo permissions). Ladies, I salute you.

Last but not least, I'd like to thank my ever-supportive husband Neil and our four totally fabulous, 100-percent Canadian kids: Julie, Scott, Erik, and Ian. Thanks for picking up the slack around the house so that I could devote so much time and energy to writing this book. I owe you guys a party pack of Timbits.

Canuck Chick Nation

We Canuck Chicks have been making our mark on the world since long before John A. Macdonald and the boys sat down to draw up the blueprints for Confederation. Not only had Frances Brooke long since penned North America's first romance novel by that time (a rather steamy story set in the frozen wilds of Quebec, incidentally): heroine and all-round gutsy broad Laura Secord had already done her bit to warn the British troops at Beaver Dams about an impending attack. (Of course, she didn't actually get any credit for that rather noteworthy achievement for the next 40 years, thanks to a Johnny-come-lately on the scene who managed to convince the military bigwigs that *he'd* been the one to save the day. Some things never change, now do they?)

That's not to say that we Canuck Chicks have exclusively specialized in virtue, of course. In fact, some Canuck Chicks, like Toronto dominatrix Terri-Jean Bedford, have made entire careers out of being bad. Likewise some of the "gifts" we've chosen to share with the world have come dangerously close to being stamped "return to sender." (For some reason, Marlen Cowpland's *Celebrity Pets* show comes to mind.) We Canuck Chicks are a decidedly motley crew of saints and sinners, good girls and bad girls, winners and losers, after all. That's what makes researching a book of this sort so much fun . . .

The Ultimate Girly Romp

Wondering what I've got in store for you? Allow me to give you a sneak peek. In addition to introducing you to some of the more noteworthy women to inhabit our part of the planet over the past 150 years or so, I'm ready to spill the beans about the sometimes hilarious lengths the menfolk went to in their efforts to keep us in our place. (They weren't too keen on letting the pre-feminist genie out of the bottle!) Of course, over time, they finally clued into the fact that their efforts to convince us to swear off smoking, drinking, and premarital sex, to abandon the fight for the right to vote, and to steer clear of the workforce had a tendency to, well, *backfire*. The more emphatically they told us *not* to do something, the greater the likelihood we would rush right out and do it. It was kind of like waving a red flag in front of a bull . . .

So if you're looking for a book that steers clear of the testosterone-soaked swampland that most Canadian history books tend to get mired in, you've found it. *Canuck Chicks and Maple Leaf Mamas* is the ultimate girly romp: a book that takes you on a wild and wonderful ride while giving you the plain unvarnished truth about what it's really like growing up female in the Great White North. You'll find out what women were wearing underneath their fancy dresses in Victorian Canada, what steamy fantasies women novelists chose to explore between the covers in generations past, and what everyday Canuck Chicks like you and me were douching with on the eve of the sexual revolution. (Think Lysol.)

Who's In, Who's Out

As you can imagine, the most challenging aspect of writing this book was deciding who and what to include and who and what to leave out. After all, had I chosen to mention every single milestone moment in the lives of Canadian women, I would have ended up with a set of encyclopedias rather than a book. As it was, my publisher ended up with a manuscript that was 50 percent bigger than the book I had been contracted to write: it's a testament to her commitment to Canadian pop culture that she decided to run with the book "as is" rather than forcing me to bid farewell to a lot of terrific material on the cutting room floor. The result is the book you're holding in your hands—an estrogen-powered hot pink Harley that will take you on a one-of-a-kind journey down the backroads of Canadian history and pop culture. Hope you enjoy the ride . . .

CHAPTER I

Spin Cycle: 100 Years of Advice to Canadian Women

Whether they were urging us to reinvent ourselves as domestic divas, happy hostesses, or suburban seductresses, the magazine editors, advice book authors, and ad agency spin doctors of years gone by certainly knew how to set the bar high for past generations of Canuck Chicks. It was pretty tough, after all, to be good in the kitchen, good at a party, and good in bed all at the same time!

Home Economics class. Archives of Ontario DIN 10005045

From "Good Girl" to "Good Wife"

Most of us grew up knowing that there were two types of girls in the world: "good girls" and "bad girls." Good girls didn't drink, smoke, swear, or run around with boys. Hell, no. They let the bad girls have all the fun.

Of course, being a "good girl" was a cakewalk compared to being a "good wife." Suddenly it wasn't enough to be youthful and beautiful. You had to know how to make a damned good meatloaf, too.

Think I'm exaggerating? Slip off those white leather gloves, reach for your fountain pen, and get ready to take the entrance exam for The Good Wife Club, circa 1900–1950. This is your chance to try to measure up to the standards set out in magazine and newspaper articles and etiquette books of days gone by. In true women's magazine tradition, you can give yourself 10 marks for each "yes" answer and 0 marks for each "no" answer. (In case you haven't noticed by now, this "good wife/bad wife" thing is an all-or-nothing proposition! Just as you can't be a little bit pregnant, you can't be a little bit good.)

Anyway, here goes . . .

Danielle Proham/June Cleaver Role
(Canadian Press: *Victoria Times Colonist*/Debra Brash)

The Good Wife Club Entrance Exam

1. Do you understand the importance of spoiling your husband?

Why, yes, of course _____ (10 marks)
Surely, you're joking _____ (0 marks)

Just in case you aren't acquainted with the benefits of waiting on your husband hand and foot, I'm going to ask "E.G." to give you a crash course in the womanly art of pampering your man. She wrote a passionate essay entitled "Why I Spoil My Husband" for the May 1931 issue of *Chatelaine*. (For some mysterious reason, the dear girl refused to allow the magazine to run the article under her full name. Perhaps she was worried about being mercilessly pursued by mobs of Canadian husbands hungry for a bit of pampering. Either that, or she was terrified of being lynched by their wives!)

You see, E.G. painted a truly heartbreaking portrait of the noble sacrifices that a man makes the moment he says, "I do." (Frankly, I get a little choked up just thinking about all the suffering men have endured for the sake of the women they love.) "When a man marries he sacrifices many things dear to the masculine heart. No longer can he play poker all night, have a fleeting but pleasant affair with a blonde waitress, or take that snappy little chorus girl out to supper." (Hey, I warned you that this was pretty heart-wrenching stuff.)

E.G. then proceeds to warn Canuck Chicks who dare to be complacent that they owe their men something in exchange for the extended free ride they are enjoying: "Some women feel that by merely saying 'I will' they have earned free board and lodging for the rest of their natural lives," she scolded. "They fasten like barnacles on a wage-earning man and take everything he has without giving anything in exchange." Her solution? "If you want to be happy . . . spoil your husband."

"It is always a man's holiday. Week days and Sundays, New Year days and Firsts of July, a woman always has the meals to get, the children to look after, the dishes to wash, the house to tidy, even if she does no extra jobs such as baking, sweeping, dusting, washing, mopping— all the thousand and one things that make up the drudgery of housework. And few men realize that their wives never get a holiday unless they go away, utterly away, from the sight of their homes."
– Philosophic Wife, "Why I Do Not Spoil My Husband," *The Chatelaine*, October 1931

2. Do you accept the fact that being married is a painful and unnatural state for a man?

Why, yes, of course _____ (10 marks)
Huh? _____ (0 marks)

Marriage isn't merely a sacrifice for men: it's a painful and unnatural state. So wrote Sidney Katz in an article entitled "Marriage Is Easy Street for Women" that appeared in the October 17, 1964, issue of *Maclean's:* "If there's anyone downtrodden in modern marriage, it's the husband. . . . Because man is a male mammal, monogamous marriage for him is a bizarre and unnatural state." Katz then went on to quote a marriage expert, American psychiatrist Russel Lee, who had this to say about men and marriage: "Other male animals . . . collect, dominate, protect and impregnate as many females as they possibly can. . . . Blocking this powerful natural instinct is a traumatizing experience and entails a certain agony." It's hard to understand how past generations of Canuck Chicks managed to live with themselves, knowing the agony they were causing members of the opposite sex . . .

3. Have you come to realize that keeping your marriage on solid ground is your problem, not his?

Absolutely _____ (10 marks)
Not on your life _____ (0 marks)

Only very foolish wives—ones who aren't generally smart enough to qualify for membership in The Good Wife Club—go into marriage expecting their men to put equal effort into the relationship. As Benjamin Grant Jefferis and James Lawrence Nichols noted in their highly popular 1894 sex manual, *Search Lights on Health, Light on Dark Corners: A Complete Sexual Science and a Guide to Purity and Physical Manhood, Advice to Maiden, Wife, and Mother, Love, Courtship, and Romance,* it's the wife's duty to keep the flames of passion burning: "The more he neglects the fire on the hearth, the more carefully must you feed and guard it," they warned. "It must not be allowed to go out. Once out you must sit ever in darkness and in the cold." And, given our climate, what Canuck Chick in her right mind would want to risk freezing in the dark?

4. Do you make an effort to look your best when your husband arrives home after a hard day at the office?

I didn't realize this was optional   _____ (10 marks)
Hell, no, he gets home before I do _____ (0 marks)

Lest you be tempted to cut corners by failing to touch up your lipstick and slip into a fresh dress shortly before that big hunk of man saunters through the front door, allow me to remind you that you could be playing Russian roulette with your marriage. After all, as Anne B. Fisher, MD, reminded *Chatelaine* readers in an article in the December 1937 issue, a wife has a certain duty to look her best for her husband: "If you look pretty and fresh, he'll soon let you know how much he loves you. . . . A fresh make-up and a comb through your wave—or just a clean apron over your regular dress will help, if you haven't time to slip into something different from what you had on in the morning." And if he's consistently beating you home because you're selfishly indulging yourself in a career, well, girlfriend, don't you think you should be counting your lucky stars that you still have a husband to come home to?

5. Do you understand that it is your wifely duty to make your home a happy place?

Yes, and I'm happy to do so _____ (10 marks)
Not exactly   _____ (0 marks)

The 1896 edition of *The Ladies Book of Useful Information* reminded Canadian women of the importance of keeping the "happy" in "happy housewife": "Many years of observation has convinced me that where a pure, industrious, and cheerful wife meets her husband with a bright smile on the threshold of her dwelling, that man will never leave the home for any other place," wrote the unnamed author. (Never mind the fact that you spent the entire day scrubbing your husband's underwear on a steel washboard in subzero temperatures. Put on a happy face!)

6. Do you agree that a man's house is his castle?

But of course _____ (10 marks)
Only if he treats me like a queen _____ (0 marks)

Depression-era housewives were warned about the dangers of inadvertently spoiling their husband's chances of climbing the corporate ladder by failing to provide him with a suitable refuge at the end of the day. "A man's home must be a refuge from everything else," noted C.L. Burton, the president of the Robert Simpson Company of Toronto, in the July 1937 issue of *Chatelaine*. "If it isn't, that wife is falling down on her job."

7. Is your emotional immaturity short-circuiting your husband's career?

Yes _____ (10 marks)
No _____ (0 marks)

In the June 3, 1961, issue of the *Financial Post,* a University of Alberta psychiatry professor warned up-and-coming executives of the threat that an emotionally needy wife posed to her husband's career. "The over-dependent woman who married because among other things, she had a strong need for her husband's continual reassurance and support will develop tensions and either irritate him or make him feel guilty," cautioned William Forster, MD. His conclusion? "The woman who has sufficient maturity to be able to lend some of her strength to her husband will do well."

8. Do you make an effort to keep up with current events so that you can be a wise and witty dinner companion for your husband?

Yes _____ (10 marks)
Actually, I insist that he entertain me _____ (0 marks)

You can hardly expect to qualify for good wife status if you think your mealtime responsibilities end with the simple act of putting a three- or four-course dinner on the table. After all, it's important to be a good conversationalist, too. "Educate yourself, as a wife, to keep up with the times sufficiently to be at least a companionable conversationalist," advised Maude C. Cooke, author of the 1896 book *Social Etiquette, or, Manners and Customs of Polite Society: Containing Rules of Etiquette for All Occasions.* "Endeavor to be as entertaining to your husband as you were to your husband-elect."

9. Are you aware of the connection between internal and external beauty?

Regrettably, yes _____ (10 marks)
Happily, no _____ (0 marks)

Beauty columnist Annabelle Lee had an important message to convey to fortysomething readers in the February 1931 issue of *The Chatelaine:* negative thoughts can make a wife ugly. "A peevish, whining, disagreeable disposition will very certainly be reflected in the expression of the face and will spoil the appearance of the most beautiful features," she warned. "A cheerful, happy disposition, and kind, loving thoughts are wonderful beautifiers.... If we remember that every time we permit an unpleasant thought to register upon our faces, we are actually helping to impress a permanent expression upon it, we will be more careful, not only with our faces, but with our thoughts."

10. If you are not yet married, are you taking steps to safeguard your virtue?

Yes, I've been retrofitted with a chastity belt _____ (10 marks)
Virtue? What virtue? _____ (0 marks)

The Ladies Book of Useful Information (1896) warned single girls of the importance of safeguarding their most valuable possession—their virtue. "No woman is fit to become a wife who is not perfectly modest in word, deed, and thought. No young man, who is worth having, would ever entertain the thought for a moment of taking the girl for a wife who is habitually careless in her conversation and displays a levity in her manners. Young men may like your free and hearty girls to laugh and talk with, but as to taking one for a wife, let me assure you they would not tolerate the idea for a moment." (Apparently, the whole concept of the "born-again virgin" had yet to come into vogue.)

How did you measure up?

100 points	You're the light of his life.
80 to 100 points	Your light is fading fast.
Less than 80 points	You're truly in the dark when it comes to marriage.

The Rules—Part I

Past generations of Canuck Chicks didn't have to spend a lot of time wondering what was involved in being "a good girl." Society was pretty clear about letting women know what was expected of them. Here are just a few of the success tips for young women that were spelled out in a 1914 textbook entitled *Manners* that was in widespread use in Ontario schools:

Remember that you don't stop being a lady just because you're riding a bicycle: "It goes without saying that [a lady] will not ride fast enough to attract undue attention; that she will not chew gum; and that she will not allow advances from strangers. . . . Neither will she ride off alone after dark, nor take long rides in the evening attended only by an escort. In the daytime, when out with a gentleman, she will avoid stopping to rest under the trees and in out of the way places."

Don't risk your reputation by entertaining potential suitors in public: "A young woman condemns herself in the eyes of good society who is observed to enter along with a young man a place of public refreshment, be the restaurant or tea room ever so select."

Try to see the best in your husband, even if that requires a great deal of effort on your part: "If a girl discovers very soon after her marriage that she has made a mistake, it is wisest for her to make the best of it; she should look for all that is good in her husband and try to forget that which she dislikes."

The Rules—Part II

The more things change, the more they stay the same. Even in the midst of the sexual revolution, Canuck Chicks were still being told in no uncertain terms what they could and couldn't do! Consider the rules for living as set out in the 1965 edition of Claire Wallace's best-selling *Canadian Etiquette Dictionary*. Here's what was expected in the sixties:

Don't insult your hostess by reaching for the salt and pepper shakers: "Guests should not season food before tasting it, implying that it is not correctly seasoned."

Remember not to take liberties with your friend's toiletries: "In the powder room at a friend's home, personal lotions, creams, and perfume in the medicine cabinet should not be used or sampled. The guests should use only those items placed out for general use."

Don't feel obliged to settle your "account" at the end of each date: "[A woman] does not need to feel that she must pay for her date at the end of the evening by kissing or necking. A date is not a sale but an evening of companionship."

Be sensitive to the feelings of "the help" when you're entertaining: "Do not discuss the household help with anyone while the help is within hearing distance."

Try not to make a nuisance of yourself when you're visiting a friend in the hospital: "The visitor should never sit on the bed, knock or kick it."

Don't get caught saying the d-word in public: Don't speak of your divorce "except legally and in conversation to personal friends." After all, there's no need to advertise this type of blemish on your person!

> "Do be careful about giving your photographs, especially to men. You would hardly like to hear the comments that are sometimes passed upon them."
> – Maude C. Cooke, *Social Etiquette, or, Manners and Customs of Polite Society: Containing Rules of Etiquette for All Occasions*, 1896

The Perils of Palmolive
(a.k.a. "What's a Nice Girl Like You Doing in an Ad Like This?")

World War I–era Canuck Chicks eagerly followed each suspense-packed installment of *The Perils of Pauline,* one of the most famous episodic films of the day. A young woman who clearly missed her calling as a *Survivor* contestant by virtue of having been born a hundred years too soon, Pauline managed to pull off narrow escapes from certain doom, week after suspense-filled week. One week it was pirates, the next it was sharks, and then—of course—there was that famous scene when she narrowly escaped being run over by a train. Hey, you've got to admire a gal with that kind of spunk!

Advertising spin doctors were only too happy to pick up on the peril theme, making it all too clear to post-Victorian Canuck Chicks that their own health and beauty—and perhaps even their children's very survival—rested in their hands. One moment of inattention—one careless misstep—and their very lives could be in peril!!! (Yes, ladies, this is one of those rare situations that calls for no fewer than three exclamation marks!!!)

Don't believe me? Here are just a few of the many dangers that a typical Canadian woman might be asked to sidestep each time she embarked on the risk-laden journey to the toiletry counter.

You might find yourself suffering from the tragedy of domestic hands.
A January 1932 advertisement for Hinds Honey and Almond Cream in *The Chatelaine* spoke of the terrible price paid by formerly carefree Nan after she developed—horrors!—domestic hands as a result of (sob!) purchasing *the wrong brand of soap.* "The Tragedy of Nan—Domestic Hands. It had been a real love match, the marrying of Nan and John. . . . Then suddenly without warning she began to change. From a vivacious, carefree bride she became furtive, self-conscious, shy. . . . Domestic hands had given her an inferiority complex."

You might unthinkingly allow your youth to slip away.
Something as simple as reaching for an inferior brand of soap could wreak havoc on your looks, according to a 1925 Palmolive soap advertisement in the

Canadian Home Journal: "Why let youth slip away, youthful radiance fade, when to keep them you need but practice a few simple rules of daily care?"

You could find yourself experiencing the heartbreak of "middle-aged skin."
One moment it was the loss of youthful radiance, the next it was the arrival of middle-aged skin—talk about a virtual parade of horrors. What woman wanted to flirt with disaster by sacrificing her girlish complexion and—by implication—her marriage, too, all for the sake of saving a couple of pennies on a bar of soap? "A wife can blame herself if she loses love by getting 'middle-age' skin!" warned a 1938 advertisement for Palmolive soap in the *New York Times*.

"The 'middle-aged woman' is fast becoming a relic of other days. Age no longer is the line of demarcation between days of charm and allure and the tasteless complacency of a chaperon's corner. Women have learned to stay young . . . "
– advertisement for Palmolive, *Canadian Home Journal Magazine*, 1925

You might notice your husband's eyes start to wander.
The spin doctors at Palmolive were no longer just warning of the dangers of allowing your good looks to fade. This time, they turned up the heat a little, drawing a clear connection between youthful skin and a happy husband. "More searching than your mirror . . . your husband's eyes. If all the women who seek to hold their husbands would first hold their good looks, editors of beauty columns wouldn't get such a large mail . . . and there would be greater chances for happiness. . . . Use Palmolive . . . twice every day . . . faithfully. Then see what your mirror reveals. See what your husband's eyes reveal," declared a 1932 advertisement in the *Canadian Home Journal*.

You might bump into Mr. Right on the wrong day.
The folks at Palmolive were also eager to make the point that skincare was a 365-days-a-year job. After all, what girl wanted to risk running into Mr. Right in the midst of an acne breakout? "A girl's complexion must be fresh, alluring every minute of the day," stated a 1942 advertisement in *Life*. "You never know when, or where, you'll meet the most attractive man!"

You might allow a substandard anti-perspirant to ruin your expensive French frock. (Assuming, of course, that you own one.)
An August 1931 *Chatelaine* advertisement for Instant Odo-ro-no anti-perspirant

spoke frankly of the awful consequences of using a substandard anti-perspirant. "Familiar Tragedies No. 2. At the races he spent . . . $30. She ruined her frock . . . $89. At the races she was charming—in a new French frock. But the day grew warm, and soon she began to perspire, under the arms. She knew the French frock was ruined, for those perspiration stains were sure to fade the color. She thought, too, of underarm odor. So gauche! Why had she trusted an ineffective preparation—when Instant Odo-ro-no, so simply and surely, would have saved her frock and her charm?"

You might experience the terrible shame of B.O.
As hard as it may be to imagine, there was an even greater horror than destroying a garment with sweat stains: the shame of B.O. "Some of our most expensively gowned women have 'B.O.' . . . Such a needless shame!" declared a 1937 advertisement for Lifebuoy in the *Canadian Home Journal*. And, lest the headline be too subtle, the advertising copywriters immediately burst into dialogue: "Please put down the window, Auntie. They freeze me every time I come here."

"Perhaps, dear, they're hinting that you're not as dainty as you might be. . . . Suggesting that you use Lifebuoy."

You might expose your darling children to Dirt Danger Days.
A 1953 *Look* magazine advertisement for Lava Soap warned mothers of the importance of safeguarding their children's health. "Mother! Guard Against 'Dirt Danger' Days" screamed the headline of the ad. The message of the advertisement was clear. Only a bad mother would fail to protect her little darlings from the perils posed by dirt and germs. And what Canuck Chick in her right mind would willingly settle for the most loathsome of labels: being pegged as a bad mother?

A 1953 advertisement for Lava Soap.
The Procter & Gamble Company. Used by permission

A Woman's Work Is Never Done

Find yourself grumbling about how long it takes to flip a load of laundry from the washer to the dryer? Well, girlfriend, you should thank your lucky stars that you weren't born a hundred years ago in the "dark ages" of housework—a scary time when appliances were woman-powered rather than electrically operated.

Housework was an all-consuming task for past generations of Canuck Chicks. Not only did it take a tremendous amount of time and energy to do battle with dirt: your very worthiness as a woman was on the line each time you picked up a broom or a mop! ("Success in housekeeping adds credit to the woman of intellect, and lustre to a woman's accomplishments," wrote the authors of *The Home Cook Book* in 1877. "No matter how talented a woman may be, or how useful in the church or society, if she is an indifferent house-keeper it is fatal to her influence, a foil to her brilliancy and a blemish in her garments.")

And while the introduction of a never-ending parade of household inno-vations promised to take some of the drudgery out of housework, most women found themselves as busy—or busier—than ever as the bar was raised ever higher when it came to the domestic arts. As Alice B. Stockham, MD, noted in the 1893 edition of her best-selling women's health book *Tokology*, "Successful housekeeping, under modern improvements, requires the combined heads of an army general and a secretary of state." Hey, this housekeeping stuff was seri-ous business . . .

History of Housework

We've come a long way, baby—or at least that's the theory. Here are some mile-stone moments in the history of Canadian housework.

1824
The first Canadian patent is issued for a "washing and filling machine." Over the next 45 years, more than 63 patents will be issued for various types of washing machines. (Clearly, there was room for improvement: most early designs failed because they were either too cumbersome to use or because they ruined clothes—a rather unwelcome feature in any washing machine.) A cen-tury later, the Maytag washing-machine company estimated that pioneer methods of doing laundry required as much energy as swimming five miles doing an energetic breaststroke, with "arm movements and general dampness supplying an almost exact parallel."

Elsa Sillanpaa using a washing machine (1927).
Archives of Ontario DIN 10005178

The Laundry Day Blues

Just how unpleasant was doing laundry in pioneer times? Unpleasant enough that upper-class households made a point of purchasing enough clothing to allow them to go for up to four months without doing laundry. Even less-well-off families made a point of having large wardrobes to draw upon: having to do laundry any more often than every six weeks was a clear indication of poverty!

To minimize the amount of laundry that had to be done, dresses were worn several times before being tossed in the laundry hamper. In order to keep dresses smelling fresh despite this extended wear, women changed their undergarments frequently—often several times a day.

It's not difficult to figure out why pioneer women were so eager to limit the amount of laundry that needed to be done. Laundry was a multiday enterprise that required a tremendous amount of hard work, and not everyone could afford to pay a servant to do their dirty work for them. Clothing had to be soaked for two to three days before it was washed and then scrubbed with a brush or washboard before being boiled. At that point, clothes were boiled for an hour and then rinsed thoroughly and hung to dry. A bluing agent was added to the rinse water to counteract the yellowing that was caused by soaps (which, incidentally, had to be manufactured at home using lye and animal fat). And because early dyes were not colourfast, garments of various colours had to be laundered separately, something that was guaranteed to give even the proverbial happy housewife the laundry day blues. (So many loads, so little time.)

1854

Catharine Parr Traill gives would-be emigrants the scoop on Canadian laundering techniques. "A washing board is always used in Canada," she explains in her book *The Female Emigrant's Guide and Hints on Canadian Housekeeping.* "There are several kinds. Wooden rollers, set in a frame, are the most common, but those made of zinc are best. These last do not cost more than the wooden ones, wear longer, and being very smooth, injure the fabric of the clothes less. In Canada no servant will wash without a washing-board."

1882

It's a banner year for breakthroughs in housekeeping technology. The electric iron is patented south of the border and the first electric cooking range is invented by Canadian inventor Thomas Ahearn.

1899

The lawn sprinkler is invented by Canadian-born inventor Elijah McCoy (a.k.a. "the real McCoy").

1907

The vacuum cleaner is invented. Initially, vacuum cleaners are mounted to wagons and kept outdoors, with huge rubber hoses extending into the house to suction dirt from carpets and draperies.

1908

Cellophane—the precursor to plastic wrap films—is invented by a Swiss chemist. Leftovers never had it so good!

1909

General Electric brings the first electric toaster to market.

1915

An electric "icebox" provides a welcome alternative to previous methods of refrigeration: storing food in cold cellars, on windowsills, or in insulated boxes chilled with a box of ice.

1916

Electric washing machines replace hand-operated washing machines, making laundry day a slightly less tortuous experience.

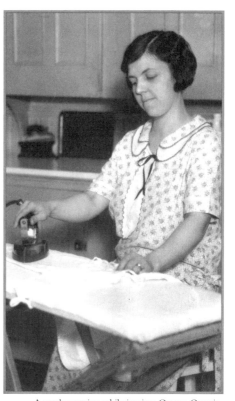

A mother resting while ironing, Ottawa, Ontario, February 1931 (E.M. Finn). National Archives of Canada NAC-PA 163915

1917

Margarine is allowed into Canada for the very first time when the large quantity of butter being exported to soldiers results in a shortage of butter on the homefront.

1918

The Frigidaire refrigerator hits the market and the first food mixer is invented.

"No washboard, no rubbing, no hand wringing. Simply place the clothes in the washer, switch on the electricity and the Trojan does the rest."
– 1918 advertisement for the Trojan electric washer

1921

The electric blanket is invented. It will be another 15 years, however, before a manufacturer invents a blanket that is capable of maintaining a constant temperature, and many more decades before an even savvier entrepreneur comes up with the concept of his and her temperature controls—something that no doubt helps to prevent many needless divorces.

1924

The margarine ban is reinstated. It lasts until 1948, at which point the Supreme Court of Canada rules that each province can decide for itself whether to allow the production and sale of margarine. At that point, a number of provinces introduce legislation that prevents margarine manufacturers from tinting margarine the colour of butter. By the early 1980s, Ontario will have earned the distinction of being the only jurisdiction in North America that does not allow the sale of butter-coloured margarine—a distinction it holds until 1995, when the ban officially ends. Then, two years later, just when the margarine lovers of the nation start to believe that it is safe to open the refrigerator door again, Quebec introduces legislation making butter-coloured margarine illegal. (Only in Canada, you say? Pity!)

Frozen food is invented by entrepreneur Clarence Birdseye following a visit to the Arctic. He admits to having been inspired by Mother Nature's "flash freezing" techniques.

1926

The pop-up toaster makes its debut, replacing the manual electric toaster. Virtually overnight, toast-making ceases to be a spectator sport.

1928

Chatelaine reassures Canadian women that canned foods need no longer be considered second rate. The product development geniuses at the country's food manufacturing companies have finally figured out that it's not profitable to can "over-ripe, under-sized, or damaged produce" and are now experimenting with a radical new concept: canning foods that people might actually want to eat!

1929

The Modern Housekeeper's Guide offers the Canadian housewife some practical tips on choosing the right location for the refrigerator: "When placing an ice refrigerator, keep in mind that icemen make tracks on a kitchen floor. Arrange to place the refrigerator near the outside door or if possible in some convenient place where the actual icing will not take place in the kitchen at all. To save trouble and labor run a pipe or rubber hose from the drip pipe to a drain or even out-of-doors. No pan-emptying is necessary and there is no danger of a troublesome overflow if this is done. An iceless refrigerator, of course, may be placed anywhere, and should be as near the kitchen worker's activities as possible."

1930

Wonder Bread—the world's first packaged, sliced bread—hits the grocery store shelves.

1931

The Chatelaine Institute Board of Consultant Housekeepers surveys Canadian women about their laundry habits. They discover that only 10 of the 316 women who partake in the survey send all of their washing out to be laundered—something that leads the Institute to reach the rather strange conclusion that "modern washing conveniences have made women realize the pleasure of doing their own laundry."

1933

Bakery owners Rose-Anna and Arcade Vachon invent a hand-sized, round, cream-filled chocolate cake. They name the cake after their two sons, Joseph and Louis. By the end of the century, pastry giant Vachon would be selling more than 100 million Joe Louis cakes each year.

The July issue of *Chatelaine* contains some important advice for women who are about to head out of town on vacation, leaving their poor husbands to fend for themselves in the kitchen. "Before you go away, show the man of the house where things are—pots and pans, bread board, clean dish towels, soap, matches, milk and bread tickets and so on," writes Helen G. Campbell, director of the Chatelaine Institute. "And, for goodness' sake, leave the can opener out

Rose-Anna Vachon. Millenium Collection. © Canada Post Corporation. Reprinted with permission in plain view; men never can find anything if they have to look for it." As a public service, Campbell goes on to provide some cooking tips for men who find themselves clueless in the kitchen, including some virtually foolproof instructions for whipping up such gourmet fare as toast and canned soup.

1935
General Electric introduces the first garbage disposal.

1937
The blender makes its debut, thanks to a moment of inspiration on the part of US big-band leader Fred Waring. That same year, Kraft Limited introduces the product for which it (and Canada) will become internationally famous: Kraft Dinner. (The bigwigs at Kraft hope that the product will mimic the success of an earlier product—Kraft Miracle Whip—which was introduced as a budget-friendly alternative to mayonnaise four years earlier.)

1938
Teflon non-stick coating is introduced by DuPont.

1940
The electric kettle is invented by Fred Moffatt for Canadian General Electric.

1940s
General Mills and Pillsbury Co. introduce the first generation of commercially manufactured cake mixes.

Bright Lights, Flush Toilets
Canadian Homes with Amenities, circa 1941 (%)

	Rural Areas	Small Towns	Large Cities
Electric lighting	20.2	75.0	99.4
Indoor running water	12.2	35.0	98.5
Refrigerator	22.2	35.0	50.9
Flush toilet	8.1	27.7	52.1
Telephone	29.3	24.7	40.3

1945
The Trades and Labor Congress Journal reports that 26 percent of urban homes and 80 percent of farm homes are still without hot running water.

1946
Hotpoint converts a bullet-manufacturing plant into a plant that will manu-

facture the appliance that every Canadian housewife yearns for—the automatic dishwasher.

Tupperware is invented by Earl Tupper. Over time, he'll come up with a powerful weapon for marketing his brightly coloured plastic containers to small groups of house-wives—the Tupperware party!

1947

The automatic electric clothes washer is invented by General Electric.

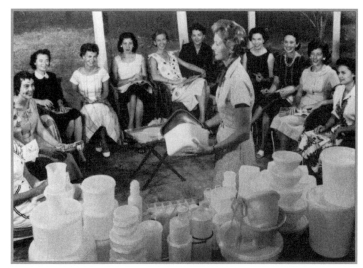

Tupperware party (Associated Press). Canadian Press

1950

A study reveals that a typical housewife puts in a 99.6-hour week. Not only is she expected to cook, sew, and clean: she's now expected to be an accomplished interior decorator, too. The Stepford Wife era has officially begun!

The Canadian National Exhibition in Toronto decides to modernize some of its competitions. Canuck Chicks will no longer be asked to strut their stuff in chair-painting, egg-cooking, salad-making, and sock-mending competitions. Instead, they're invited to participate in contests that will determine who can do her makeup the quickest, cook and serve the juiciest hamburger, and bake the best wedding cake. (Fortunately, you're not required to demonstrate all three skills simultaneously. After all, it's a rare woman indeed who is able to apply mascara while flipping hamburgers and/or icing a cake.)

"Making her home a pleasant place to live is just one of the many contributions made by the Canadian woman. For she is also a dietitian who plans good meals to keep her family fit for work or play . . . a companion who shares in her family's pleasures and problems . . . a nurse ever on call to care for her children's hurts . . . a teacher who trains her children in good citizenship. In these and many other ways she is a one-woman business contributing vitally to the welfare of her family and the stability of Canada."
- advertisement for George Weston Limited, *Chatelaine*, November 1950

The Schiefner farm near Milestone, Saskatchewan, 1956 (Richard Harrington). National Archives of Canada NAC-PA 205821

Diners Club in the United States introduces the first universal charge card for consumer purchases. North America's love affair with credit cards begins.

The green garbage bag is invented by two Canadians, thereby ushering in the era of "gift-wrapped garbage."

1953
Saran Wrap is invented by Dow Chemical.

1954
The first portable home dishwasher is introduced by General Electric.

The TV dinner makes its grand debut, packaged in a container that is designed to look like a television set. The product is the brainchild of frozen food conglomerate Swanson and Sons.

Advertisers attempt to give housework a new, sexier image by using romance to sell some decidedly unromantic products, including carpet sweepers. ("Keeps rugs spick, keeps home span, a Bissell helps her keep that man!" declares one such advertisement in *Chatelaine*.)

1955
The transistor radio is introduced by Sony.

The first generation of microwave ovens hit the US market. Microwave ovens won't make their Canadian debut, however, until 1972.

1957
A magazine advertisement designed to promote electrical appliances lists 28 kitchen appliances that every dream kitchen should contain: a dishwasher, mixer, electric range, juicer, refrigerator-freezer, waste disposer, chafing dish, food blender, food freezer, skillet, electric clothes dryer, broiler-rotisserie, air conditioner, toaster, timer, casserole, automatic washer, countertop cooking unit, food slicer, electric water heater, deep-fat dryer, electronic oven, bean pot, grill, roll warmer, kettle, built-in oven, coffee maker, and electric pressure cooker. According to the advertisement, if you have 24 or more of these wonderful gizmos, you're on easy street because "Your kitchen works instead of you." (Right.)

1962

Instant mashed potatoes are invented by Canadian Edward A. Asselbergs.

1963

The baby boom is making its presence felt in the subdivisions of the nation. Fully 20 percent of new homes have four bedrooms—a dramatic increase over 10 years ago when just 3 percent of new homes could make the same claim.

Valium (a.k.a. "mother's little helper") makes its grand debut. It's an instant hit around the world, giving bored housewives and disenchanted mothers the boost they need to survive until the next Tupperware party.

1964

Maclean's reports that Betty Friedan's book *The Feminine Mystique* has sold 70,000 copies in hardcover and 500,000 copies in paperback during its first year in print. Like their American counterparts, Canadian women are starting to whisper about "the problem that has no name"—the boredom and despair of the suburban housewife.

1965

North America's passion for electrical appliances continues: 3 percent of Canadian homes have dishwashers, 23 percent have freezers, 25 percent have clothes dryers, 69 percent have electric stoves, 86 percent have clothes washers, and 96 percent have refrigerators.

1966

Women who work outside the home are lambasted by *Maclean's* writer John Belanger for failing to measure up in the culinary department. Here's what he has to say in an article entitled "It's High Time Women Shopped Searching for Meaning—And Started Cooking Like Granny Used To" that runs in the February 19 issue of the magazine: "The Modern Woman, grim and steely-eyed behind her office desk, conveyer belt, or receptionist's chair, has left behind a kitchen full of cobwebs and a refrigerator full of Just-Thaw-and-Serve blueberry pies. . . . The tasteless meals the average Canadian woman serves up between bouts with her identity are enough to make any man blanch."

1967

Conformity becomes a way of life for Canuck Chicks who are building nests in suburbia. Residents of Etobicoke, Ontario, are required to cut their grass at least once a week, to keep hedges and fences under 2 1/2 feet high, to refrain from building backyard bird houses, and to place their garbage in plastic bags.

1968

The Chargex credit card (eventually renamed VISA) makes its Canadian debut.

1969

Chatelaine publishes a shocking exposé that lets its readers know how women who work outside the home actually manage to put dinner on the table at the end of the day. "A deli is a girl's best friend," confesses one of the women interviewed in the article.

1970

Chatelaine gives its readers the scoop on Voice of Man in Toronto (VOMIT)—an anti-feminist group whose members are committed to seeking "release from a lifetime's service as a free meal ticket for an intellectually inferior woman and the brood she forces on us." That same year, feminists discover that it's hard to sell the women's lib movement to the more affluent classes of Canuck Chicks. "To try to convince the woman who has just ankled her way through the deep-pile broadloom on her way to the two-car garage to drive away from her dream bungalow filled with every huckstered Brandname in the world by a generous, hardworking husband—to try to tell that woman she's been had at the bargaining table of marriage is to grasp the frustration of every evangelist for women's liberation," writes Barbara Frum in the November issue of *Chatelaine*. "Who in her suntanned, taut-bodied, carefully cultivated mind is going to surrender the benefits of a subsidized life for the privilege of being her own man?"

1972

The microwave oven hits the Canadian market. Six thousand units worth $3.3 million are sold in the first year at prices ranging from $450 to $650. By mid-1975, 35,000 Canadian households will have a microwave.

1973

The food processor is marketed for home use.

1975

Ziploc sandwich bags are invented by Dow Chemical.

1976

Eaton's pulls the plug on its mail-order catalogue after nearly one hundred years of publication. The catalogue had been launched in 1884 at what would subsequently become known as the Canadian National Exhibition. *Canadian Business* publishes a eulogy in its March issue: "By rights, Eaton's last catalogue ought not to be interred in the ground," writes John A. Edds. "Instead, it should be cremated and its ashes scattered over the length and breadth of Canada. For there is scarcely a square mile of Canada or a segment of Canadian society that hasn't felt the impact of . . . Eaton's mail order catalogue."

1978

No-name products make their debut in Canadian grocery stores.

1980

Homemaker's Magazine publishes an article about the feminist movement alongside advertisements that warn Canadian housewives about the embarrassment that can result from using the wrong dishwasher powder. "If your party guests looked this close at your glasses, would you worry about spots?" asks one such advertisement for Cascade.

1985

A survey conducted by *Chatelaine* reveals the shocking news that 83 percent of Canadian women do more housework than the men in their lives. But that's not the worst of it. Fully 1 percent of Canadian women admit to following in the footsteps of newly popular US author and caterer Martha Stewart by spending 30 or more hours *each week* on housework.

1996

After five years of lobbying, Carol Lees, a 51-year-old homemaker and mother of three from Saskatchewan, manages to convince the bean-counters at Statistics Canada to start collecting information about the number of hours that Canadians spend on such unpaid tasks as housework, yard work, childcare, and eldercare. Five years earlier, she had been threatened with prosecution, a fine, or imprisonment for refusing to fill out her census form because unpaid housework was not included as a category of work. "Being forced to say that I didn't work when I was putting in at least 35 hours a week on the home front made me mad. I was so angry, in fact, that I felt that I was obliged to take this action, whether it resulted in effective change or not. I guess you could say I was driven to do this for the sake of my own dignity."

2001

A Statistics Canada study reveals what every Canuck Chick knows intuitively: when both paid and unpaid labour are factored in, time-use studies indicate that a typical Canadian woman outworks a typical Canadian man by 80 hours a year—the equivalent of two weeks of full-time employment.

Kate Aitken: Canada's Own Martha Stewart

Kate Aitken: 20 good luck lunch menus.
National Archives of Canada C147274

A couple of decades before wealthy Connecticut caterer Martha Stewart tacked the word "omnimedia" to her name and set out on a mission to conquer the print and electronic media, a Canuck Chick had already made a name for herself by doing much the same thing—serving as the voice of good taste for her era. In fact, it could even be argued that this smartly dressed Canadian woman actually managed to "out-Martha" Martha, ringing up a list of career achievements that could put even Ms. Stewart to shame. The woman in question was Kate Aitken—or "Mrs. A" as she was known to the thousands of Canadians who read her newspaper columns, tuned into her radio show, and purchased her many books.

Kate Aitken got her start operating a successful home-based business, processing foods that were grown on her husband's Beeton, Ontario, farm. As demand for her products grew and she began receiving orders from restaurants and specialty shops, she hired local women to help run the small home-canning factory that was housed in her basement. Like Stewart, she used this home-grown venture as the launching pad for an exciting career that would make her one of the best-known women of her time.

Aitken's star shone particularly brightly during the war years, when she was given the title of Conservation Director for the federal Wartime Prices and Trade Board. While the position was unpaid, she took her responsibilities very seriously, encouraging Canadian women to rally around the war effort by finding creative ways to do more with less. In keeping with the campaign slogan "Use it up, wear it out, make over, make do," Aitken used her platform as a radio broadcaster to teach Canadian women how to remake a man's formal jacket and trousers into a daytime suit for a woman; and how to cut the worn feet off men's socks and join the remaining pieces together to make a children's dressing gown.

It was that practical, no-nonsense advice that became Aitken's trademark. Of course, her willingness to shoot from the hip occasionally landed her in hot water. In 1947, she created a bit of a furor when she told the readers of *Chatelaine* that there were only 7 basic recipes in the world—white sauce, yeast mixtures, plain cake, baking powder mixtures, pastry, cornstarch desserts, and custard mixtures—a rather startling admission for someone who wrote 9 cookbooks over the course of her career and who claimed to test no fewer than 12 new recipes each week!

In 1941, *Time* magazine estimated that Kate Aitken was earning approximately $25,000 a year—this at a time when $3,000 a year was considered to be a decent wage. By 1950, she was believed to be earning in excess of $52,000 a week—an almost unheard-of achievement for a Canadian woman. Kate Aitken wasn't merely known for her wealth, however: she was also known for her sense of style. Not only was she consistently named as one of the best-dressed women in Canada year after year: she was known to keep company with prime ministers and other world leaders, and to travel in the same circles as royalty every now and again.

When journalist Gordon Sinclair referred to Aitken as "the busiest woman in the world" in an article in the April 15, 1950, issue of *Maclean's Magazine,* he wasn't exaggerating in the least. At that point, she was taping 600 broadcasts a year, giving 150 speeches, commuting to and from her job as cooking editor for the *Montreal Standard* (the weekly magazine supplement to the *Montreal Gazette*), and ensuring that her staff of 21 secretaries read and responded to the more than 5,000 fan letters she received each week. On top of her day job, Aitken also found the time to write 15 books: 9 cookbooks, 2 autobiographical books, and a book each on beauty, etiquette, child-rearing, and travelling solo.

Her career also included stints as a consultant to a chain of drugstores, the publicity director for the Kiwanis Music Festival, and the Director of Women's Activities for the Canadian National Exhibition—a position she held for 14 years. (Rumour has it that the hardworking Aitken would sleep on a cot outside her office on the days leading up to the opening of the Exhibition each year. There simply weren't enough hours in a day to accomplish everything that needed to be done!) She also operated her own spa: The Kate Aitken Spa in Streetsville, Ontario, for a period of time. And, during her later years, she served on the Board of Directors of the CBC. (Never one to rest on her laurels or coast because of her age or reputation, Aitken was determined to be a hands-on director. In fact, she managed to spark a huge uproar when she took the virtually unprecedented step of sending out a questionnaire to ask Canadians what they thought of CBC programming—not exactly the way to score points with the CBC bigwigs.)

Kate Aitken died in 1971 at the age of 81. Over her lifetime she'd managed to attract quite a cult following: at the height of her broadcasting career in the 1950s, fully 32 percent of Canadians tuned into her radio show. That's not to say that she was without her critics, however: she took some heat over the years for the sing-song quality to her voice and her almost relentlessly sunny outlook on life, a point she discussed in a 1957 interview with the *Star Weekly:* "I don't mind being made fun of because life's too short to get mad at anybody. I never answer my critics. I admit my beliefs are optimistic, that I think all's right with the world. But isn't that better than not believing in the church, democracy, people, in anything good? I think it is. I'd rather be a Pollyanna than a cynic." (Or, to borrow a phrase from Ms. Stewart: Seeing the good in everyday life— it's "*a good thing.*")

Make That One-Part Martha Stewart, One-Part Ann Landers

When Canadian women wrote to Kate Aitken to ask her advice on something, she had no problem pulling an Ann Landers and telling them to "Wake up and smell the coffee!"

Here's what she had to say to a secretary who was coming dangerously close to having an affair with her boss: "If you want to sit on a red hot stove you are at liberty to do it. And if you want to cut off your hair you're your own boss. But neither of these projects are as silly as getting yourself mixed up with a married man who talks about his wife to his stenographer. Just remember when it comes to the final say-so, the average man stays with his wife and family. Many an unhappy girl who listens to the sad story has found this out for herself. If I were you I'd try to find a contented boss who isn't interested in either cheesecake or sympathy."

Martha Stewart
(Richard Drew). Canadian Press

CHAPTER 2

Maple Leaf Mamas

"Every pregnant woman should be considered as a laboratory in which she prepares a new being, to which the slightest physical or moral emotion is injurious. . . . The art of raising fine stock is almost perfect. Let us make it so with raising children."
- Annette Slocum, MD, *For Wife and Mother,* 1900

"Mother's Day roses come once a year. Not so the thorns of blame. From bed-wetting to poor table manners, no mishap in a child's life is too small to attract a barbed remark."
- Rona Maynard, "Let's Stop Blaming Mum," *Homemaker's Magazine,* May 1983

The more things change, the more they stay the same. Skirt lengths may rise and fall, but blaming Mom always seems to be in fashion. And given how high the bar was set for past generations of Maple Leaf Mamas—for much of the past century, the job of mother demanded purity of thought, word, and deed both before, during, and after pregnancy!—it's hardly surprising that so many mothers were left feeling as if they deserved to have "Canada Grade C" stamped on their foreheads. (Grade A was, of course, reserved for those perfectly coiffed, cookie-baking moms who derived great personal fulfillment from making their children's Halloween costumes from scratch, serving as Brown Owl for the local Girl Guide troop, and coordinating the penny drive for the charity du jour—superhuman beings who found the endless rounds of carpooling to be invigorating rather than exhausting, and who, after 16 hours in the motherhood trenches, somehow managed to find the energy to have an Aviance night rather than merely begging Calgon dishwashing powder to take them away.)

In this chapter, we're going to focus on the history of Canadian motherhood. We'll start out by looking at the "scientific motherhood" movement of the early 20th century and follow the inevitable swing of the pendulum from

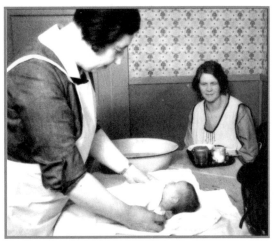

VON home visit. Glenbow Archives NA-3445-17.

"punishing" to "permissive." Then we'll consider how the experts' advice to mothers and our ideas about birth have changed over the past hundred years. (Just think of it as a crash course in bringing up baby, Canadian-style!)

Scientific Motherhood

During the years after World War I, a more scientific approach to mothering came into vogue. Rather than relying on something as unscientific as maternal instinct or—even more unforgivable!—asking other mothers for advice, Canadian mothers were encouraged to turn to the true experts—members of the medical profession. (The importance of the medical establishment in the lives of Canadian families comes through loud and clear in an advertisement in a 1933 issue of the *Nova Scotia Medical Bulletin*. "This little girl has three parents," the ad boldly declared. "The third one is the family physician.") For the better part of four decades, the message to Canadian mothers was painfully obvious: mother *doesn't* know best.

The medical establishment firmly believed that previous generations of mothers had botched the job of raising children, and that society as a whole was paying the price for their child-rearing deficiencies. It was therefore time for the experts to step in and show the next generation of mothers how to apply the principles of scientific reasoning to the child-rearing arena: "If the daily conduct of men and women could be guided by a technique as effective as that of the dentist or engineer, the age-long battle against ignorance, superstition, and prejudice would have been won," noted one US proponent of "scientific motherhood" in *Child Welfare Magazine*.

Risky Business

Poor sanitary conditions caused by rapid urban growth meant that one out of every six babies born in the City of Toronto in 1901 died before reaching his or her first birthday. By 1907, that number had climbed to almost one in five. The mortality rate in Montreal was even higher, with one in three children dying during the first year of life.

The Mother Load

Wondering why Canadian moms swallowed this argument hook, line, and sinker? Because they were desperate for information about bringing up baby, that's why.

The growing exodus from the country to the city meant that it was less likely than ever before that you'd have your mom in easy access when your own babies came along. And, to make matters worse, declining birth rates meant that you'd likely had less of an opportunity to practise your child-rearing skills on your siblings than had been possible for girls in generations past. Add to that the fact that electrical appliances such as refrigerators, washers, and dryers were eliminating some of the drudgery of housework—something that made it possible for you to devote a greater amount of time and energy to the business of child-rearing—and you can see why child-rearing "experts" found themselves with a ready-made audience each time they climbed up on the soapbox.

Time and time again, Depression-era mamas found themselves being warned about the perils of drowning their children in "too much mother love." Their duty as mothers, according to the experts? To stick to a rigid program of "habit training" that was designed to nurture good behaviour and stamp out such "strong and dangerous impulses" as dawdling, stammering, temper tantrums, thumb-sucking, and masturbation. Schedules and routines were the key to raising a kinder and gentler generation of children—or at least that's what the experts were claiming.

Since much of what the experts had to say didn't quite jive with what their maternal instincts were telling them to do, Canadian moms found themselves faced with the mother of all dilemmas: whether to follow their heart or to heed the advice of the cold-hearted doctors who warned them about the perils of spoiling their babies. (One such expert—US psychologist J.B. Watson—even went so far as to suggest that kissing and hugging be eliminated from the parent-child relationship entirely. He recommended that it be replaced with a much more businesslike handshake!)

That Was Then, This Is Now

Predictably, the pendulum soon began to swing in the opposite direction, moving from punishing to permissive. After a decade or two of telling them to stick to rigid schedules and routines, experts began dishing up the opposite advice, telling mothers that they should be taking their cues from their children. Suddenly, it was children rather than mothers who were in the driver's seat!

Of course, it wasn't just mothers who found themselves in the parenting hot seat after World War II: the new generation of fathers was being called upon to move beyond the traditional provider role and to play a more active role in the emotional life of the family. (Within a few generations, the emotionally distant father would be magically transformed into the 1990s' sensitive, new age guy!) But even if Dad did make a point of arriving home from the office in time to play a quick game of road hockey with the kids, parenting was still very much a girl thing. It was the Janey Canucks of the world, after all, who found themselves baking muffins at 11 p.m. so that their husband and kids would have something homemade to take in their lunchboxes the next day. (A woman's work is never done, remember?)

The Gold Standard

The 1950s mom was encouraged to set the bar increasingly higher for herself—to settle for nothing less than perfection. The golden age of mother guilt had arrived. Even Dr. Spock got involved in the mom-bashing act, co-authoring a book that claimed that thumb-sucking was a sign of insecurity: according to Dr. Spock and his cronies, a child only sucks his thumb "when he feels that he is not loved enough, not safe enough, not good enough."

Given the pressures that went along with being a fifties mom, it's hardly surprising that there was a stampede to the drugstore when Valium arrived on the scene. Thanks to the impossibly high standards set by the child-rearing experts, an entire generation of mothers ended up being haunted by the image of a mythical mom who never lost her cool and who was always waiting with a plate of freshly baked cookies when her children arrived home from school—the 1950s equivalent of the "supermom."

Of course, not every expert bought into the idea that raising children was some superhuman feat. Pediatrician and psychoanalyst D.W. Winnicott, author of the 1957 book *Mother and Child: A Primer of First Relationships*—offered a refreshingly different (albeit annoyingly condescending!) perspective, arguing that being a mother was mere child's play: "You do not have to be clever and you do not even have to think if you don't want to. You may even have been hopeless in arithmetic at school; or perhaps all your friends got scholarships but you couldn't stand the sight of a history book and so failed and left school early. Or you may be really clever. But all this does not matter, and it hasn't anything to do with whether or not you are a good mother. If a child can play with a doll, you can be an ordinary devoted mother."

But just in case you didn't think you could rely on your internal compass to help you make the right parenting decisions—no big surprise there, given that the experts had just spent the previous few decades trying to drive maternal instinct into extinction!—book publishing companies and the federal government were only too happy to come to your rescue, serving up a smorgasbord of child-rearing advice.

The era of the baby book had arrived.

You've Come a Long Way, Baby!

You've come a long way, baby. (And so have you, Mom.) Over the past hundred years we've watched child-rearing experts do flip-flops on all the perennial hot topics: formula-feeding, toilet-training, discipline, and more. So pour yourself a stiff cup of coffee and get ready to watch the experts reverse themselves on every issue imaginable as we push the baby carriage down Memory Lane.

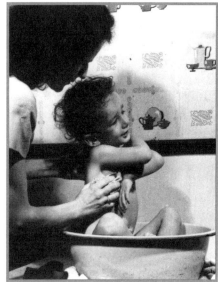

Typical Canadian family: mother bathing child.
National Archives of Canada PA 205817

Wishful Thinking Department

A Kingston, Ontario, mother of 10 who was eager to head to California to cash in on the gold rush of 1840 placed this rather optimistic advertisement in the local newspaper: "Benevolent Mothers, a young widow not yet forty, is anxious to proceed to California but is detained by the harrowing thought of leaving ten beloved children behind her. It is only the idea of separation that grieves her. But if any lady of respectability would take care of them in her absence, and promise to treat them as ten of her own family, a liberal reward shall be given on the lady's return from California, and the kindness not quickly forgotten. Answers are to be sent immediately, stating what masters and kind of table beer are kept, to Mrs. B—, Post office, Kingston."

Pye in the Sky

Never one to mince words or to shy away from taking a stand on a controversial issue, British physician and author Pye Henry Chavasse had plenty of advice for Canadian mothers and mothers-to-be. The following examples are drawn from his book *Advice to a Wife on the Management of Her Own Health*, published by the Hunter Rose Company Limited of Toronto in 1879.

On the need to recuperate during the postpartum period: "The patient should, after the birth of her child, be strictly prohibited from talking, and noisy conversation ought not to be allowed. . . . For the first 10 days or a fortnight, a lying-in woman cannot be kept too quiet. . . . A horizontal . . . position for either ten days or a fortnight after a labour is important. . . . She ought, after the first nine days, to sit up for an hour."

On the need to avoid vigorous exercise prior to nursing your baby: "A mother ought not immediately after taking exercise to nurse her infant, but should wait for half-an-hour. Nor should she take violent exercise, as it would be likely to disorder the milk."

On the importance of limiting a baby's time at the breast: "A sore nipple is frequently produced by the injudicious custom of allowing the child to have the nipple almost constantly in his mouth. Stated periods for suckling . . . ought to be strictly adopted."

On a preferred method for dealing with breast engorgement: "Some mothers object to suck-paps; they dislike having a strange woman sucking their nipples, and well they might. If my fair reader be one of the objectors, she may, by using a nice little invention, dispense with a suck-pap altogether, and with ease draw her own bosoms. The name of the invention is 'Maw's Improved Breast Glass with Elastic Tube for Self Use.'"

On the importance of avoiding prolonged breast-feeding: Pye noted that a baby who is breastfed beyond his first birthday is generally "pale, flabby, unhealthy and rickety" while his mother is usually "nervous, emaciated, and hysterical."

On the merits of good old-fashioned hard work: "The healthiest mothers, as a rule, are working-men's wives, who are employed from morning until night—who have no spare time unemployed to feel nervous, or to make complaints of aches and pains."

"It is important from the very first to accustom a child to sleep at definite hours, else the parents' lives are in danger of becoming a burden to them. To walk the floor night after night or be obliged to sit up with a healthy child and sing it to sleep is a form of martyrdom which is entirely uncalled for."
- J.P. Crozer Griffith, MD, *The Care of The Baby: A Manual for Mothers and Nurses*, 1898

History of Baby Care

Given some of the advice they received from the so-called experts over the years, it's amazing Canadian moms didn't end up throwing the baby out with the proverbial bath water.

1898

J.P. Crozer Griffith, MD, offers some practical advice on hiring a wet nurse—a woman who breastfeeds other women's babies—in his book *The Care of The Baby: A Manual for Mothers and Nurses:* "A married woman is to be preferred, but the difficulties connected with obtaining a good wet-nurse are so great, and married wet-nurses often so scarce, that it is folly to refuse to engage an unmarried one if she is qualified in other respects. Because she has made one so false a step [getting pregnant out of wedlock] does not prove her wholly bad. . . . [Besides] there is no more probability of a baby imbibing the character of the nurse through the milk which she gives . . . than there is danger of a child learning to 'moo' because it is fed on cow's milk."

1908

The Canadian Medical Association creates a milk commission to provide expert medical advice about the growing problem of tainted milk—something that poses a major threat to the well-being of Canadian children.

1914

The Toronto Department of Public Health organizes 19 ferry day trips for city-bound mothers and babies. Over the course of the summer, 1,963 mothers and 2,318 babies participate in the outings, which are designed to get children out of the city and teach their mothers about proper health practices.

Forget the old adage that says that children should be seen and not heard. Experts—including the author of a highly popular textbook on manners—are now recommending that children refrain from being children: "Children should be taught that it is rude to yawn without trying to suppress it, or without concealing the mouth with the hand; to whistle or hum in the presence of older persons; to make any monotonous noise with feet or hands, beating time, etc.; to play with napkin rings or any article at table during meal time; to pick the teeth with the fingers; to trim or clean one's nails outside one's room; to lounge anywhere in the presence of company; to place the elbows on the table, or to lean upon it while eating; to speak of absent persons by their first names, when one would not so address them if they were present; to acquire the habit of saying 'you know,' 'says he,' 'says she,' 'do you see'; to use slang words; to tattle; to hide the mouth with the hand when speaking; to point at any one or anything with the finger; to stare at persons; to laugh at one's own stories or remarks; to toss articles instead of hanging them; to leave the table with food in the mouth; to take possession of a seat that belongs to another without instantly rising upon his return; to leave anyone without saying 'goodbye'; to interrupt any one in conversation; to push; to ridicule others; to pass, without speaking, any person whom one knows, etc." The textbook neglects to explain, however, what children actually *are* allowed to do!

1915

In her book *The Four Epochs of a Woman's Life: A Study in Hygiene*, Anna M. Galbraith, MD, warns breastfeeding mothers of the importance of avoiding any emotional turmoil: "Nervous agitation may so alter the quality of the milk as to make it poisonous."

1916

Alice B. Stockham, MD, author of *Toxology: A Book for Every Woman,* informs new mothers that it is no longer considered necessary to offer a breastfed newborn "catnip tea, panada [a thick paste made from bread crumbs, flour, or rice], gruel, cracker water, cream tea, etc." while the mother is waiting for her breastmilk to come in.

1921

The Canadian Mother's Book is published by the federal government. Over the next 12 years, 800,000 copies of the book will be distributed—nearly one copy for every four babies born during this time.

1928

Chatelaine warns its readers that "only a super-woman can juggle both a family and a career."

Strained baby food is invented by Daniel and Dorothy Gerber for Fremont Canning Co.—an American firm that eventually renames itself the Gerber Products Company.

1930

Pablum is invented by three doctors at the Hospital for Sick Children in Toronto: T.G.H. Drake, Alan Brown, and Frederick F. Tisdall. Initially, they set out to invent a vitamin biscuit, but then they decide to devote their energies to inventing a nutritious, pre-cooked cereal instead.

1931

Chatelaine columnist and nurse Margaret Laine reminds breastfeeding mothers to stick with the standard four-hour schedule for feeding their newborns, making an effort to omit the 2 a.m. feeding as soon as possible. She also advises washing the nipples with boracic lotion before and after each feeding and to apply Eau de Cologne at the first sign of any tenderness. Then, in a separate article, she warns her readers about the dire consequences of deviating from baby's schedule: "When making arrangements for the baby's morning bath, it should be remembered that a certain time should definitely be set apart for it and that nothing should be allowed to encroach upon that particular time. Unless regular hours and strict punctuality are enforced, the baby cannot be well trained and most people will agree that, apart from his physical well-being, which must also suffer, a badly trained baby is a nuisance to himself and to all those with whom he comes into contact."

"When Mother's Nerves Are Healthy. What a joy are children to the healthy mother! What an irritation they are when mother is weak, nervous, and excitable!"
– from an advertisement for Dr. Chase's Nerve Food in the March 1932 issue of *Chatelaine*. Clearly Canadian moms were a nervous lot: the product was still being offered for sale in the 1961 Simpsons-Sears catalogue.

1936

John W.S. McCullough, MD, warns *Chatelaine* readers that they risk spoiling their babies if they give them too much attention: "Children under two should not be in the parents' company too much."

1942

The Canadian Mother and Child stresses the importance of starting toilet-training as soon as possible: "Usually a child, when a month old, will go to stool at a definite time of the day, or it may be trained to this by the use of soap suppositories or a rubber catheter which will act as a stimulant to bowel action. . . . Later, at about the fifth or sixth month, the child may be made to sit on a specially constructed toilet chair."

Spare the Rod, Spoil the Child

McGill University pediatrics professor Alton Goldbloom, MD, holds the distinction of having written one of the bossiest Canadian parenting books ever. He wrote *The Care of the Child* in 1945, the year after he was named chairman of the Pediatrics Department at McGill—just in time for the Baby Boom! Here are a few of the more memorable bits of parenting advice he chose to pass along in his book:

On the importance of routine: "The difference between a good baby and a bad baby, between a placid and a nervous one, is, with few exceptions, merely the difference between a baby who is on a strict and regular daily routine, and one who is not."

On the risky practice of playing with a baby: "Playing with a young baby is never necessary and is often harmful. . . . It is a good rule to leave the baby alone as much as possible."

On the health benefits of crying: "All young babies should have a crying period during each day. . . . The infant who chooses to have his crying spell during the night should be trained to have it during the day time, so that he will sleep at night. This is not difficult to achieve. Very often the mere removing of the baby from his crib on to a large bed and allowing him to move his arms and legs freely, will, if he is left in such a position for some time, give him the opportunity of exercising his lungs. . . . This is both good discipline and good exercise, and is not harmful to the baby."

Two girls playing at a wartime nursery at G.E.
Archives of Ontario DIN 10004936

1945
The Family Allowance program (a.k.a. "the baby bonus") is launched, providing monthly payments to parents with children under the age of 18.

1946
The first edition of *Dr. Spock's Baby and Child Care* hits the bookstore shelves. By the end of the century, more than 50 million copies will have been sold, making the book the second best-selling book of all time, second only to the *Bible*.

C. Anderson Aldrich, MD, and Mary M. Aldrich warn about the dangers of masturbation in their book *Babies Are Human Beings:* "Some time during infancy, a baby's wandering hands will happen to discover his genital organs. If he persists in finding this region of his anatomy pleasing, he may be termed a 'masturbator,' thus acquiring a blot on his baby reputation, one which puts him definitely in the 'bad' class and makes his family ashamed of him."

1954
Vancouver mother of seven Susan Olivia Poole invents the Jolly Jumper—a popular device that allows a baby to bounce up and down. It consists of a harness that attaches to a spring that is hooked to the top of a doorframe.

1955
Broadcaster and author Kate Aitken has some stern words for mothers who are willing to "let themselves go" after the birth of a baby: "Are you as fussy about clean hair, clean nails, becoming clothes, well-fitting shoes as you were two years ago? Maternity is no excuse for sloppiness but rather an incentive to a more attractive personality."

1956

Seven US mothers band together to form La Leache League, a breastfeeding support association—this at a time when bottlefeeding rather than breastfeeding has become the norm.

1957

Dr. Spock comments that parents have become too permissive, adding that subsequent editions of his best-selling child-rearing manual will focus more on discipline and less on giving children freedom.

1961

Pampers disposable diapers hit the market.

1962

The *Financial Post* reports on a marvellous new invention—the baby sleeper—which it describes as "a one-piece stretchable suit of nylon or a cotton-nylon combination for babies." The Canadian manufacturer for the product reports that it has managed to sell 600,000 sleepers in a single year.

1967

Mister Dressup hits the airwaves, guaranteeing Canadian mothers at least a half-hour of sanity each weekday morning.

Orders for the popular action figurine G.I. Joe nosedive by 50 percent when Dr. Spock speaks out against war toys in the latest edition of *Dr. Spock's Baby and Child Care*. The following year, Dr. Spock is convicted of assisting draft dodgers and is sentenced to two years in jail, although he never actually serves the time.

1970

The latest edition of *The Canadian Mother and Child* informs mothers that fresh cow's milk, canned evaporated whole or half skimmed milk, or powdered whole milk are all suitable substitutes for breastmilk, provided that you add granulated sugar or corn syrup to this homemade "formula."

1972

The federal government introduces changes to the income tax act that allow working mothers to deduct childcare expenses from their taxes for the very first time.

1979

Chatelaine arranges for a time management consultant to help a stay-at-home mother and a working mother to use their time more efficiently.

1983

Chrysler introduces the minivan. Virtually overnight, a flotilla of square, boxy vehicles invades the suburbs of the nation as the minivan establishes itself as the official vehicle of she-who-lives-in-suburbia.

Today's Parent magazine is founded. Ten years down the road, proud "mama" Beverly Topping—the magazine's founding publisher—pauses to reflect back on the circumstances surrounding her "baby's" birth in an article in *Strategy* magazine: "We adopted at first, a fledgling, an immature yet promising child, *Great Expectations,* back in 1983. But she was soon on her feet, as you know so well, and was quickly asking for, no, demanding, a baby sister. How could we let her down? And then, miracle of miracles, you came along, and we happily and thankfully christened you *Today's Parent . . .* "

1985

The *Toronto Star* reports that baby monitors are becoming popular with Canadian parents.

1987

The Canadian Medical Association calls for a ban on baby walkers—a product that is used by 90 percent of Canadian children and that results in 2,500 injuries and at least one baby death each year. One year later, Canadian juvenile product manufacturers agree to some tough new standards for baby walkers—standards that a federal government spokesman describes as "the most stringent in the world."

Suburban housing. Aerial photo of Levittown, New York (AP Photo/Levittown Public Library). Canadian Press.

1990

Canadian singer/songwriter Nancy White releases her landmark CD *Momnipotent: Songs for Weary Parents.* It immediately attracts a cult following on both sides of the border.

1992

Canadian journalist Marni Jackson writes *The Mother Zone: Love, Sex, and Laundry in the Modern Family*—one of the first books to tell the truth about what it means to be a mother! The book is inspired by an earlier article that Jackson wrote for *Saturday Night,* countless illegal photocopies of which could be found stashed away in the diaper bags of the nation.

1994

Mom's the Word makes its world debut at Vancouver's Women in View Festival. The play—a tribute to motherhood that is written by and for moms—is an immediate hit with audiences. The playwrights eventually sign an international rights licensing agreement that allows the play to be produced in other languages and in other countries around the world—proof positive that mother angst is a universal phenomenon.

1999

BC Children's Hospital's Safe Start injury prevention program estimates that there are still 60,000 to 70,000 unsafe baby walkers in Canada—walkers that have been kicking around in garages and basements for the past 10 years or that have been smuggled across the border from the US since Canada's more stringent baby walker guidelines came into effect.

Oh, Baby! Changing Ideas About Birth

Over the course of the past century, we've seen the birth rate drop, the percentage of babies born in hospitals rise, and outcomes for both mothers and babies improve by

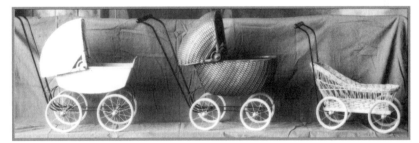

Doll carriages. Glenbow Archives NC-6-12105a

leaps and bounds. And, along the way, we've seen childbirth experts do some rather radical flip-flops and great and not-so-great birthing inventions get their proverbial 15 minutes of fame. (Who could forget the "abdominal decompression chamber" that promised to take much of the "labour" out of giving birth. It may have been invented by an aircraft manufacturer, but this is one childbirth device that never really got off the ground!) Here's what you need to know about these and other milestone moments in the history of Canadian birthing.

1879

Physician Pye Henry Chavasse all but admits that women are the superior sex in his book *Advice to a Wife on the Management of Her Own Health:* "Women are far more patient than men: it is well they are; for men would never be able patiently to endure, as women do, the bitter pangs of childbirth."

1893

The preferred method of treating morning sickness involves administering an enema. (Perhaps the unpleasantness of the enema helps to take your mind off the queasy feeling in your stomach.)

1896

Elisabeth Robinson Scovil stresses the importance of thinking happy thoughts during pregnancy in her book *Preparation for Motherhood.* "From the first the mind should be filled as far as possible with pleasant images. Interesting books should be read, beautiful pictures, or natural scenery, dwelt upon and everything that excites disagreeable emotions put as far away as possible." She's not the only expert of the day to lay the mother of all guilt trips on expectant mothers. In fact, B.G. Jefferis and J.L. Nichols offer an even more pointed warning in their book *Safe Counsel or Practical Eugenics,* declaring that, "Low spirits, violent passions, irritability, frivolity, in the pregnant woman, leave indelible marks on the unborn child."

1900

In her book *For Wife and Mother,* Annette Slocum, MD, warns expectant mothers to avoid such risky activities as "riding on horseback, riding a bicycle, or running a sewing machine."

1901

A typical Canadian woman can expect to give birth to 4.6 children over her lifetime.

1902

"Twilight sleep" (which involves administering a combination of scopolamine and morphine to a labouring woman) is introduced as a method of controlling the pain of childbirth. Although suffragists and women's rights advocates applaud its arrival on the grounds that it will give women a greater ability to control the birthing experience, there's a definite downside to "twilight sleep." Not only do women lose all memory of having given birth—something that causes many to question whether the baby in the bassinette beside them is, in fact, their own!—but they're also more subject to postnatal depression. And, from the physician's standpoint, there's another rather noteworthy drawback: "It generally renders the patient so unmanageable as seriously to hamper labour."

1908

Although some doctors are supportive of midwifery care, feeling that midwives help to ease some of the burden for the overworked family doctor, one University of Toronto obstetrics professor is a little less tolerant. In fact, he goes so far as to express his gratitude that "a kind of Providence has thus far mercilessly preserved us from the licensed midwife."

1909

The infant death rate for the City of Toronto stands at 230 deaths per 1,000 live births. According to Helen MacMurchy, MD, who is commissioned by the Ontario government to study the problem, intestinal diseases, ignorance, poverty, and inadequate medical care are to blame for the baby deaths.

1910

A British medical textbook widely read by Canadian physicians makes the startling assertion that it's okay to expose a woman's private parts while she is in labour. Apparently, this is one of those rare situations when modesty needs to take a back seat to common sense: "Presumably, when non-exposure of the vulva is adopted, it is done with the object of sparing the feelings of the patient, but, during the expulsion of the foetus, the patient is far too much occupied by her suffering to notice what is done, and, moreover, the sensible patient will object to a precaution taken for her own good, if the necessity for it is made clear to her. The patient's sentiments have in the past been too frequently considered to the detriment of the physical condition."

1911

Only one in five women going into labour has received any sort of prenatal care.

1913

Although there's a growing move to view childbirth as a normal human function, not all physicians share it: Joseph B. DeLee—a prominent American physician—expresses the countervailing view when he poses the $10,000 question of the day: "Can a function so perilous, that in spite of the best care, it kills thousands of women every year, that leaves at least a quarter of the women more or less invalidated, and a majority with permanent anatomic changes of structure, that is always attended by severe tearing of tissues, and that kills 3 to 5 percent of children—can such a function be called normal?"

1914

Childbirth is widely viewed as a "hazardous occupation" resulting from "a disease of nine months' duration."

1915

In her book *The Four Epochs of a Woman's Life: A Study in Hygiene*, Anna M.

Galbraith, MD, warns pregnant women to be prudent when it comes to doing housework and engaging in recreational activities: "The sewing-machine is a tabooed thing for the pregnant woman, because of the jarring of the pelvis which it produces. Sweeping of heavy carpets is also injurious. There must be no lifting of heavy pieces of furniture, and especially no lifting from the floor, as it interferes with the circulation in the uterus and is apt to produce miscarriage. . . . Horseback-riding and bicycling are, of course, forbidden, as are also golf, tennis, and dancing."

1925

Canadian physician Harold Atlee describes the tough-love approach that he takes to morning sickness, an ailment that be considers to be predominantly psychological in origin: "From the moment the patient enters the hospital she is denied the solace of the vomit-bowl. She is told that, in the event of not being able to control herself, she is to vomit into the bed; and the nurse is instructed to be in no hurry about changing her."

1926

B.G. Jefferis and J.L. Nichols support the idea of having fathers present at the delivery in the latest edition of their book *Safe Counsel or Practical Eugenics:* "Should the husband be at the bedside when the baby is being brought into the world? There is only one answer to this question: if the wife desires it there is no better place in all God's earth for the husband to be than at his wife's side, comforting her, and assisting her through life's most painful ordeal. It is good for man to see for himself, to know absolutely and forever, just what an insignificant part his really is in the great scheme of life, and to realize how truly, how dearly the woman pays."

1928

Chatelaine advice columnist Stella E. Pines, RN, urges Canadian mothers to give birth in a hospital that trains newborn babies to sleep through the night right away. That way, they won't have to miss out on much-needed sleep when they get home: "Nearly all babies cry for the first five or six nights," she explains. "It does them no harm unless in excess. In fact, the exercise helps to establish good lung capacity."

1930

Scientists discover that it is possible to diagnose pregnancy by injecting the urine of a pregnant woman into an immature female mouse. A hormone in the urine produces detectable changes—the so-called Zondek-Aschheim reaction. An accuracy rate of 98 percent is claimed, but most scientists agree that the test is only about 75 percent accurate in practice.

The Canadian maternal mortality rate reaches a new high: 5.8 maternal deaths per 1,000 live births.

1932

Dr. T.R. Nichols of Stratford, Ontario—the author *of Instructions for Expectant Mothers and the Care of Infants,* warns that "Riding over rough roads in an automobile may . . . bring on miscarriage." His advice to mothers-to-be who insist on travelling during pregnancy? "Drive very carefully and slowly."

1934

The Dionne quintuplets, the world's first surviving quintuplets, are born in Corbeil, Ontario, on May 28.

1937

Canadian Medical Association's Committee on Maternal Welfare notes that hospital births aren't without their dangers: "The inefficient hospital ambushes its patients with two sinister dangers: The first is cross-infection. . . . The other danger appears when the convenience of hospital equipment encourages injudicious interference and needlessly radical procedures."

1942

The Canadian Mother and Child advises pregnant women to switch from regular corsets to maternity corsets for the duration of their pregnancy.

1944

Prenatal classes come into vogue. The Victorian Order of Nurses, the St. Elizabeth Visiting Nurses' Association, the Visiting Homemakers, and public health departments across the country start offering pregnancy and childbirth preparation classes to mothers-to-be.

1945

Maclean's reports that the maternal mortality rate has dropped to just 2 to 3 per 1,000 births—a vast improvement over a century earlier when 1 out of every 5 mothers died as a result of pregnancy or birthing-related complications.

1946

Chatelaine urges Canadian women to do their patriotic duty and go forth and multiply: "Three children per married couple should be a minimum goal," the magazine declares.

1947

One of the best-selling books of the year—*Modern Woman: The Lost Sex* by Ferdinand Lundberg and Marynia F. Farnham—tells North American women that it's impossible to conceive of happiness without children. Lundberg and Farnham insist that true happiness and womanly fulfillment come only through getting married and having children. Suddenly, opting for the life of the unmarried aunt (a.k.a. the "old maid") becomes a suspect—even subversive—activity. Media images glorifying the life of the "career girl" are similarly unacceptable because they might distract a woman from her true destiny as a wife and mother.

1948
An article in the *Alberta Medical Bulletin* endorses the use of diethylstilbestrol (DES)—a synthetic estrogen used to prevent miscarriage—this despite the fact that animal studies indicate that DES could cause cancer.

1949
Prominent Canadian physician Ernest Couture advises mothers-to-be to avoid attending hockey or football games while they're pregnant. His concerns? The chill and the thrill! He doesn't want a pregnant woman to get either too cold or too excited.

1950
The baby boom begins. By the time it ends in 1965, an extra 1.5 million babies will have been born in Canada.

1960
The baby boom reaches its peak. Approximately 479,000 Canadian babies are born this year—a massive increase over 20 years earlier, when just 253,000 babies were born in a single year.

The caesarean birth rate stands at 5 percent. By the late 1980s, it will have jumped to 25 percent.

The world's first effective birth control pill—Enovid-10—hits the market, ushering in the start of the sexual revolution. It is later discovered that it contains 10 times as much estrogen as is needed for contraceptive purposes.

The *Financial Post* reports that Canadian aircraft manufacturer Canadair is developing a new obstetrical aid that is designed to speed up and ease childbirth. Known as an "abdominal decompression chamber," the device fits over the mother's abdomen and reduces atmospheric pressure on the abdominal wall to help the muscles to relax during the first stage of labour. An ordinary household vacuum cleaner is hooked up to the dome to remove air from the chamber. Unfortunately, despite some early excitement about the device, the idea never takes off.

1962
Thalidomide is pulled off the Canadian market in April, a year to the month after first being approved for use in Canada.

1963

In the latest edition of his book *Expectant Motherhood,* Nicholson J. Eastman, MD, advises pregnant women to limit themselves to 10 cigarettes per day. "It seems clear that the newborn of mothers who smoke tend to weigh slightly less than those of mothers who do not smoke. But whether this lower birth weight indicates an injurious effect has not been established."

1964

Christina Newman describes the "monstrosities" of maternity fashion to the readers of *Maclean's* magazine. "What this country needs is a good twenty-five-dollar maternity dress," she declares.

1965

A blackout in eastern North America on November 9, 1965, results in a huge jump in the birth rate nine months later. The blackout later inspires the 1968 Hollywood comedy *Where Were You When the Lights Went Out?* starring Doris Day.

1966

The *Financial Post* reports that Canada's population is made up of a larger proportion of children than any other Western nation: 34 percent of Canadians as opposed to just over 20 percent of Americans are 15 years of age or younger.

1967

Maclean's reveals that fathers are welcome in the delivery room at one Canadian hospital, St. Joseph's in Hamilton, Ontario. Not all obstetricians are enthusiastic about having fathers present at the birth, however: "It's true the husband is present at the laying of the keel, but I'm damned if I think he has any right to a place at the launching," declares one Montreal obstetrician.

1970

The Canadian Mother and Child advises expectant mothers to check with their doctors to see if they will be conscious for the delivery: "Some mothers wish to be conscious when the baby is born while others prefer to have an anesthetic. Whether or not an anesthetic is necessary and what kind of anesthetic [is used] are things your doctor will decide. Your safety and that of your baby are his responsibility. You should discuss this matter with him ahead of time so you will know what to expect."

1972

Chatelaine reports on the growing home-birth trend.

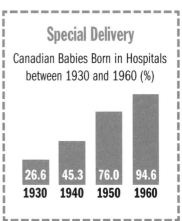

Special Delivery

Canadian Babies Born in Hospitals between 1930 and 1960 (%)

| 26.6 | 45.3 | 76.0 | 94.6 |
| 1930 | 1940 | 1950 | 1960 |

1974

Paul Anka's hit single, "You're Having My Baby" enrages US feminists so much that the National Organization for Women (NOW) awards the Canadian singer/songwriter its annual "Keep Her In Her Place Award," claiming that the song glamorizes unplanned pregnancy.

1977

Warner-Lambert introduces the world's first home pregnancy test.

1978

The world's first test-tube baby, Louise Brown, is born in Britain.

Ultrasound technology provides a welcome alternative to x-rays.

1980

Homemaker's Magazine informs its readers that fathers-to-be who participate in prenatal classes and play a role in their wives' pregnancies are less likely to be subject to "womb envy" than other expectant fathers.

1982

Researcher Ronald Melzack of McGill University warns *Chatelaine* readers that natural childbirth advocates who promise "painless" childbirth may be whitewashing the truth a little.

1983

Statistics Canada reports a big increase in the number of women giving birth after age 30. There are 88,043 births to women over 30 this year as compared to 65,698 a decade earlier.

1992

Equinox publishes an article on the role that doulas (professional labour support assistants) can play in providing support to labouring women. It's the first Canadian article about doula care to appear in the mainstream media.

1993

Childbirth classes are now a pregnancy rite-of-passage for 60 percent of Canadian women.

1997

The fertility rate drops to the lowest level in Canadian history—1.6 children per woman.

1998

America's Health Network—a cable TV channel—carries what is hailed as "the first Internet birth." The four-hour broadcast culminates with the birth of a 7 1/2-pound baby boy.

The birth control pill is advertised on television for the very first time.

No Sex Please, We're Pregnant

Pity the poor Canuck Chick of a century ago who found herself thinking lustful thoughts while she was "in the family way." The experts of the day made it painfully clear that sex was to be avoided during pregnancy: "Incalculable benefits would be derived if married people imitated the lessons of lower animals in this matter—thereby conserving all forces for the benefit of offspring," wrote Alice B. Stockham, MD, in the 1893 edition of her book *Tokology*.

Sex during pregnancy was linked to all sorts of evils, including morning sickness—a point that B.G. Jefferis, MD, and J.L. Nichols made rather emphatically in the 1893 edition of their book *Safe Counsel or Practical Eugenics*: "Morning sickness . . . is the result of an irritation in the womb, caused by some derangement, and it is greatly irritated by the habit of indulging in sexual gratification during pregnancy. If people would imitate the lower animals and reserve the vital forces of the mother for the benefit of her unborn child, it would be a great boon to humanity."

And, as if morning sickness weren't enough to dampen a woman's ardour, the certain knowledge that she was sentencing herself to an extra painful delivery by virtue of her wantonness might do the trick. "During pregnancy intercourse should never, or at least rarely, be indulged in," wrote Anna M. Galbraith, MD, in her 1915 book *The Four Epochs of a Woman's Life: A Study in Hygiene*. "At this time the mother needs to conserve all her strength and energies for herself and child; and any sexual relations during this time increase the sufferings of the mother and impair the vitality of the child. It has even been suggested that much of the pain during partition [childbirth] would be avoided by entire continence during pregnancy."

Clearly not someone who was afraid of raining on anyone's parade, Galbraith had some additional words of warning for any woman who was looking forward to a little post-delivery romance: "A woman should never be subjected to coitus until three months after delivery. During lactation intercourse should never, or at least very rarely, be indulged in; as the function of lactation makes a heavy drain on the strength of the mother, and anything which would further weaken her would tend to impoverish the quality of the milk and thus the child would suffer." (Who knows? Perhaps this ban on sex during breastfeeding helps to explain the popularity of the wet nurse!)

It wasn't until the eve of the Great Depression that Canadian women finally got the official go-ahead to make love during pregnancy. Here's what Canadian physician Harold Atlee had to say as he lowered the checkered flag: "We have now given up on the preposterous belief that two healthy and loving young people will sleep for weeks in the same bed without moving toward the middle. There seems no clear evidence that this does any harm, but a considerable amount that its deprivation does no good, since not all sex-starved husbands are content to lower their libido by merely taking cold baths." (Naturally, Dr. Atlee forgot to consider the effect of prolonged sexual abstinence on all the sex-starved pregnant women! Typical . . .)

CHAPTER 3

What's Up, Doc?

"This little organ seems to embody the most delicate sensibilities, and affords a nucleus from which, owing to the intimate nervous connection with the rest of the sexual system, and with the latter, the general system, nervous shocks can be produced by its titillation which must prove very detrimental to [a woman's] well-being. Like a pole to a battery where the electrical energies are concentrated and given off with such damaging force, this point affords an exit to the combined nervous energies, leaving the human battery just so much weaker thereby."

– Dr. E.C. Abbey, describing the clitoris in his 1882 book *The Sexual System and Its Derangements*

Dr. Abbey wasn't the first guy in history to be positively awestruck by the sexual power of the human female. Nor did he prove to be the last. Venus envy has, after all, been a fairly common phenomenon over the years. But what Abbey and other physicians of his day didn't seem to understand was that it was possible for a rendezvous behind the proverbial woodshed to top up rather than drain a woman's sexual batteries. (Clearly, the North American medical establishment had not yet clued into the fact that Mother Nature had designed the clitoris to function as the world's first rechargeable battery!)

But, to be fair, you'll have to excuse Abbey for his rather limited knowledge of the workings of the female anatomy. He was, after all, practising medicine at a time when the female body was positively shrouded in mystery. Not only did the medical textbooks of the day focus almost exclusively on the male anatomy, viewing the female body as an aberration by virtue of the fact that it was not male: medical students were repeatedly warned of the damage that could be done to their own reputations as well as the reputations of their patients if they failed to respect their patients' modesty and actually took a peek at their patients' genitals while they were conducting gynecological exams. (It kind of makes you wonder what Abbey and his contemporaries would have thought of the modern-day full-stirrup gyno exam now, doesn't it?)

In this chapter, we're going to be talking about changing ideas on women's health. We're going to start out by looking at the history of gynecological health in Canada, zeroing in on noteworthy inventions and eavesdropping on some of the outlandish advice that was dished out to past generations of Canuck Chicks. Then we're going to discuss a subject that was only whispered about by "good girls" in generations past: s-e-x.

And Now for My Next Trick . . . Delivering a Baby Blindfolded!

Here's a bit of medical magic that could have put even Harry Houdini to shame. Most nineteenth-century doctors mastered the art of performing gynecological examinations on fully clothed patients.

More often than not, these examinations were done with the patient standing in an upright position. The doctor simply slipped his hand up the woman's skirt, taking pains to turn his head the other way during the examination so as to avoid making eye contact or doing anything else that might offend her tender sensibilities.

Of course, using a speculum was pretty much out of the question. While this particular gynecological instrument had been available to physicians since the start of the century (it was invented in France in 1801), the American Medical Association had been advising against its use since 1851, noting both the embarrassment that a vaginal examination might cause to the woman and the "hazard" it might cause to the doctor's reputation and status.

There was also considerable debate about whether it was appropriate for the attending physician to see a woman's genitals while she was giving birth—or whether it would be best for all concerned if he draped the patient in order to safeguard her modesty and then simply reached under the sheet to assist in the delivery as the baby's head started to crown.

Tampon Nation

It's no wonder they called it "the curse." Getting your period was no fun at all before the advent of modern-day sanitary protection. (Forget the television set and the personal computer: I would argue that the two most noteworthy inventions of the 20th century were the tampon and the disposable adhesive pad!) So grab your party hat and noisemakers: it's time to celebrate these and other noteworthy milestones in the history of women's gynecological health.

1896

Johnson and Johnson introduces the world's first disposable sanitary pad, but the product proves to be a total flop. The reason? No one feels comfortable talking about it, let alone marketing it. It's not until after nurses in World War I start using cellulose surgical dressings as menstrual pads that commercially manufactured disposable sanitary pads start to gain public acceptance.

1921

Kimberly-Clark introduces Kotex, the world's first commercially successful disposable sanitary pad. Kotex comes dangerously close to flopping, too, but then retailers discover the secret to selling the product to ultra-shy consumers: making sanitary pads a self-serve product. Sales really take off when women are given an alternative to dealing with a sales clerk: grabbing a box of pads, depositing money in a box designated for the purpose, and then exiting stage left.

1926

B.G. Jefferis and J.L. Nichols—authors of the best-selling book *Safe Counsel or Practical Eugenics*—remind their readers that douching is just as important as taking a bath and that douching is thought to cure "barrenness or other diseases of the womb."

1929

Advertisements for disposable sanitary pads stress the freedom that these exciting new products offer to women: The modern girl "will not tolerate the drudgeries that held her mother in bondage" declares an advertisement for Modess sanity pads in *Saturday Night* magazine.

1930

A Kotex advertisement encourages *Chatelaine* readers to send away for three free samples of Kotex—a product that is designed to be used during those unmentionable times of "hygienic distress." (It'll be years before the word "menstruation" appears in any such ad, so Canuck Chicks quickly learn to read between the lines.) The company promises that the pads and an accompanying book, *Personal Hygiene,* will be shipped in a plain envelope, thereby eliminating the need to hide from your mailman as he goes about his route.

Ads for Lysol proudly declare that it's not just possible to use Lysol to clean your toilet: you can also use it as an antiseptic douche. Apparently, Canadian women appreciate the product's rather remarkable versatility: Lysol becomes the leading feminine hygiene product on the market—a distinction it holds until into the 1960s.

1931

The first tampon hits the market sans applicator. Five years later, an American businesswoman purchases the rights to an applicator tampon called the Tampax tampon from an American doctor for $32,000 US. Tampax sales are initially sluggish, both because pharmacists are too embarrassed to stock the product and because churchmen denounce the product on moral grounds—something that leads a generation or two of Canadian women to secretly worry that they may have unwittingly lost their virginity to a tampon! This particular worry is so widespread that tampon manufacturers go to great lengths to set the record straight: time and time again they patiently remind Canadian women that there's only one way to lose your virginity, and it has nothing to do with your choice of sanitary protection.

> "Never would I put such a strange article inside a woman. Don't discuss this with anyone because some damn fool will want to put it on the market and you'll be in trouble!"
> – Kimberly-Clark medical consultant Dr. George H. Williamson's reaction when his son showed him an early prototype for a tampon that he had developed: a condom punctured with holes and filled with the same highly absorbent material used in disposable sanitary pads

1932

Kotex runs ads for the new Phantom Kotex—a product that is "designed to fit so perfectly it leaves no telltale lines or wrinkles under the thinnest, the smoothest-fitting frocks." Canadian women sleep better at night knowing that they no longer have to deal with "the haunting dread" of telltale outlines that positively scream to the world, "I'm on my period!"

1935

Kotex distributes a booklet entitled *Marjorie May's Twelfth Birthday* that is designed to explain the mysteries of menstruation to young girls. (A quick plot summary: Marjorie May's mother gives her the gift that every 12-year-old girl longs for on her birthday: a heavy-duty mother-daughter talk about the mechanics of menstruation and the many related joys of womanhood. Lucky, lucky girl.)

1937

In her book *The Intimate Side of a Woman's Life,* Leona W. Chalmers informs North American women of the important role that douching can play in keeping a couple out of divorce court: "An internal bath, or douche . . . should be included in the woman's cleansing habits, not only as a prophylactic measure against possible infection, but it should be used after the menstrual period, and most certainly should follow the intimacies and responsibilities of marriage. Why do so many women fail to realize this? . . . Failure to obey the natural laws of cleanliness is probably one of the principal reasons for so many marriages going on the rocks." Chalmers then goes on to warn of the dangers of leaving one's most prized treasure—one's "irrigation apparatus"—unguarded: "Let no one touch it, and keep it under lock and key when not in use. This may save a lot of heartaches."

1944

Kotex runs a series of advertisements encouraging women to buy Quest—the Kotex deodorant powder. "Smart girls choose Quest," an advertisement in the *Star Weekly* declares. "They know that a powder deodorant is best for sanitary pads, because it has no moisture resistant base . . . doesn't retard absorption. And Quest was especially created just for this purpose. It's soft . . . soothing . . . safe . . . and it destroys odors completely. You can be sure with Quest."

1961

The country's two biggest mail-order catalogues are positively bursting with all things gynecological. The Simpsons-Sears catalogue features hot-water bottles that double as douche bags and a "feminine syringe set" that comes complete with hexachlorophene douche solution to "subdue bacterial odor." The Eaton's of Canada catalogue also delivers the goods, gynecologically speaking. It features a Cyklo-test thermometer "to help determine ovulation days," liquid Lysol to douche with, three brands of vaginal suppositories, and three brands of sanitary belts to hold your sanitary napkins in place.

1970

Belted sanitary pads begin to go the way of the do-do bird as adhesive pads find their way into the marketplace. Canuck Chicks rejoice: it's no longer necessary to spend a week a month with a hammock slung inside your underwear!

1971

Sales of feminine hygiene sprays reach $68 million. Sales will nosedive the following year, however, when hexachlorophene—a key ingredient in most sprays—is found to be toxic.

1976

Douche sales skyrocket when manufacturers replace flavoured douches (ranging from champagne to strawberry) with a new generation of "fresh" scents. At the same time, they launch advertising campaigns designed to make women feel less than clean if they don't douche on a regular basis. Their key message? A little douche will do ya!

"Feminine hygiene is an important part of every woman's daily grooming routine. Just as you apply deodorant each morning before dressing, so should you spray a light mist of feminine deodorant spray to your vaginal area . . . F.D.S. (feminine deodorant spray) was designed with the purpose of neutralizing and absorbing these embarrassing odors."
- *On the Go: A Beauty Guide for the Active Woman*, published in 1982 by Alberto-Culver Canada Inc.

1980

Tampons are linked to toxic shock syndrome.

1982

Ontario premier Frank Miller decides to take his life into his hands by extending provincial sales tax to feminine hygiene products for the first time in the province's history. The outcry is so strong and so immediate that Miller is forced to overturn the tax. ("By what possible stretch of his mean, male-minded imagination could [the premier] impose a tax on tampons and sanitary napkins—which is a direct tax to the women of this province?" outraged Liberal MPP Sheila Copps asks on the floor of the legislature.)

1991

Canadian women are similarly outraged when the federal government decides to apply the newly introduced goods and services tax to feminine hygiene products, but this time the tax sticks.

1992

The tampon briefly emerges as a romantic object and the public's respect for the monarchy hits an all-time low when a cellphone call between Prince Charles and his mistress Camilla Parker Bowles is intercepted and he is heard expressing his wish that he could be reincarnated as a tampon. ("Never mind the old chestnut of how difficult it is supposed to be to imagine the Queen on the lavatory," writes Polly Sampson in the London *Sunday Times*. "It's picturing the King as a tampon that I find perplexing.")

1994

It's still open season on Prince Charles. This time, his infamous cellphone conversation with his mistress is being reenacted nightly in a Manhattan theatre production called *Loose Lips*.

1995

Feminine hygiene product manufacturers are now offering so many different types of maxipads, minipads, panty liners, and tampons that hunting down your favourite brand and type starts to feel a bit like a Girl Guide scavenger hunt. After decades of having almost no choice, suddenly there's too much choice.

1999

Minipads designed to be worn with thongs make their debut.

2002

Black panty liners take their place alongside white panty liners on the drug-store shelves.

Ontario MPP Marilyn Churley calls upon the federal government to get rid of the GST on feminine hygiene products, noting that an average woman will ring up approximately $350 in GST charges over the course of her reproductive years: "It's an unfair tax and its discriminatory. It taxes a bodily function that is central to womanhood and family life." Churley takes a bit of heat from Gwen Landolt, vice-president of REAL Women of Canada—an anti-feminist lobby group. Landolt complains that the feminists are expecting the federal government to act as "their sugar daddies" by picking up the tax on feminine hygiene products. After all, she argues, aren't men expected to pick up the tab for the GST on their shaving cream?

Doctor's Orders

Some of the medical advice we've received about our gynecological health over the years is every bit as creepy as Canadian filmmaker David Cronenberg's gynecological flick *Dead Ringers*. Here's the lowdown on some of the zaniest advice we Canuck Chicks have received over the past century or two.

1880
Physician-induced orgasm is considered to be a valid treatment for hysteria because the condition is believed to be triggered by sexual deprivation. The symptoms of this dreaded condition include genital swelling, "excessive" vaginal lubrication, and a tendency to indulge in sexual fantasies. Some doctors find themselves devoting more than three-quarters of their practice to treating this particular "disorder." Because it can take up to an hour for certain patients to reach orgasm—time that many busy physicians decide they simply don't have—doctors begin to experiment with "clitoral stimulators" that are fuelled by pressured water, steam, and other devices in an effort to free up their hands. Eventually, a desperate physician invents the vibrator so that women can "treat" themselves at home, and, by 1900, more than a dozen manufacturers are producing various electric or battery-powered vibrators. The era of the self-serve vibrator has arrived.

1882
Physicians pin much of the blame for nymphomania on monomania—an addiction to masturbation. They view excessive masturbation as the first step on the slippery slope that will inevitably lead to sexual degeneracy and even death. In his book *The Sexual System and Its Derangements,* Dr. E.C. Abbey warns of the horrors that await a woman who allows herself to become addicted to

sex: "deafness, noises in the ears, impairment of the mental faculties, headache, dizziness, blindness, husky voice, constant desire to clear the throat, emaciation, timidity, fits, and a general destruction of the mental, moral and physical faculties." It's enough to scare you off sex for life. (Hey, maybe that's the point?!!)

A Victorian Horror Story

While modern-day Canuck Chicks may get a little freaked out if their period is delayed, they can barely even imagine the panic that their great-great-grandmothers experienced when faced with a similar fate. Women were warned that a missed period could lead to "hemorrhage from the nose, lungs, or stomach . . . and often from the nipples, mouth, eyes and rectum." Our favourite doomsayer, Dr. Abbey, had this to say on the subject: "No more dangerous condition can the woman be placed in than that of suppressed menses, for unless restored, death, sooner or later, is the result."

Desperate times called for desperate measures, and—for a time—it was commonplace to treat an absence of menstruation by placing leeches directly on a woman's cervix to induce bleeding. And if that isn't a bad enough mental image to conjure up, consider this: sometimes a leech would find its way into the woman's uterus. (I don't know about you, but I think this has the makings of a *really* freaky David Cronenberg flick.)

Fortunately, by the early 20th century, this particular method of treatment had gone out of vogue and the new generation of health experts was doing its best to reassure women that it was no longer necessary to hit the panic button if your period happened to be late: "Our grandmothers taught that the absence of the menses was always greatly to be feared, the prevailing idea being that serious results would follow to some vital organ," wrote Alice B. Stockham, MD, in the 1916 edition of her book *Tokology*. "This is a mistake."

1915

Menstruation is still being treated as illness. In her book *The Four Epochs of a Woman's Life: A Study in Hygiene,* Anna M. Galbraith, MD, warns about the dangers a woman faces if she has the misfortune of being caught in a rainstorm during her menstrual period: "If the woman has been so unfortunate as to be caught out in a heavy rain so that her clothes have been wet through or if in the cold weather she should come into the house thoroughly chilled, the best thing to do is to take off her wet things as quickly as possible, be well rubbed down with hot, rough towels, drink a cup of hot tea, go to bed at once, and place a hot-water bag over the abdomen. She should remain in bed until the next morning. . . . If this exposure should have caused the cessation of the flow, a hot mustard foot-bath should be taken."

1916

Alice B. Stockham, MD, recommends a mind-over-matter approach to any woman who is troubled by menopausal symptoms. Rather than spending your time "bewailing [your] real and imaginary woes," you should "plant your foot down with emphasis and say . . . 'Get thee behind me, Satan . . . I will not be your slave, you cannot dominate my life and chain my energies.'" (Clearly, Stockham believes that there's a lot more to menopause than just raging hormones!)

1926

B.G. Jefferis and J.L. Nichols, authors of *Safe Counsel or Practical Eugenics,* advise menstruating women to avoid everything from cold baths to overexertion to "athletics of any kind." The two spoilsports also warn of the dangers of masturbation, noting that it is at the root of "almost every disease and symptom of disease known to the human race," including vision problems, epilepsy, and insanity. Of course, if male readers are looking for any guidance on what they shouldn't be touching, they're going to find such knowledge sadly lacking: the illustration of the male reproductive system has been carefully cropped to avoid including anything as indelicate as a penis. (Wouldn't Loretta Bobbitt have been proud?)

1958

Five years after British physician Katharina Dalton coins the term "premenstrual syndrome" to describe the physical and emotional complaints that many women experience in the days leading up to their period, *The Canadian Medical Association Journal* states that women who complain of premenstrual symptoms are guilty of denying their femininity and envying men.

1981

Two-thirds of respondents to a survey on attitudes towards menstruation believe that menstruation is an unsuitable topic for social gatherings or at the office, and one-quarter believe it is an unacceptable topic even at home.

Our Mirrors, Our Selves

In 1969, The Boston Women's Health Collective publishes the first edition of *Our Bodies, Our Selves*—the gynecological health instruction book that Mother Nature forgot to include. Suddenly North American women find a new use for their makeup compacts: the do-it-yourself gynecological exam!

Your Top Five Victorian Sex Questions Answered!

No respectable newspaper or magazine would have even *considered* carrying a sex column during the late 19th or early 20th centuries. After all, if it was highly improper to even think the word "sex" to yourself, it would have been nothing short of scandalous to air your dirty lingerie in public. But assuming there *had* been a Dr. Ruth around the turn of the century, here are a sampling of the types of questions she might have been asked to answer and her likely replies.

Q: *I have thirteen children at home and am not sure if I want any more. I tried telling my husband that the nightly romps in the hay were going to have to stop, but, naturally, he's eager to exercise his conjugal rights. My best friend tells me that I can reduce my changes of becoming pregnant if I drink mercury, swallow carrot seeds, ingest diluted copper ore, mix myself a beaver testicle cocktail, and/or find a spot where a wolf has urinated and circle the spot three times. Is there any truth to what my friend is telling me?*

A: A century ago, your friend would have been considered to be a very wise woman indeed. In fact, she probably would have been writing this column! But the times have changed and we now know that these birth control methods are somewhat ineffective. It's a shame that your husband fails to understand that intercourse is intended for reproductive purposes only. As one of my most trusted reference books (the 1896 edition of *The Ladies Book of Useful Information*) notes, "Husband and wife . . . are to live in marriage chastity, not in lust and uncleanness." I suggest that you show him this column.

Q: *My husband tells me that he read somewhere that the withdrawal method of birth control can be physically injurious to both the husband and the wife. I bet him a fresh, home-baked apple pie that he's wrong. So what do you think, Dr. Ruth? Should I pick up some apples on my way home?*

A: You should definitely plan to swing by the orchard. And I must tell you you're going to be eating more than just apple pie, dearie. You're going to be eating a rather hefty serving of humble pie.

Your husband is quite wise to point out the awful dangers associated with the so-called withdrawal method of birth control. As Anna M. Galbraith, MD, notes in the 1915 edition of her book, *The Four Epochs of a Woman's Life: A Study in Hygiene*, "Perhaps the most frequent method used to prevent conception is withdrawal before the ejaculation of semen. While this is most injurious to the husband—debility, nervous prostration, and even paralysis are said to ensue—the health of the wife also suffers. . . . The generative organs become engorged with blood, but are not permitted to enjoy relaxation consequent upon the full completion of the act. . . . The nerves become shattered, and the woman will be fortunate if she contracts no serious womb trouble."

So the next time you decide to engage in a little bit of betting, you might want to ensure that you have your facts straight. Hope your husband enjoys the pie!

Q: *A really attractive woman has moved into the farm next to ours. Suddenly, my husband has taken to venturing over there every couple of hours to offer to lend her some sort of tool. Should I be concerned?*

A: You don't mention in your letter whether you make a point of dressing nicely and paying attention to your personal hygiene. If you don't, your marriage could be on the rocks. If you do, your marriage is likely on solid ground. As my trusted reference book, the 1896 edition of *The Ladies Book of Useful Information,* notes, "These attractions [cleanliness and dressing nicely] will act like a magnet upon your husband. Never fear that there will be any influence strong enough to take him from your side." My advice to you? Instead of paying so much attention to what your husband is doing, start paying a little more attention to what you see in the mirror!

Q: *I spend a lot of time riding horses. I'm concerned that I may no longer be, well, you know, intact. What man would want to marry a woman who no longer appears to be a virgin?*

A: As long as you're still a virgin in thought, word, and deed, you needn't worry about the physical effects of all that horseback riding. As physician Hannah M. Thompson once noted, it's time we ladies got over all this silliness about the hymen: "If the hymen was intended as a guarantee of moral character, and for moral protection . . . would we not have some reason for reflecting on the wisdom and righteousness of a Creator who has failed to make equal provision, and to give a like guarantee of an uncorrupted manhood?" So until the menfolk can give us some sort of guarantee of purity, I would advise that you put this particular concern out of your pretty little head.

By the way, don't feel silly about being a little vague on the whole concept of virginity. If you follow the news much, you'll know that Marie Carmichael Stopes—a British academic with no fewer than two PhDs to her name (one in science and one in philosophy)—was so unclear about what sex was all about that it took her six months to figure out that her marriage had not yet been consummated. She went on to write a book, *Married Love* (1918), to prevent other women from making the same mistake. If it could happen to Marie, it could happen to you . . .

Q: *My grandmother keeps telling me stories about going bundling with young men. I'm not sure what she's talking about and I don't feel that it's my place to ask. Can you give me the inside scoop?*

A: The term "bundling" was used to describe a common courting ritual enjoyed by Confederation-era couples. Basically, couples who were courting would climb into bed with their clothing on and enjoy a bit of a cuddle. Now lest you think that there was a lot of monkey business going on between your grandmother and your grandfather in days gone by, allow me to set the record straight. There was a board placed down the centre of the bed to prevent things from getting too hot and heavy. So unless your grandfather was eager to get splinters and/or a concussion, your grandmother's virtue was safe. Hope that helps to answer your question.

Sex Canadian-style: 100 Years of Being Hot and Bothered

Wondering what was going on between the sheets from one decade to the next? Here are some of the ups and downs in the history of sex.

1882
It becomes illegal to sell or advertise birth control in Canada. Suddenly, the birth control options that have been available up until now—douching or using such contraceptive devices as medicated sponges, condoms made from animal intestines, and/or "womb veils" (diaphragms) made of rubber or cotton—are driven underground. For the most part, Canadian couples who want to avoid pregnancy have to rely on the most troublesome method of all: abstinence!

Clock. National Archives of Canada PA-179922

1905

A German doctor named Sigmund Freud publishes *Three Essays on the Theory of Sexuality*—a controversial book which suggests that there are two types of female orgasm: the immature clitoral orgasm and the more mature vaginal orgasm. Canuck Chicks find themselves faced with an unspeakably difficult choice: chase after the elusive vaginal orgasm or admit their immaturity by settling for the less prestigious clitoral orgasm.

1926

Readers of *Safe Counsel*—the best-selling "marriage manual" of the day—are warned that you *can* get too much of a good thing: "Sexual excess weakens the vitality, lessens the resistance, and paves the way for many dread diseases," authors B.G. Jefferis and J.L. Nichols caution.

1928

British writer Radclyffe Hall writes *The Well of Loneliness*—a "scandalous" lesbian novel that is subsequently banned under article 1201 of the Customs Tariff. (Hey, the authorities can't start allowing *that sort of stuff* to make its way across the border, now can they?)

1930

Scientists discover to their amazement that ovulation occurs in the middle of the menstrual cycle, not during menstruation, as had previously been believed—a landmark discovery that helps to even the playing field for couples who are hoping to avoid pregnancy by avoiding intercourse at a woman's most fertile times. A little bit of knowledge can, after all, take you a long way.

1932

Canada's first birth control clinic opens its doors in Hamilton, Ontario.

1938

Chatelaine writer Lorna Slocombe offers the magazine's readers some tips on seduction, Canadian-style: "Every date have something new as a surprise for him. . . . Curl your eyelashes, wear your sweater backwards—anything!" She then notes that it's also important to come up with a list of questions to prevent the conversation from grinding to a halt: "Do you like Greta Garbo?" . . . "Were you ever in an automobile accident?" . . . "Do you really enjoy cutting up frogs?". . ."Tell me, what are you planning to do after you graduate?" If all else fails, Slocombe suggests that would-be seductresses whip up a batch of scrambled eggs for their dates: "It's a grand opportunity for you to radiate domesticity and charm . . . with a becoming apron tied on your evening dress—that Myrna Loy combination of glamor and comradeship."

1942

An advertisement for Ivory Soap lets men in on an exciting secret: guys who use soap are rewarded with more action in the bedroom.

1946

Girls who are willing to go "all the way" with their dates find themselves stuck with the less-than-desirable label of "psychologically maladjusted juvenile delinquent." It's enough to make them nostalgic for the days when they would simply have been known as "bad girls."

Maclean's Magazine reports that the average girl is "engaged about twice before she is finally sure of her mate" and that petting has become the norm for courting couples: 9 out of 10 people engage in petting before marriage today as opposed to just 6 out of 10 back in 1909. The magazine stresses, however, that the explosion in the amount of petting cannot necessarily be blamed on the even more common practice of necking: "Necking is no more the cause of petting than an automobile is the cause of wrecks," the magazine insists. "It is not the car that makes the wreck, it is the driver."

1950

Condoms are now available in Canadian drugstores, but they're kept in drawers under the counter. If you want them, you have to ask for them. And since it's illegal to sell condoms for contraceptive purposes, you have to fudge your reason for needing them. Fortunately, the product label states explicitly that they are to be "sold in drugstores only for the prevention of contagious diseases"— a wonderfully convenient built-in excuse!

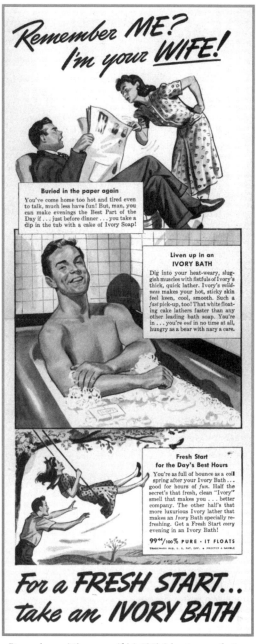

Remember me? I'm your wife! A 1942 Advertisement for Ivory Soap. The Procter and Gamble Company. Used by permission

1951

A group of scientists led by Stanford University chemist Carl Djerassi extracts norethindrone from Mexican yams—the first step towards creating a pill to manage infertility and menstrual disorders. Over time, they discover that norethindrone combined with another similar steroid can prevent ovulation, creating a revolutionary new form of birth control—the Pill.

1953

Alfred C. Kinsey writes a landmark report on female sexuality that leaves North American men feeling hot and bothered. The book sends shockwaves through North American society by revealing high rates of sex outside marriage and low rates of frigidity, by documenting the speed at which women can reach orgasm, and by providing iron-clad evidence of the clitoral orgasm. Kinsey also delivers another shocking revelation: while fully one-third of women born before 1900 routinely make love with their clothes on, only 8 percent of younger women are similarly modest. Clearly, the world is going to hell in a hand basket—assuming, of course, it hasn't arrived already. Kinsey pays a considerable price for his frank talk on sex: he loses funding from the Rockefeller Foundation for his research and is accused by the US Congress of aiding Communism by trying to undermine traditional American morals. (Of course, this puts him in rather good company. It seems that half of Americans are in hot water with Senator Joseph McCarthy and the House Committee on UnAmerican Activities for one reason or another.)

The first issue of *Playboy* hits the newsstands. It features a full-colour nude photo of sex goddess Marilyn Monroe.

The latest edition of Roy Dickerson's best-selling US sex education guide *So Youth May Know* makes a clear distinction between the good girls and the bad girls: "The first woman a man thinks of for a petting party is not often the first one he thinks of for a wife. She may be all right for his good times, but ordinarily he does not want secondhand goods or a woman who has been freely pawed over for a sweetheart, wife, and mother of his children."

1956

Dr. Marion Hilliard, chief of obstetrics and gynecology at Women's College Hospital, makes a case for the fake orgasm in her book *A Woman Doctor Looks at Love and Life:* "A man can feel kinship with the gods if his woman can make him believe he can cause a flowering within her. If she doesn't feel it, she must bend every effort to pretense. . . . Thousands of women who have begun this sort of benign sham have discovered that their pretended delight rapidly became real." Just don't hold out for *le petit mort* each and every time, Hilliard advises, noting that no two orgasms are alike: "A sneeze is an orgasm of the nose. . . . Some sneezes are kitten-soft and others can be heard for two blocks."

Millions of Canuck Chicks park themselves in front of the tube to catch US rock 'n roll star Elvis Presley's much-talked-about appearance on *The Ed Sullivan Show*. If the Canuck Chicks in question were hoping for any sort of X-rated performance, however, they end up being sorely disappointed. Presley is considered to be such a threat to the moral well-being of North American youth that the cameraman is ordered to shoot him from the waist up only: his pelvic gyrations are thought to be too hot for even a late-night TV audience.

1959

Sidney Katz informs *Maclean's Magazine* readers of a recent news poll indicating that 82 percent of parents are opposed to having their daughters going steady. These parents have a powerful ally in their court—the Roman Catholic Church. Going steady "places too much strain on the moral fibre of the individual," notes one church spokesman.

1960

The Margaret Sanger Research Bureau interviews 9,000 American women and concludes that one in four women is "sexually anesthetized"—in other words, she takes no pleasure in sex.

The world's first truly effective birth control method—the Enovid-10 birth control pill—hits the market, ushering in the start of the sexual revolution. One year later, the Canadian government approves it for sale in Canada. It is later discovered that Enovid-10 contains 10 times as much estrogen as what is needed for contraceptive purposes, leading *Toronto Star* writer Robin Harvey to com-

Birth control pills
(*Maclean's*/Christina Strong). Canadian Press

ment that using early formulations of the pill was "like using a fire extinguisher to put out a candle."

A Montreal bookseller is convicted of peddling obscene material when he is caught selling copies of D.H. Lawrence's critically acclaimed novel *Lady Chatterly's Lover.*

1961

The Eaton's of Canada spring and summer catalogue isn't just selling pastel housedresses: it's also selling sex. The catalogue features six different vibrators, including the rather intriguing Douglas massage unit that promises to "help circulation in scalp, muscular sore spots, *etc.*"

The Canadian Woman: A Manual of Personal Hygiene warns brides- and grooms-to-be to keep their expectations low when it comes to their wedding night. "Satisfactory sexual relations on a wedding night may be more the exception than the rule. Newlyweds who try to force themselves on this point may create nothing but a fiasco of the whole affair, and begin their marriage with resentment toward each other and disgust with themselves."

1962

Montreal city council overturns a 1929 bylaw that makes it illegal to display in a public place any photographs or drawings depicting nude or semi-nude female bodies. Over the years, Montreal merchants have been forced to remove or alter the covers of *Time* magazine (banned for featuring a small drawing of an African woman breastfeeding her baby), *Mademoiselle* (banned for featuring a model in a two-piece bathing suit), and *Popular Mechanics* (banned for featuring a motorboat containing a little girl in a two-piece bathing suit). To ensure that they stayed on the good side of city council, magazine distribution companies routinely assigned office clerks the task of blotting out any offending images with black felt pens.

1963

Pierre Berton scandalizes the readers of *Maclean's Magazine* by speaking out in favour of teenage sex. He complains about "the Great Twentieth Century Hoax, whereby every adolescent is taught that sex is the key to everything—but he can't enjoy it for another ten, fifteen or twenty years." Berton continues: "Having goaded the infants into a state of emotional and romantic frenzy, to which intercourse, rather than cold baths, must be the obvious release, we are going to have to accept teenage sex as matter-of-factly as we now accept the other facets of togetherness. . . . I would rather have them indulge in some good, honest, satisfying sex than be condemned to a decade of whimpering frustration brought on by the appalling North American practice called 'petting.'" The response from readers is fast and furious: "Who is Pierre Berton that you honor him by squandering a whole page on the trash he writes?" asks a reader in Stockholm, Saskatchewan. Another reader says simply, "I would like to offer my sincere sympathies to Mr. Berton's wife." Berton's column stops appearing in the magazine shortly thereafter.

The *Financial Post* reports that there's a new birth control pill in the works for men, and that this one seems to offer more promise than previous formulations: "This one does not have the undesirable side effect of an earlier pill which made a man's face go bright red when he took a drink of alcohol after he had taken the pill."

1965

Marion Hilliard, MD, warns *Chatelaine* readers of the hazards of kissing: "Not enough mothers warn their daughters that kissing is intended by nature to be an appetizer, not an entire meal." She also cautions these innocent damsels about the frightening power of the female reproductive system: "Femaleness . . . is savage. Woman is equipped with a reproductive system that, even if she never uses it, dominates her fibre. It has vicious power that can leap out of control without the slightest warning, while a man and a woman share a companionable chuckle or happen to touch hands."

Quebec City police chief Gerard Girard sends 50 patrolmen out to enforce a law that says that women aren't allowed to display their thighs in public. Women are given written warnings that tell them to "cover your thighs or risk a fine of $100 or three months in jail."

1966

Canada gets its first topless dancers at the Cat's Whisker bar in Vancouver.

1967

Maclean's Magazine writer Douglas Marshall describes the effect the birth control pill is having on Canadian society: "Today nearly a million women in Canada and more than eight million other women throughout the world are happily swallowing the pill and wondering how on earth their mothers, let alone their grandmothers, ever managed to lead reasonably normal lives without it. They are part of the first generation in history in which women have been given a real choice about when to marry and when to have children. The pill has freed them from the tyranny of pregnancy—the oldest, the most natural, and thus the harshest tyranny of all."

Children at creche. Glenbow Archives ND-3-6623

1968

The CBC refuses to air a Penman's men's underwear commercial on the grounds that "no treatment could make a men's underwear commercial acceptable at the present time." Barry Donnelly, assistant supervisor of the CBC's commercial acceptance department, explains the ruling to *Maclean's Magazine:* "We've opened up to the extent that we'll accept brassieres and foundation garments, but still no panties or men's underwear I'm afraid."

1969

Contraceptives become legal for use in Canada—and on Canada Day, no less! (Bet the fireworks were pretty spectacular that night.) Doctors no longer have to pretend that they're prescribing birth control pills to their patients to help regulate their cycles or manage cramping. It's *okay* to take the pill for contraceptive purposes.

Pierre Elliott Trudeau makes his famous statement about the state having no business in the bedrooms of the nation and ushers in legislative changes removing some of the restrictions against homosexual relationships between consenting adults.

1972

The *Financial Post* reports that there are now two franchised sex shop chains operating in Canada—The Garden in Montreal and Lovecraft in Toronto.

Alex Comfort's *The Joy of Sex* is one of the year's hottest best-sellers.

Toronto's CityTV airs the notorious *Baby Blue Movies*—a series of soft-porn flicks the likes of which the viewing public has never seen before.

1973

Chatelaine announces that it won't be following in the footsteps of *Cosmopolitan* magazine by publishing a nude male centrefold.

Born-again Christian Marabel Morgan redefines what it means to be a woman in her best-selling book *The Total Woman*: "It is only when a woman surrenders her life to her husband, reveres and worships him, and is willing to serve him, that she becomes really beautiful to him. She becomes a priceless jewel, the glory of femininity, his queen!" And lest a woman mistakenly assume that this surrendering business is in any way a bum deal, Morgan is quick to set the record straight: "A Total Woman is not a slave. She graciously chooses to adapt to her husband's way, even though at times she desperately may not want to. He in turn will gratefully respond by trying to make it up to her and grant her desires. He may even want to spoil her with goodies."

1974
The Dalkon Shield—an IUD—is pulled off the shelves after being linked to the deaths of 16 American women.

1975
June Callwood—one of the contributors to *The Chatelaine Guide to Marriage*—reports that there's a growing chill in the bedrooms of the nation: "A quarter to a half of all marriage beds in this country are cold, lonely places," she writes. Callwood then goes on to quote "an attractive, unusually free-living housewife in her early forties," who has this to say about the lack of sizzle in married sex: "Sex with your husband is comfortable, like house slippers. . . . For that sense of intense and delicious excitement that you once enjoyed when sex was new, you have to look outside the marriage." At this point, Callwood asks Dr. Stephen Neiger, a former psychologist at the Toronto Psychiatric Hospital, to weigh in with his two cents. He helpfully points out that female orgasms are a bonus rather than a right: "The female orgasm of any kind is far from a universal or natural trait, as some marriage manuals suggest," he insists.

1976
No longer satisfied with merely being a *Total Woman,* US sexevangelist Marabel Morgan writes *Total Joy,* a book that asserts a wife's right to clitoral stimulation.

Chatelaine tells its readers how to go about choosing a sex therapist.

1982
Flare magazine runs its first condom ad.

Homemaker's Magazine reports that pornographic videotapes are outselling non-pornographic videotapes three to one.

1983
Playgirl holds auditions for a "Men of Canada" calendar. The men who turn out

for the audition are disappointed to find out that the magazine is offering just $750 to male centrefolds—this at a time when *Playboy* Playmates are routinely walking away with $10,000. Finally, the Canadian male has a chance to experience the glass ceiling for himself!

1993
A Canadian sex toy manufacturer invents and registers a product called "The Tongue." More than one million units are sold around the world over the next eight years.

1994
Norplant makes its Canadian debut.

A study commissioned by the Confectionery Manufacturers Association of Canada reveals that 27 percent of women would prefer to have chocolate more often than sex as compared to just 8 percent of men.

Josey Vogel's sex column, "My Messy Bedroom," debuts in Montreal's *Hour Magazine*.

1995
The birth control pill is the contraceptive method of choice for 38.2 percent of Canadian women between the ages of 15 and 34—something that amounts to about $150 million in sales for Pill manufacturers each year.

1997
It's a banner year for birth control. Both Depo-Provera and the female condom make their Canadian debut.

1999
Health Canada approves the emergency contraceptive pill (sometimes called "the morning after pill").

A *Maclean's* survey finds that 53 percent of Newfoundlanders are satisfied with their sex lives as compared to just 44 percent of Canadians nationwide. Writer John DeMont comments that at least part of the credit for the spicier sex lives of Newfoundlanders can be attributed to simple geography, noting that it's a place where even the place-names—Dildo, Come By Chance, and Conception Bay—sound suggestive.

Chatelaine publishes an uncharacteristically frank article about sex toys. Writer Buffy Childerhose offers some reassuring words to Canadian women who are deathly afraid of death by vibrator: "Most battery-operated toys are no more dangerous than your Walkman. It's possible to electrocute yourself if you bathe with your plug-in, but the same is true of a hair dryer. So unless you're the type who thinks it's wise to use your electric shaver in the tub, it's unlikely that your buzzing distractions will power you into the great beyond."

Flare reports that the average Canadian woman has sex 70 times per year and an Angus Reid study reveals that sex in a public place is the number one sex fantasy for women.

2000
The birth control pill is advertised on television for the very first time.

2001
A survey by a Canadian condom manufacturer finds that 9 percent of men and 3 percent of women claim that eating chocolate is better than sex. Sadly, the researchers neglect to ask these chocolate devotees the obvious follow-up question: Would sex be a little more tolerable for you if you could enjoy it *while* eating chocolate? As a result of this single moment of inattention, the window slams shut on this rare opportunity to get to the heart of the crucial sex-chocolate link, thereby setting back this groundbreaking Canadian research by another few years at least. It's a tragedy of almost epic proportions.

CHAPTER 4

Fashion Femmes

You have to wonder if journalist Eric Nicol was going through a bit of a rough patch in his personal life when he decided to write an article questioning the sexiness of Canadian women. After all, it's one thing to pick a fight with your wife or girlfriend if you're feeling a little grumpy because your favourite hockey player just got traded: it's quite another to take on *seven million* Canuck Chicks at one time!

The article—which appeared in the February 1957 issue of *Chatelaine*—asked a rather pointed question: "Why Aren't Canadian Femmes More Fatales?" Nicol started out by describing the problem as he saw it: Canuck Chicks simply couldn't hold a candle to French *Mesdemoiselles* or Spanish *señoritas:* "The Canadian girl has the connotation of clean living, of outdoor activity," he complained. "We don't associate her with any pursuit that can't be made on skis. Any suggestion of sex appeal is buried under a snowdrift of wholesomeness."

The response to Nicol's article was understandably heated. Two gals from Hamilton, Ontario, were only too happy to jump to defend our collective honour, placing the blame for any cold front that happened to be passing through the bedrooms of the nation squarely at the feet of Nicol and other members of his sex: "The *Mesdemoiselles* sizzle for their French lovers, the *señoritas* simmer for their dashing *señors*. We fizzle for our Canadian men."

Oh, La La!

Writer and broadcaster Gordon Sinclair sang the praises of the women of Quebec in the February 15, 1950, issue of *Maclean's Magazine:* "The girls of Quebec do know how to be entertaining," he enthused. "Perhaps it's the shrugs, pouts, hand waves and other bits of showmanship that I enjoy. Perhaps the ever-changing angle of the hip, shoulder, or eyebrow. . . . Any Canadian male over the age of 12 can recall incidents in which 'She's French' has goaded his anticipation to a new high."

In this chapter, we're going to consider our ever-changing ideas about beauty, zeroing in on the many milestone moments we Canuck Chicks have experienced both on and off the fashion runway. Then, we'll wrap up the chapter by looking at the history of dieting—a subject that will give you plenty of food for thought and/or a bad case of indigestion. Bon appetit!

The Great Debate

Think the brains vs. beauty debate is a relatively recent phenomenon?
Think again.

This particular debate has been raging since pre-Confederation days. One of the first to weigh in with an opinion on the issue was pioneer chick extraordinaire Catharine Parr Traill. Here's what she had to say on the subject in her 1854 book *The Female Emigrant's Guide and Hints on Canadian Housekeeping:* "Every young woman is prized in this country according to her usefulness; and a thriving young settler will rather marry a clever, industrious girl, who has the reputation for being a good spinner and knitter, than one who has nothing but a pretty face to recommend her."

Three-quarters of a century later, journalist Marceline D'Alroy added her two cents to the debate in an article in the January 1930 issue of *The Chatelaine:* "To earn the title of being an 'interesting woman' is not easy, but it is worthwhile," she wrote. "To make one's self interesting means hard work. And to do it, three things are necessary: effort, brains, tact. Of course, one can be an 'attractive woman' with much less effort, a great deal less brains, plus the same amount of tact."

D'Alroy's article sparked a rather heated retort by Nan Robins, who penned an article entitled "I Would Rather Have Beauty Than Brains" for the February 1931 issue of *Chatelaine.* (The magazine had recently dropped its "The.") "Correct spelling will bring me in twenty-five dollars a week, perhaps, but a cute nose will give me a meal ticket to punch for the rest of my life," she declared.

More than a quarter century later, the debate was still growing strong. Journalist McKenzie Porter no doubt managed to ruffle more than a few feathers by making the case in the *Financial Post* that a beautiful wife was more likely to be a liability than an asset to her husband: "A beautiful woman combines an exquisite physical configuration with a sensitive nature and a vital mind. She stands out against an assembly of merely attractive women by virtue of a stunning silhouette, a manifest aesthetic sense, and eyes that are illuminated by the unmistakable effulgence of intellect. She prostrates almost every civilized man she meets. . . . Eventually, the husband may resent the compliments paid to his wife by other men. . . . This can result in a form of impotence that is limited to relations with his wife. Disaster is implicit in such a situation."

The final score in this round of the debate? Brains, 3; Beauty, 1!

Clothes Call

Wondering what the best-dressed Canuck Chicks were wearing in generations past? Let's take a peek inside the dressing rooms of the nation . . .

Bathing beauties, Muskoka.
National Archives of Canada NAC-PA 161586

"My sister-in-law assured me that I needn't be at all particular about my dress, but being a little desirous of displaying my Old Country finery and my own gentility, I dressed myself in silk and lace, thin shoes, and the finest thread stockings . . . Of course, going through dense woods and swamp I soiled my silk pelisse and dress, tore my fine lace veil and pelerine scrambling along wet logs, and fnally lost one of my shoes in a mudhole."

– Catharine Parr Traill, describing her first Canadian fashion faux pas in "Forest Gleanings" (a series of articles that appeared in *The Anglo-American Magazine* in 1952-53).

1890–1900

Corsets are *de rigueur* for any self-respecting woman. To do without is to be perceived as having "let yourself go." However, underneath those oh-so-prim corsets, many Victorian ladies have a rather shocking secret. According to Kate Mulvey and Melissa Richards, authors of *Decades of Beauty: The Changing Image of Women—1890s to 1990s,* "Tiny gold or jeweled rings were fixed on nipples . . . to improve the bustline, make it curvier, and produce a pleasant sensation brushing against fabrics."

While Amelia Bloomer's divided skirt (a.k.a. "the bloomer") is initially viewed as slightly scandalous, the growing popularity of the bicycle helps to guarantee its acceptance. After all, it's pretty hard to go cycling if you're wearing a long skirt.

1900–1910

Fashions become looser and more feminine, but Canuck Chicks aren't ready to throw away their corsets just yet—this despite many rants from members of the medical profession. "If women had common sense, instead of fashion sense, the corset would not exist," declares Alice B. Stockham in the 1893 edition of her book *Tokology*. "There are not words in the English language to express my convictions upon this subject. The corset, more than any other one thing, is responsible for woman's being the victim of disease and doctors."

Necessity proves to be the mother of invention once again. New York socialite Mary Phelps Jacobs makes a bra out of silk handkerchiefs and ribbon in 1913 in an effort to avoid wearing her bulky corset underneath her evening gown. One year later, she patents the backless brassiere, eventually selling her patent to Warner Brothers Corset Co. She's not the first person to invent a bra-type garment, but she's the first to secure a patent for a bra.

Feathered hats are so popular that some newspapers run articles warning about the impending extinction of certain types of birds because of the large number of feathers being used to decorate hats.

1910–1919

Frivolous, fussy fashions may be on their way out, but there are still a few areas of indulgence. Canuck Chicks who can afford to do so treat themselves to fur-trimmed lingerie and nightgowns. (Hey, living in a frosty climate has its privileges!)

Women reject the aptly named "hobble skirt" when it makes its debut at the end of World War I. After spending the war years in practical clothing that allowed for freedom of movement, women aren't about to squeeze themselves back into some form-fitting skirt that barely allows them to take baby steps.

Every well-dressed woman owns at least one pair of gloves and makes a point of following "glove etiquette" to the tee: gloves stay on during theatrical and opera performances but come off when you're sitting at the dinner table or playing cards. (According to one etiquette book of the day, wearing gloves while playing cards is "an affectation of elegance." In other words, it will merely succeed in making you look like trailer trash!)

The metal-toothed zipper is invented in 1913. It doesn't manage to find its way into clothing other than galoshes until after 1934, when the then Prince of Wales asks to have zippers sewn in the flys of his trousers. Eventually, the zipper will find its way into women's clothes as well, but, for now that's all pie in the sky.

1920–1929

The "flapper" look is officially in vogue. Women purchase special bras with side-lacings that allow them to bind their breasts in order to minimize their curves and achieve a slimmer, sportier, more boyish look. Skirt lengths get chopped, as does the length of women's hair. Not everyone is a big fan of the flapper, however: those die-hard spoil-sports B.G. Jefferis and J.L. Nichols, co-authors of *Safe Counsel or Practical Eugenics,* express their disgust at the way in which the flapper "glories in the lustful looks and vulgar comments which her appearance calls forth on the street. If people turn to stare in horror stricken amazement, her costume is a success," they declare.

Vogue magazine makes fashion history by including maternity fashions in its pages for the first time. Who knew it was possible to be both pregnant and fashionable?

The invention of the first generation of hand-held electric hair dryers allow for greater creativity in the hair department, as does society's newfound acceptance of hair dye.

"The fashions of today have never been so sane. Take the length of the average skirt, the comfortable neck, the freedom of the sleeve which all tend toward health and happiness. They are a reflection of the occupations and enjoyment of the people of today."
- *Toronto Star*, 1922

1930–1939
Warners makes brassiere history when it starts selling bras by the cup size and the corset makes a comeback—albeit in a much sexier, less matronly way.

Trousers finally come into their own. Women wear them for sport, evening, and casual wear—basically anywhere, anytime.

1940–1949
Nylon stockings hit the market at $1.15/pair. Four million pairs are sold in the US over four days when they make their debut in 1940. Unfortunately, everybody's favourite fashion accessory is hard to find during the war years. Women take to painting their legs with makeup and drawing a seamlike line down the backs of their calves instead.

Velcro and permanent press fabric are invented.

Elizabeth Arden introduces a waterproof white velvet gas mask for evening wear—arguably the oddest fashion accessory of the decade.

Rose Marie Reid of Vancouver—swimsuit designer and operator of a 200-employee swimsuit manufacturing plant—is spotlighted in *Maclean's Magazine.* Journalist Lotta Dempsey notes that Reid specializes in creating bathing suits for real women rather than "the Hollywood-type glamour girl or the Florida

Chamber of Commerce lovely" and that Reid makes a point of incorporating uniquely Canadian designs into her line of swimwear. "Why do a print with a Hawaiian frieze or a South American fiesta when we've got Indian totem poles and teepees, maple leaves, wheat fields, trilliums, and all the rich clear colors we can find here?" Reid explains.

Reid's company gets a run for its money when the bikini makes its debut in 1946. It takes its name from a tiny, South Pacific island where the US Army is doing weapons testing at the time. At first, the bikini is considered slightly scandalous: the Paris fashion designer who invents it can't find any models who are willing to wear it down the runway, so he is forced to hire a nude dancer to model it instead. Even a decade later, the bikini is still getting a lot of flack from mainstream society: *Modern Girl* magazine in the United States writes it off entirely, noting that "it is hardly necessary to waste words over the so-called bikini since it is inconceivable that any girl with tact and decency would ever wear such a thing."

1950–1959
Femininity and refinement are back in vogue and fashion designers choose to accentuate rather than downplay womanly curves.

The strapless bra becomes the must-have fashion accessory in the era of the backless ballgown.

The Très Secrète bra features something that's, well, *très secrète*: a plastic straw that allows you to inflate the cups of the bra if you feel that Mother Nature shortchanged you in the bosom department.

The invention of spandex in 1958 leads to a complete revolution in the world of undergarments. By the early 1960s, there's something other than white cotton briefs in a typical Canuck Chick's underwear drawer.

Pantyhose provides a welcome alternative to the inconvenience and discomfort of garters and girdles. It hits the street in 1959—the same year that Barbie is born.

1960–1969
The fashion world is rocked by the invention of the miniskirt—proof positive that less can be more. The topless bikini (or monokini) and the see-through dress also make their mark. (Chandler's on Bloor Street in Toronto reportedly manages to sell 2,000 of these risqué garments—and this at a time when Marlen Cowpland is just nine years old.)

Montreal's Canadelle company invents the push-up bra in 1964.

Nancy Sinatra's 1966 hit song "These Boots Are Made For Walkin'" helps to move truckloads of white leather go-go boots. On our side of the border, fashion designer Marilyn Brooks is contracted to supply go-go costumes to *A Go Go '66*, a CTV musical variety show.

The *Financial Post* publishes an article in 1966 linking market trends to the length of women's skirts: "Put aside your graphs and stock charts and concentrate on the fall trend in hemlines when trying to figure out which way the market will go," journalist Amy Booth advises.

North America's fixation with space travel carries over into the fashion arena as designers begin to emphasize a new, more modern look. They turn to so-called space-age fabrics (a.k.a. man-made synthetics) for inspiration and come up with unisex fashion lines that would have been unthinkable up until now. (This hot new fashion trend provides the older generation with a fun, new pastime: trying to guess the sex of the young people they meet on the street.)

Have Tiara, Will Travel

While the younger generation is busy rewriting the rules of fashion, members of the older generation prefer to live by the traditional rules. Many of those rules are spelled out in the 1965 edition of Claire Wallace's *Canadian Etiquette Dictionary*.

Diamond watches and tiaras are no longer *de rigueur* at state functions. According to Wallace, the appropriate garb for a formal state function is a long or ballet-length evening dress, a fur wrap or some other glamorous evening coat, a pair of sixteen-button, white-kid gloves, a snazzy evening bag, and your very best jewellery. You can accent your outfit with a diamond watch and a tiara in the hair "if desired."

Don't be tempted to wear your tiara on the golf course. "In golfing, a single strand of pearls may be worn, but other jewellery is not advisable with sports outfits."

Reserve your slacks for such activities as gardening or sports. "Slacks are not always becoming and should be worn with discretion, preferably not on the street or for shopping."

When in doubt, err on the side of caution. "It is always in better taste to wear plain things than to be overdressed." (Unless, of course, there's a tiara at stake.)

1970–1979

The seventies are the era of the platform shoe—heavy, chunky contraptions that feature heels as high as seven inches. One legendary pair even features a glass heel filled with water and a live goldfish.

Bad taste is definitely in vogue. Over the course of the decade, we're subjected to such fashion atrocities as hot pants, toe socks, clogs, disco-wear, gauchos, and the toga party.

The string bikini is popular with the handful of women who have the figures required to carry it off.

A black model appears on the cover of *Vogue* for the very first time in 1974.

French movie star Brigitte Bardot travels to Newfoundland to protest the seal hunt in 1977.

Quaint and demure *Miss Chatelaine* morphs into feisty and sexy *Flare* magazine in 1979.

1980–1989

Madonna makes it fashionable to parade around in slinky undergarments. The material girl shows a decided preference for the missile-inspired, cone-shaped bras that were all the rage in the 1950s.

Fitness wear comes out of the gym. Suddenly, it's okay to go grocery shopping in your Lycra workout clothes.

Canadian adults show up in orthodontic offices in record droves. It's now fairly commonplace to see someone over the age of 20 wearing braces.

Everyone wants to look like a CEO. Corporate chic has arrived!

1990–1999

The grunge look emerges to challenge corporate chic. Red flannel shirts and other "hoser"-esque fashion accessories are no longer reserved for weekends at the cottage: hip young Canuck Chicks proudly wear them anywhere, anytime.

Alfred Sung's 1990 fashion show features more than 500 pieces, uses 50 models, and attracts 8,000 spectators. The hottest number in the line? A pleated twill trench coat that is described by a fashion insider as "the most knocked-off garment in Canadian history."

Canuck Chicks are spending more money on luxurious undergarments than ever before. And plus-sized clothing manufacturers have finally caught on to the fact that large women like sexy things, too: voluptuous, full-figured gals have never had it so good.

Eye-print tunic by Montreal designer Jean Airoldi. Designer Tunics (Moe Doiron). Canadian Press

Noting the increasing number of Canadian models showing up on runways around the world, *Chatelaine* declares that "beautiful women are threatening to replace softwood lumber as Canada's greatest export."

The Ten Most Memorable Moments in Canadian Fashion History

1. Marlen Cowpland—wife of Corel entrepreneur Michael Cowpland—makes it into the *National Enquirer* after showing up at a company gala wearing a million-dollar, form-fitting Italian lamb-leather jumper that features a 24-karat gold breastplate adorned with a 15-carat diamond poised on her left nipple. (1997)

2. Marlen Cowpland displays what the *Toronto Star* describes as "plumber-worthy butt cleavage" at her 43rd birthday bash. Her birthday cake features a Barbie doll wearing an equally butt-bearing outfit—a rather bizarre case of art imitating life. (2001)

3. Candypants make their Canadian debut. The *Financial Post* reports that the panties are available in banana-pineapple flavour (the cherry-raspberry flavour so popular south of the border is banned by the Canadian government over concerns about the safety of the red food dye that it contains). A licorice drawstring ensures that one size truly does fit all. The Canadian public eats them up, purchasing $1.5 million worth of Candypants in less than one year—this despite the fact that there are some drawbacks to wearing Candypants on the dog days of summer: "Stride off to work on a July morn, comfortable in your candy knickers, and chances are that by sweltering noon they'll have melted," warns the *Financial Post*. Apparently the winter weather can also cause a problem: "When it's cold, the licorice drawstring can snap." (1977)

4. *FashionTelevision* (a.k.a. FT) makes its debut with host Jeanne Beker at the helm. Ten years after FT makes its debut, the show's co-creator, Jay Levine, acknowledges to *Maclean's* that there may be something to that long-standing rumour about the show's popularity amongst prison inmates: "I'm sure that if you were in prison and there were a lot of sexy girls on TV, you'd watch that show," he admits. Unfortunately, US prisoners looking for a peek at the bare breasts for which FT quickly becomes famous are simply out of luck. Apparently, the US TV networks aren't quite as liberal-minded as their Canadian counterparts.

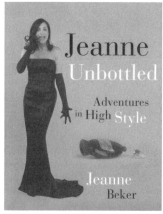

Jeanne Unbottled: Adventures in High Style by Jeanne Beker (Stoddart, 2001)

5. Victoria fashion designer Trish Tacoma introduces a line of women's underwear featuring Pierre Elliott Trudeau. She intends the underwear as a tribute to the former prime minister, telling the Canadian Press that the panties depict Trudeau in the way that most Canuck Chicks remember him—as the handsome, playful, charismatic, and sexy bachelor he was at the height of 1960s Trudeaumania. (2001)

6. A study indicating that girls who wear miniskirts develop more fat on their thighs than those who wear longer skirts sends terror into the heart of every Twiggy-wannabe. "There are few things outside the woodshed that scare young women so formidably as the news that they're getting fatter," notes the *Financial Post*. "[The news that] miniskirts will give them thighs like a wrestler should send hemlines in Droitwich rattling down like venetian blinds." (1969)

7. Canada gets its first jet-set supermodel, Linda Evangelista. (1988)

Linda Evangelista on a Paris runway (Remy de la Mauviniere). Canadian Press

8. Vancouver ophthalmologist Jean Carruthers pioneers the cosmetic use of the muscle-paralyzing agent Botox along with her husband, dermatologist Alistair Carruthers. The technique doesn't receive Canadian government approval until 2001 and U.S. Food and Drug Administration approval until 2002, so it's a while before Botox starts doing battle with the wrinkles and other woes of boomers on both sides of the border. Of course, perfect beauty doesn't come without a price: such adverse effects as headaches, respiratory infections, nausea, flu-like symptoms, droopy eyelids, double vision, and corneal ulceration are noted in clinical trials—a message that seems to be lost on American boomers who are now holding "Botox parties" rather than "Tupperware parties!" (1987)

Marcia Kilgore of Bliss Spas
(*Maclean's*/Phill Snel) Canadian Press

9. In 1992, Outlook, Saskatchewan–born Marcia Kilgore launches Bliss, a spa in downtown New York that becomes the hottest destination for the celebrity set. Three years later, she sells it to LVMH Moet Hennessy Louis Vuitton for a reported US$30 million. (1992)

10. Expatriate Canuck Chick Barbara Amiel is named the fifth best-dressed woman of the year by Britain's *Tatler* magazine while Ontario Lieutenant-Governor Hilary Weston is named the country's best-dressed woman by the *Toronto Star*. The following year, Weston will share best-dressed honours with none other than hockey aficionado Don Cherry— he of the trademark plaid blazers. (2000)

Hilary Weston in 1995 (*Toronto Star*). Canadian Press

Model Citizens

Here's the lowdown on just a few of the many (super) models who have made
names for themselves—and Canada—over the years.

Linda Evangelista: A proud Canuck Chick, Evangelista scored big points with Canadians by carrying a Canadian flag down a Paris runway in 1993. She is best known, however, for once having said that she wouldn't get out of bed for anything less than $10,000 a day. That and the fact that *Vogue* editor Anna Wintour once called her "the camera's greatest collaborator" have made her Canada's best-known supermodel.

Yasmeen Ghauri: A Montreal native, Ghauri became one of the best-known models of the early 1990s—this despite the fact that the Canadian fashion establishment was initially resistant to her exotic good looks. (She's of Pakistani and German descent.)

Dayle Haddon: Haddon's 15 minutes of fame arrived in the 1970s, when she landed lucrative contracts modelling for both Revlon and Max Factor—this after turning down an invitation to join Les Grands Ballet Canadiens.

Shalom Harlow: Harlow became known for her waiflike look—a look made famous (or infamous) by British model Kate Moss.

Tricia Helfer: Helfer was a winner of Ford Model's Supermodel of the World competition—an achievement that helped her to land plenty of high-profile modelling gigs.

Lana Ogilvie: Ogilvie made history by becoming the first black woman to land an advertising contract for Cover Girl cosmetics.

Kirsten Owen: Owen successfully made the transition from avant-garde runway model to mainstream model—no small feat, that.

Kim Renneberg: Renneberg's main claims to fame were her extensive editorial coverage in *Mirabella* and her flashy campaigns on behalf of designers Krizia and Emporio Armani.

Eve Salvil: Salvil made her runway debut in the fall of 1992. Almost overnight, her distinctive shaved and tattooed head was everywhere.

Monica Schnarre: Schnarre found herself stepping into the international limelight after winning the Supermodel of the World title in Los Angeles in 1986—a pretty impressive accomplishment for a fourteen-year-old high school student from Scarborough, Ontario.

Estella Warren: A sweet young thing in her early twenties, Warren has already made a name for herself as an athlete, model, and movie actress. She started out by competing internationally as a synchronized swimmer. Then she made the switch to modelling and—more recently—acting, making her film debut opposite Sylvester Stallone in *Driven*, a racing movie filmed in Toronto.

Judy Welch: Welch was 1956's Miss Maple Leaf (later known as Miss Canada). She subsequently founded one of Canada's most famous (and occasionally infamous) modelling agencies.

Skin Deep: The History of Cosmetics

Here's a quick rundown of how our taste in cosmetics has evolved from one generation to another.

1890–1900

It's socially acceptable to wear cologne, "shade" your bosom to give the appearance of a more amble bustline, and you might even be able to get away with using a bit of hair powder, but dipping your fingers into the rouge pot is risky business indeed—an indication that you might be (gasp!) a fallen woman.

"The daily use of oil or pomatum, with which a few grains of carbonate of lead, lead plaster, or trisnitrate of bismuth, have been blended by heat and careful trituration, has generally a like effect on the hair to ferriguinous solutions; so also has a leaden comb, but its action is very uncertain. None of these last are, however, safe for long-continued use. Atrophy of the scalp, baldness, and even local paralysis, have sometimes, though rarely, been caused by them."
– hair-care tips from *The Ladies Book of Useful Information*, London, Ontario, 1896

1900–1910

The pale look is in. In fact, it's commonplace for women to paint pale-blue veins onto their skin in the hope of making it look a little more delicate and translucent. And, if you happen to suffer from problem skin, there are now a growing number of arsenic-based preparations available to help you do battle with pimples, freckles, wrinkles, blackheads, and other marring facial imperfections.

1910–1919

Wearing cosmetics during the war years isn't just politically incorrect: it's downright unpatriotic. After all, aren't Canuck Chicks supposed to be trying to do more with less? But that doesn't stop women from indulging in the odd bit of high-priced skin cream or face powder for "health reasons"—or from loading up on the cosmetic world's latest and greatest invention: solid lipsticks.

1920–1929

Suntan oil makes its debut and twist-up lipstick becomes the hallmark of the flapper—a "fast woman" who is notorious for her short hair and short skirts and for her predilection toward smoking and wearing makeup in public.

1930–1939

Dyeing or perming your hair comes into vogue, nail polish is invented, and cosmetics become both more sophisticated and more widely used. By the end of the decade, Canadians are spending $20 million on toiletries annually.

1940–1949

A shortage of such key ingredients as alcohol, oils, and glycerine leads to less-than-satisfactory cosmetics for the duration of the war. Such wartime sacrifices are rewarded by the emergence of a whole new generation of cosmetic products after the war: artificial eyelashes, fluid eyeliner, eye shadow sticks, and more.

1950–1959

Hair dye goes mainstream. Three out of ten brunettes dye their hair blonde, apparently taking Marilyn Monroe's claim that "Gentlemen prefer blondes" to heart. By the middle of the decade, Canadians are spending $80 million on cosmetics each year.

1960–1969

False eyelashes make their debut. Initially, they're custom-made—the esthetician applies them lash by lash—but, over time, they are mass-produced in rows. In keeping with the psychedelic mood of the times, some Canuck Chicks opt for false eyelashes made of foil or glitter. Groovy . . .

1970–1979

Glam rockers such as KISS and David Bowie popularize face painting, but Canuck Chicks are more likely to try to carry off the tanned and toned California look. An ever-growing selection of self-tanning products gives us women of the Great White North at least a fighting chance of looking like California girls despite our anything-but-toasty climate.

Elizabeth Arden: Canada's First Lady of Cosmetics

Within 10 years of opening a salon on Fifth Avenue in New York in 1910, Canadian-born Elizabeth Arden (originally Florence Nightingale Graham of Woodbridge, Ontario) managed to build what was, at that time, the most powerful beauty brand in the world.

It wasn't just her famous bright red door that set her apart from the competition: she was a pioneer and an innovator in every way. It was Arden who first came up with the idea of "the makeover"—a simple concept that quickly became a beauty industry institution. She also pioneered the idea of the "total look"—coordinated eye, lip, cheek, and nail colours. And she had a lasting impact on the industry as a result of her lifelong campaigns to make cosmetics safe and socially acceptable.

In 1930, Arden turned down a $15 million offer for her company—no small change in those days. When she died in 1966 at the age of 89, she left behind an $11 million estate. She was buried in a gold lamé gown that famed designer Oscar de la Renta had made for her prior to her death, but that she insisted on saving for a special occasion. That occasion ended up being her funeral.

1980–1989
Blonde highlights and elaborate hairdos become *de rigueur* for trophy brides—women who have perfected the art of marrying well. And even if you aren't floating in quite the same social circles as the Ivana Trumps of the world, chances are you still have "big hair." It's kind of an eighties thing . . .

1990–1999
Liposuction and cosmetic surgery become almost commonplace and tattoos and pierced navels are definitely in.

2000 and beyond
A survey by a leading hair dye manufacturer reveals some regional differences when it comes to the hair colour preferences of Canadian women: while blonde hair is most popular in British Columbia, red hair is most popular in Alberta, and brown hair is most popular in Atlantic Canada. The survey also notes that while 47 percent of Alberta women dye their hair to give their self-esteem a boost, only 16 percent of Quebec women dye their hair for the same reason. *Vive la difference!*

The Cure For What Ails You

Troubled by such beauty woes as forehead wrinkles, unruly eyebrows, or scraggly eyebrows? Here's how Kate Aitken recommended these problems be dealt with in her 1951 book *Lovely You: A Blueprint for Beauty*.

Problem	Solution
Forehead wrinkles	Pull a strip of adhesive tightly across the wrinkles before going to bed and leave the adhesive in place while you sleep. You can use the same piece of adhesive night after night.
Unruly eyebrows	Brush nightly using an old toothbrush and mild soap.
Scraggly eyelashes	Soften with salad oil each night before going to bed.
Tired eyes	Keeping your eyes wide open, dip your face into a bowl containing one quart warm water and one teaspoon boracic acid. Swish the warm water in and around your eyes and eyelids.
Makeup that runs on a hot day	Stick your head in the refrigerator to give your makeup a chance to set.

Three women on a beach.
Archives of Ontario DIN 10004622

The Dirt on Diets

Think dieting is a relatively recent phenomenon—a product of the post-Twiggy, post-bikini era? Think again! We Canuck Chicks have been engaged in some heavy-duty navel (and thigh) gazing for well over a century.

Dieting first came into vogue in the 1830s when US Presbyterian minister Sylvester Graham began preaching against the evils of overeating. He argued that gluttony was the first step on the slippery slope to sinful living: one day, you'd give into that craving for an extra serving of dessert: the next, you'd be indulging your craving for The Boy Next Door. The result? Nothing less than lust, sexual perversion, and social chaos! (It seems kind of ironic, don't you think, that Graham's descendants were responsible for inventing the honey-flavoured crackers that bear his name. I'm sure Sylvester would have preferred instead to have his name attached to a much blander type of food—say pre-chewed soda crackers.)

Following close on the heels of Graham was the nineteenth century's next big-name diet guru: William Banting. A British casket-maker by trade, Banting was inspired to write a diet book after dropping 46 pounds from his 202-pound frame. The book went on to sell 58,000 copies—no small feat in the days before Oprah's Book Club. (Of course, sales were no doubt helped by the fact that Graham's diet plan prescribed a couple of alcoholic beverages per day in addition to the main staples of his program: lean meat, dry toast, and soft-boiled eggs. After all, it's a heck of a lot easier to say no to dessert if you've got a martini in one hand!)

The next weight-loss expert up at bat was Horace Fletcher, an American who felt that the key to weight-loss success was to focus on "the science of chewing." He argued that chewing each bite of food 20 times or more guaranteed weight-loss success. Not only would your food be broken down to the rather unappealing consistency of infant cereal: your jaw would conk out long before you could consume enough food to do any serious damage to your waistline. Bottom line? Over time, you'd begin to think of eating as an unpleasant chore rather than an enjoyable activity. And, according to Fletcher, this was *a good thing.*

Think Fletcher sounds like a bit of a flake? You ain't heard nothing yet! Apparently, he was every bit as obsessed with what came out of his body as with what went in: he was in the habit of weighing and cataloguing his feces. He even went so far as to mail some of his feces to a Yale University researcher who was studying weight loss. (It kind of gives you a whole new level of respect for postal workers, now doesn't it?)

Of course, it was only a matter of time before the "chew your food to death" fad was replaced by the "don't chew anything at all" fad—one of investigative journalist Upton Sinclair's less noteworthy contributions to the world. In 1909, Sinclair penned an article on the merits of fasting for *Cosmopolitan* magazine, noting that doing without food for days at a time left him feeling healthy and alert. The article helped to kick-off a North America–wide fasting trend.

John Harvey Kellogg—a member of the cereal-manufacturing family of the same name—was also in favour of some rather extreme weight-loss measures. The weight-loss regime that he recommended at his sanitarium in Battle Creek, Michigan, included cold rain douches and plunge baths! (Brrrr!!!) He also lent his name to "Kellogg's Safe Fat Reducer"—an anything-but-safe weight-loss product that put your thyroid into overdrive, triggering such unwelcome side effects as nervousness, heart palpitations, sweating, weakness, insomnia, and—in some cases—permanent damage to the nervous system. (Hey, no pain, no gain, remember?)

Of course, Kellogg's Safe Fat Reducer was downright safe as compared to other early 20th-century diet preparations. Popular ingredients in the growing number of diet products on the market included laxatives, purgatives, washing soda, Epsom salts, arsenic, dinitrophenol (a powerful insecticide and herbicide), human chorionic gonadotropin (a hormone found in the urine of pregnant women), and amphetamines. Not all weight-loss preparations were laced with hormones and chemicals, however. One quick-thinking con artist managed to sell "fat-burning water" to an unsuspecting public; another managed to charge top-dollar for a fancy package containing plain, old-fashioned pink lemonade.

As the century marched on, North Americans began purchasing a motley assortment of products: the Slendro Massage Table (a gizmo that promised to jiggle away your fat), Slim-skins (inflatable rubber trousers that were hooked up to a vacuum cleaner), astringent body wraps and sweat-inducing rubber garments that caused dehydration, an Astro-Trimmer sauna belt that promised to take inches off your waistline, earrings that were supposed to eliminate hunger pains, and a rolling pin with suction cups that promised to help you slim down. And then there were my two personal nominees for The Weird Weight Loss Products Hall of Shame: an electric fork that contained flashing green and red lights that were supposed to tell you when it was okay to start and stop eating and an obnoxious electronic device that would remind you to just say no to the cheesecake each time you were tempted to open the fridge.

Dreams for Sale

Here's a quick rundown of some of the weight-loss-related products that were offered for sale in the Eaton's of Canada and Simpsons-Sears mail order catalogues during 1961.

MOVERS AND SHAKERS

A Home Steam Bath: Trust me, this sounds a lot more luxurious than it was in real life. It consisted of a vinyl plastic canopy, cap, slippers, and vaporizer, and promised to "melt" your fat away. Basically, it was like having a pup tent strapped around your neck with a vaporizer inside. Oh well, the price was right: a mere $6.95.

The "Lithe-Line" by Helena Rubenstein: The catalogue described this gizmo in terms that were vague enough to keep you guessing: "A strong rubber exerciser to help figure control in an easy, invigorating way. Also helps to tone muscles. Instruction sheet shows a variety of interesting exercises." Again, it was one of your more affordable options. Your total investment? $4.50.

Belt Massager: Described as a vibrator-belt massager that was designed for the modern family, this product was designed to be lightweight and portable. It promised to help reduce tension, tone muscles, and aid in reducing. It was designed to be used on the hips, abdomen, and the back and featured a heavy canvas belt and two massage cycles—high and low. This one didn't come cheap. It retailed for $69.95.

De Luxe "Firm Line" Massage Belt: This massage belt promised to provide the important daily exercise you need to keep you looking and feeling your best. It featured a sturdy frame as well as a removable foam-upholstered seat—something that justified the rather hefty price, I suppose: $129.95.

Dual "Firm Line" Massage Lounge With Heat: The advertisers really went to town on this one: "Our best home-reducing plan"—the ad copy proclaimed, boasting of the product's amazing four-way massaging action and other bells and whistles. "Yes, in the comfort and convenience of your own home . . . for only a fraction of the cost. . . no time-consuming travel . . . no disrobing . . . you can now have all the advantages of a professional salon. . . . We also send you 'Firm-Line' Dietary Plan tablets and low-calorie yet varied menus." The cost? A mere $249.

"Chic" Figure Glorifier: This electro-massage unit promised to help you maintain a trimmer, youthful silhouette while soothing the fatigue caused by muscular tension. Not a bad deal for $12.95.

MAGIC LITTLE PILLS

Metrecal by Mead Johnson: The best-known liquid diet plan of the era, Metrecal billed itself as "a supplementary diet especially prepared for those on a reducing plan." It also promised to help you maintain a normal weight after reducing. (Once a customer, always a customer.) A three-day supply could be had for $4.77.

Vita-thin Reducing Plan: A dietary supplement that was to be taken in the place of two of the daily meals, the Vita-thin reducing plan would set you back $3.95 for a 10-meal supply.

Larson's Swedish Milk Diet: Whatever was in the can was mixed with milk to provide a liquid meal replacement. The cost? $1.98 for a one-week supply.

Ben Weider Protein Tablets: These tablets were a "supplement to reduce fatigue due to protein deficiency." The price of combatting fatigue? $3.50.

Ayds: While the catalogue described Ayds as "candy rich in vitamins and minerals," you had to use your imagination to convince yourself that what you were eating was candy. It was chewy, foul-tasting stuff that invariably failed to satisfy your appetite. And whether you opted for vanilla or chocolate, you needed to fork over $3.49 for 104 pieces.

Slendor Reducing Plan: A box of 63 tablets would cost you $2.50. Apparently, that's all you needed to know. (The catalogue description wasn't exactly forthcoming!)

Meltoway Reducing Plan: Another mysterious weight-loss product. You could purchase a five-day supply for $2.95.

Melozets: These were described as "menthyl-cellulite wafers, low in calories, to help appease hunger." A box could be had for $1.50.

Bal-Cal meal replacement: This product certainly made a lot of promises: "Lose weight without feeling hungry. 900 calories a day satisfy your appetite while you reduce. Simply, safely, effectively . . . the youthful, attractive figure you have always wanted can be yours—almost automatically. No more calorie counting, no more charts and measures, no more temptations on your path back to beauty." The damages? 85¢ for a one-day supply.

Metrecal Plan: "From Mead Johnson, makers of Pablum, comes a new concept in weight control" the catalogue declared. Your cost? $4.77 for a three-day supply.

Through Thick and Through Thin

Of course, being skinny wasn't always in vogue (although it's hard for us modern Canuck Chicks to keep that fact in mind, given that it hasn't been chic to have ample thighs since Louis St. Laurent was prime minister!) Here's the skinny on some great—and not-so-great—moments in the history of dieting.

1890

American actress Lillian Russell, widely considered to be the most voluptuous woman of her era, weighs in at a hefty 200 pounds. Known for her flawless skin, her round cheeks, her plump figure, and her long, golden hair, Russell was considered to be far more attractive than the French actress Sarah Bernhardt who was openly mocked for having a skinny body. (Cartoonists had a heyday at Sarah's expense, depicting her as a broomstick or a boa constrictor, or showing her body as being made from water pipes.)

1895

Artist Charles Dana Gibson's paintings of tall, athletic, self-confident "Gibson Girls" redefines the female ideal. The measurements of his fantasy girl? 38–27–45.

1918

Food rationing causes most Canuck Chicks to drop a few pounds: the girlish silhouette of the flapper is on its way . . .

1932

Overweight women aren't the only ones taking some heat in the body image department. Underweight women also face increasing pressure to conform to the figure ideal du jour. A *Chatelaine* advertisement for the Canadian Ironized Yeast Company promises womanly curves, a clear complexion, glorious pep, perfect health, and romance to underweight women who purchase ironized yeast pills.

1934

Chatelaine beauty writer Annabelle Lee reminds her readers that it's important to drop those excess pounds: "No woman can be in the best of spirits when she's carrying around with her a burden of ten, twenty, or thirty extra pounds."

1935

Taskmaster Annabelle Lee offers *Chatelaine* readers some additional slimming advice. This time she's ready to do battle with the dreaded double chin. "Massage and exercise are your twin salvations. The massage may take the form of vigorous slapping with the back of your hand from the point of the chin all the way along the jaw line. Or you can clench your fists . . . kneading away the double chin. . . . . Exercise is simple, but must be as faithful as your massage. Rotate the head on the shoulders. . . . Then throw the head back and bite the air several times."

1945
Wartime rationing combined with the need to save gasoline by walking or biking encourages a leaner female physique.

1946
Maclean's Magazine offers its readers a no-nonsense approach to weight loss. "There are only two satisfactory reducing exercises," declares W.W. Bauer, MD. "Either one taken by itself is effective. Used together they can't fail. Here they are: (a) while still hungry, place your palms against the edge of the dining table and push yourself steadily away; (b) when offered a second helping, move the head vigorously from side to side. Repeat as required."

1950
Womanly curves are back in style—but that doesn't mean you can "let yourself go." Kate Aitken advises newly married women to resolve to check their figures and reduce any bulges as they appear and to "have the strength of mind enough to diet if necessary and exercise each and every night."

"Figures don't lie. A man wants to take out a girl whom the other lads eye with envy. He wants a slim (not skinny) lass well set up with adequate hips, shoulders, and legs. . . . Says our marriage broker, 'Sweat it off, girls! Ten minutes daily does the trick!'"
- Kate Aitken, *Lovely You: A Blueprint for Beauty*, 1951

1959
Barbie makes her debut at the American International Toy Fair in New York. One of the earliest Barbie dolls comes packaged with a bathroom scale permanently stuck at 110 pounds. Over the next 40 years, enough Barbies will be sold to circle the earth three-and-a-half times. If Barbie were a real person, her measurements would be 39–21–33.

1964
Chatelaine begins publishing first-person dieting success stories.

1965
Entrepreneur Mark Eden makes a name for himself by bringing a number of "figure enhancing" products to market, including the Mark Eden Bust Developer (a contraption that promises to increase the size of your bust), Trim

Jeans (inflatable shorts that promise to slim your hips), and Vacuum Pants (pants that are supposed to "vacuum away" your fat).

1966

The miniskirt arrives from Britain—a look made popular by an underweight 17-year-old British fashion model named Twiggy who is 5'6" and weighs just 89 pounds.

1969

Chatelaine publishes weight-loss tips from such celebrities as future Prime Minister John Turner, athlete Nancy Greene, broadcaster and future Governor General Adrienne Clarkson, actor Bruno Gerussi, and journalist June Callwood in its April issue. Later that same year, it publishes "The Thinking Woman's Diet," a 914-calorie-a-day exercise in deprivation!

1973

Chatelaine recommends a two-week, 700-calorie-a-day crash diet to its readers. "We think a few headaches and a few hunger pangs . . . and a dull menu for two weeks are small prices to pay for a short time when there's such an encouraging result," writes Barbara Croft in an article that's rather aptly entitled "That Hateful Diet."

1974

A pair of American researchers rock North American's image of the full-figured gal by revealing the shocking results of their research: a woman with a hearty appetite for food is likely to have a hearty appetite for sex. "One of the best predictors of a woman's being able to enjoy sex is her ability to enjoy food," they note.

1981

Plus-sized model Jacqueline Hope launches Big, Bold, and Beautiful—a modelling agency and plus-sized women's clothing company that is founded on the then-radical belief that the worth of a woman is measured by more than her dress size.

1982

Jane Fonda brings out the first in what will be a string of celebrity workout videos.

1983

The bookstore shelves are overflowing with weight-loss books. There are now 360 diet books in print.

Homemaker's announces that it's okay to have an athletic body, but notes that not all men are enamoured with the new lean-and-mean feminine ideal. One

Fit TV

Here's the scoop on three of the most popular fitness programs
to show up on Canadian television over the years.

The Bonnie Prudden Show: Bonnie's workout show aired from 1965 through 1968. Her claim to fame was that she was "a grandmother with the body of a chorus girl." Nobody cared that she was American: the show managed to attract a cult following of Canadian housewives in search of tighter abs.

Kareen's Yoga: *Kareen's Yoga* was a staple of daytime TV throughout the 1970s. Kareen's voice was every bit as relaxing and soothing as the soft music and potted palms that soon became her trademarks. I guess you could say hers was the official workout show for the Stepford generation!

:20 Minute Workout: *:20 Minute Workout* was taped and directed in Toronto in the early 1980s by American Ron Harris—a creepy guy who went on to direct *Totally* *Nude Aerobics* and to run an Internet site that offered up the eggs of models to would-be parents! ("This is Darwin at its very best," he claimed.) *:20 Minute Workout* attracted a large viewership during its two seasons on the air and its many years in reruns. While 85 percent of the audience was female, Harris was the first to admit that some of the show's viewers were men: "We also get 'men-in-the-penitentiary' type letters. They write to say [the show] is the greatest thing since the bikini." The show's production work was done by Nelvana, a Toronto film production and distribution house that later made a name for itself doing animation featuring such well-loved children's characters as Babar and Franklin.

man quoted in the article declares: "Anything that sweats or has sweated or is about to sweat does not interest me sexually." Another has this to say about fitness guru Jane Fonda: "She has a body like wood. You don't want to stroke her, you want to sand her down."

1984
The Abdominizer—a home fitness device—is invented by Canadian entrepreneur Dennis Colonello.

1985
Health and Welfare Canada reports that 65 percent of Canadian women want to lose weight.

1990
The supermodel look comes into vogue—a look that some people refer to as "heroin chic" because of the sickly, bone-thin bodies of the supermodel set. While the average American woman is 5'4" and 144 pounds, the average model is 5'9" and 123 pounds.

1992

Registered dietitian Linda Omichinski writes *You Count, Calories Don't*—the first Canadian book to challenge the wisdom of dieting.

1993

Writing in *Chatelaine*, journalist Suanne Kelman describes the struggles that she and other Canuck Chicks experience each time they step foot on a scale: "We've invested weight with so many meanings that numbers on the scale have become a shorthand for self-worth. Slenderness is not just beautiful; it proclaims that you are feminine, self-disciplined, well-adjusted, sexy. Fat, on the other hand, reveals that you're sloppy and self-indulgent, out of control, and out of the running as a human being."

1995

There are more than 700 weight-loss books in print.

1996

Plus-sized fashion model and entrepreneur Jackqueline Hope writes *Big, Bold and Beautiful* and Canadian journalist Terry Poulton writes *No Fat Chicks: How Women Are Brainwashed to Hate Their Bodies and Spend Their Money*. In her book, Poulton describes what it was like to wage her battle with weight on the pages of *Chatelaine* in 1982—and then subsequently regain that weight: "There's something only Oprah Winfrey and I know from actual experience: Hell is having to show up fat when the whole country knows you're supposed to be thin."

2002

Jackqueline Hope states that the plus-sized movement has come a long way—but that we've still got a long way to go: "It shouldn't matter if you're a little sedan or a luxury car. We should all be at peace with ourselves."

Terry Poulton. Reprinted with the permission of Key Porter Books (2002). Photo Credit: Jim Allen

"Beauty does not stop at a size 14. . . .
A beautiful woman is someone who oozes self-confidence, has her own personal style, believes in herself, walks with poise, and shows the world that beauty can't be measured.
There are no limits."

– Jackqueline Hope, *Big, Bold and Beautiful*

Jackqueline Hope
(*Toronto Star*/Ken Faught). Canadian Press

CHAPTER 5

Canuck Chicks

"Canadian girls are so pretty it is a relief to occasionally see a plain one."
- Mark Twain, quoted in Lena Newman's book *An Historical Almanac of Canada* (1967)

"Some girls have so much beauty, charm, sex appeal, or talent that they will be sought out by men even though they hide themselves in the wilderness."
- Isabel Turnbull Dingman, "Can She Manage Alone?" *Chatelaine*, April 1932

Forget all the hype about Hollywood starlets and California girls. The most beautiful women in the world can be found right here in the Great White North. After all, hasn't Canada proven itself time and time again to be the favourite hunting ground for none other than *über* Playboy Hugh Hefner?

While we Canuck Chicks have every right to declare ourselves the eighth wonder of the world, it's unlikely that our message is going to get much media play any time soon. Yet again, our much-talked-about Canadian modesty gets in the way. You won't catch any Canadian songwriters following in the foot-steps of the Beach Boys, writing impassioned tributes to Canadian woman-hood, nor do you find our various tourist authorities revealing the truth about the much-lauded natural beauty of Canada. (There's more to our country's natural beauty than just pristine lakes and towering trees, after all!)

This chapter is my attempt to defend the honour of every little Canuck Chick who has ever cried herself to sleep, convinced that she was doomed to be uglier than those much-celebrated California girls or much-sighed-over French women, by virtue of mere geography. Who says that you have to hail from Los Angeles or Paris to be beautiful? Just try to tell that one to the residents of Ladysmith, British Columbia; Timmins, Ontario; and Peterborough, Ontario, the birthplaces of three women who are widely considered to be among the sexiest in the world: mega-babe Pamela Anderson, country rock star Shania Twain, and up-and-coming sexpot Estella Warren.

Dance hall girl in Klondike.
National Archives of Canada NAC-PA

Belgian Queen—Klondike.
National Archives of Canada NAC-PA

Northern Lights

Of course, Pamela, Shania, and Estella aren't the only noteworthy beauties to call Canada home—nor were they the first Red Hot Canuck Chicks to show up on the international radar screen. Here's an A-to-Z roundup of just a few of the many women who've made a name for themselves—and Canada—over the past one hundred years.

Pamela Anderson

Unquestionably the Grand Babe of Canada, Pamela Anderson's story is a classic rags to riches success story—but in this case, the "rags" are a Labatt's beer T-shirt and the "riches" are the royalties she's earned on her million-dollar breasts. Anderson first found herself in the spotlight when she wore the now-famous beer T-shirt to a BC Lions football game in 1989. One of the cameras panning the crowd zeroed in on Pamela, broadcasting her image on the jumbo-sized screen. The reaction of the highly appreciative crowd caught the attention of beer executives, who immediately offered her a contract to be the Labatt's Blue Zone Girl—a major career breakthrough for an almost-unknown Vancouver-based fitness instructor. Then, lightning struck again. A *Playboy* magazine editor spotted her in the crowd at a fashion show and asked her if she'd be interested in posing for the magazine. She ended up being featured on the cover of the October 1989 issue of the magazine. That cover helped to launch a career that has included numerous *Playboy* video appearances as well as starring roles on both the big screen and the small screen, including her best-known role as a curvaceous lifeguard on *Baywatch* (a.k.a. "Babewatch").

Pamela Anderson-Lee (Michael Probst).
Canadian Press/Associated Press

Babe Watch

Here are some of the more noteworthy milestones in the life and career of the world's most famous Canuck Chick, Pamela Anderson.

1967: Pamela Anderson makes her grand debut on Canada's 100th birthday—July 1, 1967. Because she's the first centennial baby in her hometown of Ladysmith, BC, Anderson ends up being headline news from the day she is born—literally. (She shares her July 1st birthday with another famous Canuck Chick, by the way—Edmonton North MP Deborah Grey, who was born on Canada Day, 1952.)

1989: Anderson appears on the cover of the October 1989 issue of *Playboy*.

1991: Anderson makes her debut as Lisa The Tool Time Girl on the hit US TV show *Home Improvement*.

1992: Anderson begins a five-year run as lifeguard C.J. Parker on *Baywatch*—a role that will make her a household name around the world, including in China. (*Baywatch* was the first American TV show to be broadcast in that country.) The role also allows Anderson to realize a childhood dream: in the yearbook for her 1985 graduating class at Highland Secondary School in Comox, BC, she'd noted that her ambition was to become "a California beach bum."

1995: Anderson marries bad-boy rocker Tommy Lee of Mötley Crüe after a whirlwind four-day courtship in Cancun. Reportedly, the bride wore an ultra-teeny white bikini and sunglasses while the groom wore cutoffs. The happy couple makes an X-rated honeymoon video that is later stolen from their home and pirated around the world. Lee later had this to say about his brand new bride: "On ecstacy, Joan Rivers looks like Pamela Anderson, so imagine what Pamela Anderson looked like."

1996: Anderson plays a leather-clad futuristic bounty hunter in the feature film *Barb Wire* and then gives birth to her first child.

1997: Anderson gives birth to her second child.

1998: Responding to widespread criticisms that she's little more than a larger-than-life version of Barbie, Anderson defends the Barbie way of life, telling *Cosmopolitan* magazine, "I like being a Barbie." That same year, she makes her debut as bodyguard Vallery Irons, owner of Vallery Irons Protection, in *V.I.P.*—the TV show she left *Baywatch* to develop.

1999: *Saturday Night* magazine reports that there are more than 3.3 million Internet searches of Anderson's name each year and that more than 145,000 web pages contain the words "Pamela Anderson." This is also the year when Anderson opts to have her breast implants removed. (She had had them implanted in 1989, shortly after the first of her six *Playboy* appearances.)

2000: Canadian News Online reports that there's a Pamela Anderson videogame in the works based on Anderson's *V.I.P.* character, Vallery Irons.

2001: Eruptor Entertainment introduces the PortaPam—"a sizzling wireless entertainment version of Pamela Anderson" for hand-held PalmPilots. Designed to function as a digital pet, digital Pam apparently requires feeding and protection from the paparazzi and "nasty tabloid headlines." In exchange, users are rewarded with the opportunity to take peaks at her in the shower, in her bedroom, or at the gym.

2002: Anderson announces that she's flirting with the idea of giving up her acting career to work as a stripper on new boyfriend Kid Rock's rap concert tours. She also tells New York gossip columnist Liz Smith that she's planning to follow in the footsteps of Martha Stewart and develop lines of branded merchandise—in her case hair and makeup products, bikinis, lingerie, and bed linens. She's also taken the plunge into magazine journalism: Her debut "Pam, Honestly" column in *Jane* magazine focuses on domestic abuse.

Teri Austin

Toronto–born actress Teri Austin is best-known for her role as smart but sexy Jill Bennett on the hit eighties TV show *Knots Landing*—a character who, according to Austin, was "flirting with one man, sleeping with another, and having shady contacts with a third"—a series of events that would ultimately torpedo her relationship with good guy Gary Ewing (played by Ted Shackelford). She managed to steam up the screen and do Canada proud during her four-year run on the show by dissing the Americans every now and again. Her description of Hollywood in a 1986 interview with *TV Guide:* "Well, it's sort of like Mississauga without the culture and charm."

Lee Aaron
Lee Aaron was originally the name of a Canadian bar band that made the rounds in the late 1970s. Over time, the band's lead singer, Karen Greening, decided to ditch her own name and take on the band's name instead. By the late 1980s, Lee Aaron was firmly entrenched as Canada's metal queen, having achieved great commercial success with a series of hard-rocking tunes, including the controversial "Metal Queen" video—which ran into trouble with the censors in Australia and Britain, but that miraculously made it on to Canadian TV—and the super-sexy "Whatcha Do To My Body"—a song that won her MuchMusic's highly coveted Best Video award for 1990. She recently reinvented herself as a jazz artist, but is still better known for her late eighties bad girl persona. (Once a bad girl, always a bad girl . . .)

Liona Boyd
Likely the only classical guitarist in the world who managed to catch the eye of former Prime Minister Pierre Elliott Trudeau—a man renowned for his appreciation of beautiful women—Liona Boyd certainly warrants a mention in the Canuck Chicks Hall of Fame, even if she does have rather odd taste in neighbours. Her Beverly Hills home is located directly across the street from Ozzy Osbourne's place!

Genevieve Bujold
Genevieve Bujold made a name for herself by looking sexy and scared in such feature films as *Coma, Earthquake,* and *Dead Ringers* (definitely the creepiest "gyno flick" ever made). She started out planning to be a nun, but was expelled from convent school at the age of 15 after being caught reading Marcel Pagnol's *Fanny*—a steamy drama about a woman who marries an elderly man after becoming pregnant by her lover. (Not exactly convent-approved reading, it would seem.)

Neve Campbell
Her girl-next-door good looks made her a natural for the role of Julia Salinger in the award-winning Fox series *Party of Five,* but Neve Campbell is better known as the scream queen in the cult classics *Scream, Scream 2,* and *Scream 3.* The Guelph, Ontario–born starlet made *People* magazine's list of the 50 Most

Beautiful People in both 1998 and 2000 (guess she had a Bad Hair Year in 1999) and was once romantically linked to Pat Mastroianni (yes, the very same Pat Mastroianni who played the cheek-pinchingly cute Joey Jeremiah on *Degrassi Junior High*). Aww . . .

Kim Cattrall

British-born but Canadian-raised bombshell Kim Cattrall has made a career out of being sexy. While she is best known for her role as the libidinous Samantha Jones on hit TV show *Sex and the City,* she also made a name for herself in the Canadian-made 1980s sexploitation flick *Porky's,* when she played a sex-crazed fitness instructor. Recently she co-wrote a sex manual with her husband, jazz musician Mark Levin. Its title? *Satisfaction: The Art of the Female Orgasm.*

Erica Ehm

One of the most recognized women in Canada throughout much of the 1980s, MuchMusic VJ pioneer Erica Ehm was the subject of many a schoolboy fantasy. Since then, the woman whom CITY-TV founder and president Moses Znaimer once described as "a feisty, happy, Yiddish-Montreal version of a Valley Girl" has evolved into an accomplished writer and proud mama—a mama who was so proud, in fact, that she agreed to pose semi-nude for Toronto photographer Helen Tansey while she was pregnant with her son Joshua. The photos—which are reminiscent of Demi Moore's groundbreaking 1991 *Vanity Fair* photoshoot—later appeared in *Flare Pregnancy* and the *Toronto Star.* Like Moore before her, Ehm proved without a doubt that a pregnant body can be a very sexy thing indeed.

FHM Magazine/Nelly Furtado
(Dave Caulkin). Canadian Press

Nelly Furtado

After soaring to stardom with her hit single "I'm Like A Bird" from her debut album *Whoa, Nelly!,* Nelly Furtado made the British men's magazine *FHM's* list of the 100 sexiest women of 2002. (In fact, they went so far as to dub her "Canada's sexiest export.") Furtado went ballistic, however, when she got wind of the photo that the magazine was running on its cover: "There I am with a shirt that has been digitally altered to go to just below my chest, with a stomach that I don't recognize," she complained to BBC Radio 1, noting that she had neither posed for the magazine nor given her permission for them to use any existing photos of her. As a source close to Furtado told the *London Sun,*

"She's not a men's magazine kind of girl." (Of course, some Canuck Chicks *are* men's magazine kinds of girls: six months later, the cover of *FHM* would feature a photo of another Sexy Canadian Export—in this case, Pamela Anderson.)

Natasha Henstridge

Natasha Henstridge created a bit of a sensation when she appeared on the cover of the French edition of *Cosmopolitan* at age 15. She then went on to star as a sex-starved alien in the critically panned cult flicks *Species* and *Species II*— roles for which she would become famous.

Sass Jordan

A sizzlingly sexy eighties rock bad girl whose raspy voice earned her comparisons to Melissa Etheridge and Tina Turner, Jordan once got a *Toronto Star* reporter hot and bothered by taking off her blouse in the middle of a telephone interview. Lucky for him, it was before the dawn of the videophone.

Ruby Keller

You have to flip a bit further back in the history books to find mention of Canadian-born twenties starlet and tap dancer Ruby Keller. At the height of her career, this popular performer—who was married to American entertainer Al Jolson—was pulling in $5,000 a week and receiving "carloads" of fan mail.

Diana Krall

Known as the glamour girl of jazz, sultry singer Diana Krall was named one of the 25 most intriguing people of 2001 by *People* magazine. She can reportedly count both Elton John and Clint Eastwood among her many fans. (Go ahead. Make his day.)

Mitsou

A sex kitten known for her snug-fitting clothes, sultry looks, and racy videos, Mitsou established herself as a household name in 1980s Quebec.

Monika Schnarre

Canada went a little crazy over its first-ever Supermodel of the World, Monika Schnarre. Even the

Diana Krall (Paul Chiasson).
Canadian Press

Globe and Mail got in on the lovefest, describing the Scarborough schoolgirl as an almost impossibly beautiful creature who had the genetic good fortune to be blessed with "cheekbones like the white cliffs of Dover, a mane of brunette hair as thick as a coat, a complexion as clear as rain, tumescent lips that make you think of tropical rain forests, and a six-foot-tall body from which any outfit hangs as if it grew there." Not bad PR, eh?

Meg Tilly
Nominated for a Best Supporting Actress Academy Award for her role as a pregnant nun in *Agnes of God,* but best remembered for playing the girlfriend of the decreased in the 1983 blockbuster hit *The Big Chill,* Meg Tilly is known for playing the innocent but sizzlingly sexy ingenue.

Jennifer Tilly
Known for her provocative sex kitten roles, Jennifer Tilly—Meg Tilly's sister— is most recognized for her role as a wannabe actress in Woody Allen's 1994 flick *Bullets Over Broadway.*

Shania Twain
Country superstar Shania Twain is probably the only Canuck Chick who can claim to have received an official Department of National Defence seal of approval, but that's just what she ended up with in late 1998. The bureaucrats in this particular government department arranged to ship copies of Shania's CBC Christmas special *Shania Live!* to all military personnel serving overseas. It wasn't her first such high-profile endorsement, of course: three years earlier, *People* magazine had named her one of the 25 most intriguing people of 1995.

Estella Warren
She may not be picking up any Oscar hardware anytime soon (she was awarded a worst-of-class Golden Raspberry or "Razzie" Award performance for her role in *Planet of the Apes,* in fact), but she's already established herself as one of the most recognizable Canadian women in the world. In fact, *Flare* magazine named her its pick for "future sexpot" in its June 2001 issue.

Bunny Brigade

Although Pamela Anderson is undoubtedly Canada's best-known *Playboy* Playmate and arguably the best-known Playmate in the world, she's not the only Canuck Chick to have found fame and (to a lesser degree) fortune on the pages of Mr. Hefner's well-known men's magazine. Here's the scoop on other famous—and infamous—Canadian Playmates.

Kimberly Conrad

Atlanta-born, Vancouver-raised Kimberley Conrad may hold the distinction of being the first Canuck Chick to have had children with Hugh Hefner, but she certainly can't claim to be his first Canadian paramour. Conrad's relationship with Hefner came on the heels of his much-publicized liaisons with Canuck Chicks Shannon Tweed and Carrie Leigh. ("There must be something going on in the Great White North," Hefner admitted to *Maclean's* in 1994.) Clearly, Hefner's love of all things Canadian ran deep: he and Kimberley (a 1989 Playmate of the Year) exchanged vows on Canada Day 1989. Unfortunately, there weren't to be any happy endings for Hugh and the latest Mrs. Hefner. Although their marriage lasted for almost a decade and produced two children, the two ultimately decided to part ways in January of 1998.

Pamela Anne Gordon

Pamela Anne Gordon holds the distinction of being the first Canadian Playmate ever. She strutted her stuff on the pages of *Playboy* in March of 1962 and never looked back. When she was later asked what had led her to take a job as a bunny girl at the Chicago Playboy Club, her answer was simple: she did it for her country. "I think it's a marvelous thing. Not for myself—for Canada," she exclaimed. Other civic-minded Canuck Chicks had their chance to follow in Gordon's patriotic footsteps the following year when *Playboy* published its first "Women of Canada" issue. (The magazine would hold off on publishing subsequent "Women of Canada" issues until 1980 and 1990.)

The Great Impersonators

Pamela Anderson, Celine Dion, Alanis Morissette, and k.d. lang may attract their fair share of celebrity impersonators, but none of them can hold a candle to Canada's most impersonated female celebrity, Shania Twain. Twain keeps one Toronto-area impersonator, Donna Huber, busy performing as many as 120 shows per year for crowds of up to 14,000. "I think she's going to be the next Elvis," says Huber, who bills herself as "Shania Twin."

Not every celebrity impersonator can afford to specialize in a single celebrity, of course—but American impersonator Rosalinde, who specializes in impersonating Pamela Anderson, has also managed to pull it off. American impersonator Sally Davis has three stars in her repertoire: Celine Dion, Shania Twain, and Cher. And renowned celebrity impressionist Ennio Marchetto runs through an entire laundry list of celebrities when he hits the stage to do his paper cutout-assisted impersonations. According to Marchetto, his impression of Celine Dion is a perennial crowd pleaser: "I don't like her and that *Titanic* song is horrible. But when I do her, and she transforms into a ship, people seem to like it."

Danielle House

Another high-profile Canadian Playmate, Danielle House was able to command top dollar from *Playboy* for appearing on the December 1997 cover thanks to the truckloads of free publicity she received after being stripped of her Miss Canada International crown. (For some reason, the Miss Canada International pageant officials thought it would be unseemly to have her continue in the role of Miss Canada after she was convicted of beating up her ex-boyfriend's new girlfriend in a St. John's campus bar in 1996.) House was pleased with the deal her agent was able to cut with *Playboy:* she was reportedly paid $500,000—five times as much as supermodel Cindy Crawford had apparently been paid for her *Playboy* debut. And heaven knows she didn't have to spend a lot of money on her wardrobe: she appeared on the cover of the magazine wearing nothing more than red and green boxing gloves and a tiara. House also managed to lever-

Danielle House (Jonathan Hayward). Canadian Press

age her proverbial 15 minutes of fame into a guest spot on *The Tonight Show,* an opportunity to fire the chicken cannon on *The Royal Canadian Air Farce,* and a one-episode appearance on the CBC sitcom *Dooley Gardens.*

"This isn't a nation of wimps. This is a country where an ambassador's wife once slapped her social secretary . . . [and] where the prime minister once throttled a chanting protester."
- dethroned Miss Canada International winner and one-time *Playboy* Playmate Danielle House, expressing her mystification about the furor surrounding her assault charge to *Globe and Mail* columnist Jan Wong

Carrie Leigh

Hell hath no furry like a Canuck Chick wronged. In 1988, former Playmate Carrie Lee launched a $35-million palimony suit against her ex-lover, Hugh Hefner, alleging that he had broken a promise to marry her and "store a sufficient amount of his own sperm in a sperm bank in order to impregnate (Leigh) in case he became too old to father children." She eventually dropped her suit, but then went on to launch legal action on two other occasions, alleging that *Playboy* had published photos of her without her permission.

Dorothy Stratten

In 1980, 20-year-old Vancouver-born Dorothy Stratten became the first Canuck Chick ever to earn the title of Playmate of the Year. Like Pamela Anne Gordon before her, she was very proud of her Canadian connections: "I'll always be a Canadian at heart, and I'm very, very proud to be the first Canadian Playmate of the Year," she declared. Unfortunately, she didn't get to indulge in much flag-waving: within a matter of months, she was murdered by her ex-husband, Paul Snider, who was jealous of her new romance with American film director Peter Bogdanovich. Her Marilyn Monroe-like innocence and the tragic circumstances surrounding her death transformed her into a pop culture icon. Her life story has inspired two movies (Bob Fosse's feature film *Star 80* and the made-for-TV movie *The Death of a Centerfold: The Dorothy Stratten Story*), two songs (The J. Geils Band's "Centerfold" and Bryan Adam's "The Best Was Yet to Come"), at least two books (*The Killing of the Unicorn: Dorothy Stratten—1960 to 1981* by Peter Bogdanovich and *Dorothy L'Amour*, a novel by Toronto writer Lynn Crosbie), and a special edition of the *Psycho Killers* comic book series entitled *Celebrity Stalker*. That's not the most bizarre part of the Dorothy Stratten story, however: her former lover Peter Bogdanovich was so obsessed with Dorothy that he ended up marrying her younger sister, Louise Beatrice Hoogstraten. Their marriage lasted for 13 years.

Shannon Tweed

Newfoundland native Shannon Tweed was *Playboy's* Playmate of the Year for 1982. She had a highly publicized relationship with Hugh Hefner before becoming involved with KISS singer Gene Simmons and having two children with him. Although she's made her fair share of guest appearances on such TV shows as *Frasier, Highway to Haven, Cagney and Lacey, L.A. Law,* and *Wings* and has landed recurring roles on both *Falcon Crest* and *Days of Our Lives,* she is better known for her roles in erotic thrillers, many of which were direct-to-video productions. Her most memorable role was as feminist studies professor Dr. Margo Hunt in the ludicrously titled 1988 B-movie *Cannibal Women in the Avocado Jungle of Death*: "They're an ancient commune of feminists, so radical, so militant, so left of center they . . . they eat their men," the movie promos proclaimed. (Believe it or not, this less-than-critically acclaimed flick was written by the same screenwriter who went on to write the movie that launched Julia Roberts' career: *Pretty Woman.* I guess we all have to start somewhere.) Tweed's other claim to fame was the fact that she posed nude for *Playboy* with her older sister, Tracy Tweed, in 1991. Talk about family togetherness . . .

Cara Wakelin

Cara Wakelin had to miss her graduation from McMaster University in Hamilton, Ontario, because she was off in Chicago doing a shoot for *Playboy*. The photos ran in the November 1999 issue of the magazine. She had this to say about the experience of posing for *Playboy:* "It gives you an unconscious sense of power. You become every man's fantasy. For one month." Wakelin was also recruited to The Playmate Radio Team—a group of six Playboy Playmates who fill in for radio hosts who are away on holidays or otherwise unavailable. (Clearly, someone has lost sight of the fact that radio isn't exactly known for being a visual medium.)

Beauty, eh?

Danielle House may be Canada's most famous dethroned beauty queen, but she's certainly not the *only* Canuck Chick to have her title yanked or to have faced controversy over the years. Here's a behind-the-scenes look at the Canadian beauty pageant circuit then and now.

1937
Beauty contests make their Canadian debut at the Canadian National Exhibition in Toronto.

1954
Former Miss Canada Marilyn Reddick tells *Chatelaine* readers what it takes to win the title of Miss Canada. Her recipe for success? Combining "the appearance of a musical-comedy actress with the ethics of a Girl Guide . . . [and] the constitution of a Clydesdale mare." She also notes that a Miss Canada contestant would do well to have a fairly tough skin, a lesson Reddick apparently learned while representing Canada at the Miss America pageant in Atlantic City: "Miss Alabama actually sneered at my legs," she complains.

1976
Feminists disrupt the Miss Canada pageant. (Six years earlier, feminists had staged a similar protest at the Miss American pageant in Atlantic City, tossing makeup, hair curlers, high heels, girdles, and bras into a waste receptacle that had been dubbed "the freedom trash can.")

1983
Homemaker's Magazine reports that an estimated three million viewers tune into the Miss Canada pageant each year.

1992
Nicole Dunson—who completes her reign in October of 1992—earns the distinction of being the last Miss Canada. The Miss Canada pageant is cancelled when sponsors start to drop off. In the politically correct 1990s, it's no longer a wise move to have your corporate brand name linked with something as tacky as a beauty pageant.

1997

It's a tough year for beauty queens. Danielle House, Miss Canada International, is stripped of her title after being convicted of assaulting her ex-boyfriend's new girlfriend in a St. John's bar. Meanwhile, Gabriella Petivoky, Miss Canadian International, is stripped of her title when organizers of that pageant discover that she's taken a job as a waitress at a Hooters restaurant.

1998

The new Miss Canada International—Emily Ryan—is stripped of her title when she and the competition's organizers run into conflicts over obligations and remuneration.

1999

Things go from bad to worse on the beauty queen circuit. Seven of 28 contestants drop out of the Miss Canada International competition to protest the way the competition is being managed and the previous year's winner—Leanne Baird of Stoney Creek—is prevented from crowning her successor.

"It might not be the fifth at Greenwood but the Miss World contest sure is a horse race!"
– *Toronto Sun* reporter Jean Sonmor's impressions of the Miss World contest, quoted in Penney Kome's article, "Beauty and the Big Bucks" in the April 1983 issue of *Homemaker's Magazine*

The Art of Marrying Well

You have to wonder if Marlen Therrien and Anne-Marie Sten happened to be big fans of the 1953 hit movie *How to Marry a Millionaire* during their growing-up years. After all, if ever there was a movie that spelled out the advantages of marrying well, this was it. And like their big-screen counterparts—Lauren Bacall, Betty Grable, and Marilyn Monroe—Therrien and Sten managed to leverage their considerable physical assets to attract great wealth. The dynamic duo managed to catch the eyes of two of the country's wealthiest eligible bachelors: Corel founder Michael Cowpland and the Bank of Montreal's Matthew Barrett.

Marlen Cowpland

Anyone who writes Marlen Cowpland off as a traditional trophy wife is doing her a tremendous disservice. As University of Ottawa sociologist Diane Pacom explained to *Herizons* magazine writer Anita Lahey, not only is Marlen Cowpland a little bit too old to pull off the whole trophy bride thing (she's

Marlen Cowpland
(*Ottawa Citizen*/Dave Chan). Canadian Press

fast-approaching 44), but she's also a bit too flamboyant. After all isn't the whole raison d'être of the bona fide trophy bride to make her husband look good? "Trophy wives were the jewels on which the light of the powerful, rich husband would shine. But she outshines the husband. If she were a real trophy wife she would not have a purple dog."

Just in case you're not in the habit of tuning into Marlen Cowpland's TV show, *Celebrity Pets,* on a regular basis, allow me to give you a bit of background on the purple dog. The pooch in question is Bunny, Cowpland's much-pampered Maltese dog and co-star. Bunny has been dyed both purple and hot pink since the TV show hit the air in the fall of 2000—something that has landed Marlen in hot water with veterinarians and animal rights activists alike. It's also cost her at least one big-name guest—actress and animal rights crusader Betty White. Cowpland hasn't had difficulty attracting other celebrities to the show, however: past guests have included actress Phyllis Diller, classical guitarist Liona Boyd, psychic Jo-Jo Savard, singer Jann Arden, wrestler Bret (the Hitman) Hart, comedian Mike Bullard, and movie producer Gary Marshall.

Although her TV show has attracted its fair share of media coverage—after all, stories about purple dogs can provide a welcome break from all the squabbling on Parliament Hill—Marlen is better known for the outlandish outfits she wears off-camera. (Okay, she's never entirely off-camera, but you get the picture.) In addition to her two best-known outfits (the million-dollar leather number that landed her on the front page of the *National Enquirer* back in 1997 and the butt-baring Barbie outfit that she wore to her 43rd birthday bash), she also attracted a fair bit of attention in a four-ply silk gown with a plunging neckline and a thigh-high slit when she was invited to Buckingham Palace to meet the Queen. ("I call it my Jessica dress after the cartoon character in *Who Framed Roger Rabbit,*" she later explained to the *Toronto Sun.*) And then there was the rather memorable photo that appeared on the invitations for her 43rd birthday bash: an army-fatigue-clad Marlen straddling a Rottweiler. ("The Bitch is having a party," the invitations proclaimed.)

Of course, Marlen Cowpland's flamboyance isn't confined to the fashion arena alone. She and hubby Michael—whom she met in the Hull, Quebec, hotspot Chez Henri back in 1986—were once christened "Ottawa's most glamorous couple" by the *Ottawa Sun*. (Hey, it's hard *not* to get noticed when you've got a 30,000-square-foot mansion with his-and-her Porsche 911s parked in the driveway.)

That's not to say that she's without her critics. While the news staff at the *Ottawa Sun* may have given Marlen the royal treatment over the years (they declared her "Ottawa's Queen of Style" in 1998), the paper's readers haven't always been quite so appreciative. Two years ago, they named her the "most overexposed local personality."

And, if the rumours swirling around Parliament Hill are to be believed, Aline Chrétien isn't among her biggest fans either. The prime minister's wife made a point of switching fashion designers when her previous fashion designer, Richard Robinson, started designing clothes for Ottawa's other "Mrs. C"— Marlen Cowpland. ("I don't think she wanted to be associated with the same designer that designs clothes for Marlen," Robinson told the *Ottawa Sun*.)

Anne-Marie Sten

Anne-Marie Sten's first brush with fame came when she made an appearance as a *Toronto Telegram* "Sweetheart of the Week" in 1971—a coup she managed to pull off while she was still attending Woodbridge High School. Then, the year after graduation, she showed up wearing a fur bikini as a *Toronto Sun* Sunshine Girl. For the next few years, she flirted with a career in modelling and acting, appearing as a lingerie model and doing a topless scene in a low-budget movie. But then, in 1977, she stumbled upon her true calling in life by becoming a career socialite—a career change that necessitated a move to Paris.

Anne-Marie Sten and Matthew Barrett
(*Toronto Sun*/Alex Urosevic). Canadian Press

Shortly after arriving in France, Sten managed to find her way onto the radar screen of multimillionaire jetsetter Adnan Khashoggi, a Saudi businessman and arms dealer. Referring to Sten as his "pleasure wife," Khashoggi picked up the tab for an eight-bedroom apartment off the Champs Élysées, an extravagant wardrobe, jewellery, and other goodies.

It was a pretty loosey-goosey arrangement as far as most mistress gigs go. Their relationship was decidedly non-exclusive right from the start. Khashoggi was reportedly supporting 12 different mistresses in various parts of the world and Sten was apparently seeing other men as well. At one point she was romantically linked with the lead singer of a high-profile Swedish rock band and at another point she was rumoured to be dating Pierre Elliott Trudeau. (Trudeau and Sten had apparently met on the ski slopes in Vail, Colorado, in 1979, shortly after Trudeau's marriage fell apart.) Sten's romance with Khashoggi ended, however, when he married one of his other mistresses—the one who happened to be pregnant with his child.

Sten resurfaced on the streets of New York City on the arm of a John Heimann, a respected New York banker who was only too happy to keep her in the style to which she had become accustomed. But that relationship didn't last either. After that, she was briefly married to Canadian banker Matthew Barrett, who was at the time heading up the Bank of Montreal. The two parted ways around the time that Barrett received an offer to head up Barclays Bank in Britain, but reportedly the relationship had been on the rocks for a while.

Writing in the February 2000 issue of *Toronto Life*, Sarah Hampson had this to say about the fascination that Anne-Marie Sten holds for the various men who have passed through her life: "She has always completed the men she is with, reflected their accomplishments, their wealth, their lifestyle, their sexual prowess. She is a walking, talking Porsche."

Saints and Sinners

While feeling morally superior to the Americans is a proud Canadian tradition that ranks right up there with drinking beer, playing hockey, and hitting the curling rink, not every Canuck Chick is a candidate for sainthood. While we definitely have our fair share of saints, we've also got our quota of sinners. Here's what you need to know about both.

Saints

1. Kateri Tekakwitha: You have to conduct your life in a downright saintly fashion in order to find yourself in the running for sainthood more than three hundred years after your death, but that's exactly what Kateri Tekakwitha (who lived from 1656 to 1680) has managed to pull off. In 1980, she was beatified by Pope John Paul II—an important step on the road to officially being declared a saint. If Tekakwitha succeeds in becoming a saint, she'll have the distinction of being the first aboriginal Canadian woman and the third Canadian woman ever to obtain this distinction, joining Marguerite Bourgeoys (1620–1700), the co-foundress of Montreal and foundress of the Congregation of Notre Dame, and Marguerite d'Youville (1701–1771), the foundress of the Sisters of Charity (the so-called "Grey Sisters"), as female Canadian saints. If Kateri does manage to gain entrance to the ultimate Good Girl's Club (you know, the one operated by the Catholic Church), it'll be because of her work caring for the poor and the sick and for her strong faith.

Mère d'Youville, 1978, #768. © Canada Post Corporation, 1978. Reprinted with permission

2. Madeleine de Verchères: Another early Canadian heroine, Madeleine de Verchères (1678–1747) disguised herself as a man and ran ahead of an approaching posse of Iroquois warriors to warn residents of her village—aptly named "Fort Dangerous" because of its vulnerable position on the Richelieu River—of an impending attack. As a result of her actions, numerous lives were saved.

3. Laura Secord: Laura Secord (1775–1868) made a name for herself during the War of 1812. After overhearing a group of American officers discussing a plan to attack the British position at Beaver Dams, she decided to sneak off to warn the British troops about the impending attack. It took her almost 18 hours to make the 32-kilometre trek through streams and snake-infested waters and up the Niagara Escarpment (hey, someone please do me a favour and name a marathon after this gal!), but, in the end, a man took all the credit for saving the day. The scoundrel in question? Lieutenant James FitzGibbon, the British commander at Beaver Dams. It would be another 40 years before Secord's bravery was formally recognized, but, from that point onward, she became widely known as a great Canadian heroine. A monument was built in her honour in Niagara Falls, Ontario, in 1901—the first public monument to a woman to be erected in Canada.

4. Pauline Vanier: Montreal-born Pauline Vanier worked tirelessly on behalf of a number of different humanitarian causes over the course of her remarkable life. During World War II, she helped to coordinate the return of refugees to newly liberated France—an act that earned her the *Légion d'Honneur* from the French government. When her husband, Georges, was appointed Governor General in 1959, she earned a reputation as one of the most hardworking First Ladies the country had ever seen. And in her retirement years, she worked alongside her son Jean, founder of l'Arche, a community north of Paris for mentally challenged adults. In 1967, Pauline Vanier became one of the first recipients of the Order of Canada.

5. Doris Forbes: In June of 1939, a nine-year-old Red Deer girl named Doris Forbes found an orphaned beaver on the banks of the Waskaso Creek and nursed him back to health. The story captured the attention of the international media, making Mickey the beaver the most famous beaver in the world. Repeated attempts to return Mickey to the wild didn't pan out, so Doris and her parents ended up keeping him as a pet. Almost overnight, he turned into Red Deer's hottest tourist attraction. More than 20,000 people flocked to Red Deer to see Doris and Mickey before Mickey died in his sleep in 1948.

Inmates in cells.
National Archives of Canada NAC-PA 27437

Sinners

1. Karla Homolka: She is without a doubt the most notorious female serial killer in Canadian history—a woman who not only pleaded guilty to manslaughter in the deaths of two St. Catharines, Ontario, teens, but who also reportedly played a role in the rape and killing of her own sister, a crime that occurred in her parents' basement on Christmas Eve 1990. (Homolka received immunity from prosecution on that charge as part of the highly controversial "deal with the devil" that Crown prosecutors made in exchange for Homolka's testimony against her equally monstrous fellow serial killer ex-husband, Paul Bernardo.) The fact that she has shown up in newspaper photographs partying inside the prison walls with other notorious female inmates, including a woman convicted of sex crimes involving children, hasn't exactly helped to endear Homolka to the Canadian public. In March 2001, a National Parole Board ruled that she must remain behind bars because she has the potential to kill or injure someone: "The board is satisfied that, if released, you are likely to commit an offence causing the death of or serious injury to another person before the expiration of the sentence you are now serving."

2. Evelyn Dick: Evelyn Dick was pretty much the Karla Homolka of her generation—a gal the Canadian public loved to hate. Her trial for the grisly 1946 "torso slaying" of her husband John Dick was, after all, one of the most sensational trials that the country had ever seen. Not only were there the rather gruesome details of the circumstances surrounding the murder to contend with (the headless, limbless body had to be identified on the basis of an undescended testicle because so much of the body

Karla Homolka (Frank Gunn). Canadian Press

was missing): the townsfolk of Hamilton, Ontario, also had to wrap their heads around the fact that Dick had managed to sleep with half the men in town, including the son of the presiding magistrate. Despite Dick's very creative attempts to come up with a convincing story that would help to explain the blood that was found in the back seat of her car around the time her husband was murdered, the jury found her guilty. Her execution was set for January of 1947 in order to avoid the unpleasantness of a festive season death. At the eleventh hour, she ended up being freed on a technicality, and because whiz kid lawyer John J. Robinette had managed to convince the trial judge to rule all of Dick's statements to police as inadmissible during any subsequent trial on the grounds that she hadn't been warned about the advisability of making such statements, the prosecution's case quickly fell apart. She still ended up doing some time, however, for what was considered to be an even greater crime, the murder of her newborn baby boy. While they were investigating the murder of John Dick, police investigators had stumbled upon the body of a full-term baby encased in concrete inside a suitcase. Dick was found guilty of manslaughter and ended up serving 11 years in Kingston Penitentiary for her crime before being released from jail and given a new identity.

Lili St. Cyr. National Archives of Canada

3. Lili St. Cyr: Although Lili St. Cyr wasn't ever convicted of any crime, she was widely considered to be one of the bona fide bad girls of her day. She managed to achieve international fame as a burlesque performer at a time when taking off one's clothes in public was still considered rather risqué. St. Cyr left little to the imagination with her trademark performance, stepping out of an onstage bubble bath. She achieved her career breakthrough during the years she spent performing at the Gayety Theatre in Montreal in the mid-1940s, but she eventually took her act south of the border, too. Her big break, so to speak, came when she was charged with indecent exposure during an onstage bubble bath at Ciro's nightclub on Hollywood's Sunset Boulevard. In the end, she beat the charge and was able to use the resulting publicity to turn herself into a headline act. She also ventured into B-films and—in her later years—ran a mail-order lingerie firm. Her personal motto? "Sex is currency. What's the use of being beautiful if you can't profit from it?"

4. Gillian Guess: Vancouver resident Gillian Guess holds the rather dubious distinction of being the only juror in Canada—perhaps the only juror in the world—to be convicted of sleeping with one of the accused during a jury trial. And he wasn't just any accused, by the way: he was Peter Gill, a convicted drug dealer on trial for murder. Although Guess proclaimed her innocence, arguing that she could hardly be faulted for not knowing that sex with the accused was a no-no since the trial judge had failed to spell that out in his instructions to the jury, she ended up being convicted and sentenced to 18 months in jail for obstruction of justice. She only ended up spending four days in the slammer before being released pending an appeal. Of course, Gillian Guess isn't the only Canuck Chick to exhibit some bad-girl behaviour in court. Josée Dubreuil—a former exotic dancer who was convicted of stealing $124,000 worth of sports betting tickets from her millionaire pro gambler boyfriend—winked and made suggestive mouth gestures in court during her preliminary hearing. The result? Ex-boyfriend Terry Leblanc fainted right in court.

5. **Kathryn Gannon:** Another West Coast bad girl, Miss Nude B.C. 1981, Kathryn Gannon, proved beyond the shadow of a doubt that loose lips don't just sink ships: they can also torpedo careers. She was recently convicted of passing stock tips from one lover—Wall Street investment banker James McDermott—to another—New Jersey businessman Anthony Pomponio. Although she initially proclaimed her innocence—"For God's sake, I'm an adult-movie actress. I'm not a professor of economics. Would the world give me a break here?"—in the end she decided to change her story. She ended up giving up her fight against extradition to the US and pleading guilty to insider trading.

Millennium Mama

At one point Kathryn Gannon—the adult-movie actress who was recently found guilty of insider trading scandal—had plans in the works for a very special millennium celebration. Her plan? To stage an event that would have allowed her to have sex with 2,000 different men.

Terri-Jean Bedford (Jeff McIntosh). Canadian Press

Oui, Madame!

It would hardly seem fair to wrap up this discussion of bad girls without at least touching upon the rather remarkable career of Toronto dominatrix Terri-Jean Bedford (a.k.a. "Madame de Sade").

Bedford found herself thrust into the media spotlight in the mid-1990s after being arrested at her place of business—Madame de Sade's House of Erotica—a suburban house that subsequently became known as "the bondage bungalow." Her crime? Running a common bawdy house.

While Bedford—a former prostitute—tried to argue that the bondage and sado-masochistic role-playing sessions that she provided to her clients did not constitute sex, the judge wasn't prepared to buy that particular argument. In the end, she was convicted and fined $3,000.

While some gals might have thrown in the towel at that point, Bedford wasn't ready to call it a day. She decided to embark on two new business ventures: the Millicent Farnsworth Sissy Maid Academy and Charm School and Madame's House—a downtown bed and breakfast for fetishists that rents rooms by the hour or by the day.

Needless to say, journalists across the country have had a heyday with Bedford, coming up with ever-juicier headlines to describe her activities. (Hey, it's not every day that you get the chance to write headlines about bondage and kinky sex, after all!) Here are just a few of the many headlines that could very well have earned these hardworking headline writers a place in the Canadian Newspaper Headline Hall of Fame:

"Dominatrix Says She's Been Punished Enough"—Canadian Press, October 16, 1998

"Dominatrix Slapped"- *Toronto Sun*, March 24, 2000

"Appeal Gets Boot"- *Toronto Sun*, October 13, 2000

"Dominatrix Won't Tie Up Court Business"- *Ottawa Sun*, October 13, 2000

"Dominatrix Beaten in Bid for an Appeal" - *London Free Press*, October 13, 2000

"New Bondage Hotel Whipped Into Shape" - *Calgary Sun*, June 3, 2001

The First Wives Club

For a country that's only been around a little more than 130 years, we've certainly had our fair share of colourful prime ministers' wives. Here's the scoop on a few of the more noteworthy women to call the prime minister's residence home.

Susan Agnes Macdonald

Susan Agnes Macdonald—the second wife of Canada's first prime minister, John A. Macdonald—scandalized the Conservative party bigwigs who accompanied her and her husband on their maiden train voyage through the Canadian Rockies. She insisted on riding on the cowcatcher at the front of the train so that she would have an unobstructed view of the scenery.

Annie Thompson

Annie Thompson was an enthusiastic letter writer, as was her husband, Canadian Prime Minister John Thompson. Long before they were married, Thompson had taught her how to write in shorthand so that they could exchange relatively torrid love letters without Annie's mother picking up on any inappropriate overtones. Oh, la la!

Margaret Trudeau

A hippie flower child who managed to win the heart of Canada's sexiest prime minister ever, Pierre Elliott Trudeau, Margaret Trudeau managed to alternately enchant and infuriate Canadians. She certainly left her mark on Ottawa and the country as a whole: the role of Canadian prime minister's wife has never fit quite the same way since she tried it on for size.

Maureen McTeer

Frequently criticized for sticking with her maiden name rather than adopting the last name of her husband, Joe Clark, and initially considered by Tory insiders to be her husband's greatest political liability, Maureen McTeer managed to win the hearts of even the most anti-feminist of critics. By the 1980s, a sizeable number of Canadians were convinced that she—rather than Clark—should be running for prime minister!

Catherine Clark and Maureen McTeer (Jacques Boissinot). Canadian Press

Mila Mulroney

Mila Mulroney was both revered and reviled for her sense of style. While Canadians took great pride in the way she represented us at international summits—the *Toronto Star* cattily noted on one occasion that she stood out from the other more matronly G7 wives "like a Lamborghini in a Volkswagen showroom"—we were also quick to criticize if she seemed to be spending the taxpayers' money a little too freely. Canadians went ballistic when word got out that she had spent $1.8 million renovating the official residences during Brian Mulroney's first 18 months as prime minister. And she didn't take too kindly to press comments about her shopping habits, apparently: when outspoken journalist Claire Hoy quipped that she had earned a black belt in shopping at the age of five, he found himself rather unceremoniously dumped from the Mulroney Christmas card list.

Aline Chrétien

Unlike many of her predecessors, Aline Chrétien has tried her best to steer clear of the political limelight. For the most part she's succeeded, although she did end up attracting a fair bit of attention when she managed to ward off the knife-wielding intruder who found his way into 24 Sussex Drive back in 1995. (The prime minister reportedly grabbed a soapstone carving for protection.)

Matchmaker, Matchmaker

Margaret Trudeau
(Fred Chartrand). Canadian Press

In July of 1969, *Chatelaine* published an article entitled "Whom Should Trudeau Marry?" The journalist writing the piece sought out the services of a matchmaker to help him to come up with a recipe for the ideal mate for Trudeau. The matchmaker told him that the future Mrs. Trudeau should be someone who is "not too racy" as this might be too much for him to handle, and that "she must not present a threat by being a scientific sophisticate. . . . She really shouldn't have a PhD cum laude." At the same time, she should be "reliable, steady, quiet, rather than extravagantly flamboyant, hotheaded or scatterbrained." She might be a dancer, a skater, or an artist, or "Perhaps better still, she should excel auditorily rather than visually, and be a musician of sorts—a harp player?" Most important of all, she should be "independent enough . . . to be a challenge, but not so wild or unusual as to be impossible to tame."

Whether Trudeau read the article before he met his future bride is anyone's guess, but if he did read it, he certainly didn't take the matchmaker's advice to heart. On March 4, 1971, Trudeau married 22-year-old Margaret Sinclair, the daughter of veteran Liberal James Sinclair.

Margaret was a stunning hippie princess with a bit of a wild streak—someone who was famous for her love of dancing, going barefoot, and wearing flowers in her hair. She was the youngest woman ever to be married to a Canadian prime minister. While her youthful verve appeared to be an asset at first—in fact, her campaigning on her husband's behalf is widely thought to have swayed the vote in his favour in 1974—she became increasingly more outspoken as the years went by. *Maclean's* writer June Callwood wasn't that far from wrong when she predicted in August of 1974 that the prime minister could very well find himself being relegated to the status of "second most interesting resident of 24 Sussex Drive" over time.

There's no denying it: Margaret Trudeau certainly had a knack for attracting attention to herself. Whether she was issuing a rather pointed declaration of independence ("I don't intend to be just a rose in my husband's lapel," she told one radio show host in 1976), running around with members of the bad-boy rock group the *Rolling Stones* ("After six years, I have had enough. I abdicate," she declared, when asked if she was having an affair with either Mick Jagger or Ron Wood), or scandalizing Canadians by telling *People* magazine about her "strong sexual urges" and her fondness for garter belts and stockings (not exactly standard interview fare for the wife of a prime minister!), she became the stuff of which headlines were made—both at home and abroad. Unfortunately, her increasingly flamboyant lifestyle took its toll on her marriage to the prime minister and, on May 27, 1977, the Prime Minister's Office issued a simple statement announcing the Trudeaus' intention to part ways.

While some admired her free spirit, others labelled her as merely self-indulgent. And still others seemed to miss the boat entirely. Consider the rather harsh indictment the *New York Times* made of Margaret Trudeau in 1981: "Poor Canada! Other countries may produce national heroines who are the stuff of legend, but there's no such luck in recent times for our dear neighbor to the north. Instead of, say, Jacqueline Kennedy Onassis . . . Canada has had to make do with Margaret Trudeau, a First Lady whose public antics are likely to live on in the archives of *People* magazine, not history books. To be sure, Mrs. Trudeau has been a mildly intriguing figure during her trot across the world stage—but no one could ever accuse her of having launched a thousand ships."

Well, maybe not a thousand *American* ships . . .

CHAPTER 6

Should a Woman Work?

Canada's Call to Women.
National Archives of Canada NAC-C137978

"**W**arning! The contents of this magazine may be hazardous to the health of any wife or mother who is employed outside the home. Because the health risk increases with the number of issues consumed, women who are employed for reasons other than dire financial need are advised to limit their exposure to such reading material. Significant health gains can be realized by avoiding newsstands entirely."

Just think of all the time, money, and aggravation previous generations of Canuck Chicks might have been saved if the magazine and newspaper editors of the day had been required to slap this Surgeon General-style warning message on the front page of their publications. Instead of stumbling through the front door after a hard day at the office to find yourself being trashed by some magazine or newspaper writer with an axe to grind against working women, you could carefully sidestep the publications that were most likely to send your blood pressure shooting sky-high!

"Working for the Frills"

What the magazine writers and editors of the day seemed to lose sight of was the fact that some of the women they took such delight in bashing had little choice but to seek paid employment. In many cases, a working-woman's income was the only thing that was keeping food on the table and the collection agencies at bay. In an article entitled "I Quit My Job to Save My Marriage" that appeared in the June 1955 issue of *Chatelaine,* born-again homemaker Dorothy Manning accused working women of "working for the frills." She then went on to run through a laundry list of goodies that supposedly motivated the average Canadian woman to head off to work each day: "They're working for a car, for a home, for a television set, for a new chesterfield, for a fur coat, false teeth or a holiday in Florida," she insisted.

Pass the ammunition.
National Archives of Canada NAC-C142649

Of course, Manning wasn't the first *Chatelaine* writer to chastise women for supposedly working for such extras—or to hint at the terrible price that a woman might be forced to pay for wanting a career. In an article entitled "Live With a Man and Love It" that ran in the December 1937 issue of *Chatelaine,* Anne B. Fisher, MD, warned women who were working "just to get extra clothes" that their selfish insistence on having money of their own to spend could put their very marriages at risk. "If that is the reason [you are working], look out! [Your husband will] resent doing part of your work, like having to wash dishes or peel potatoes or make the beds when he comes home. . . . At first he won't say anything—but the little boil will be there under the skin, and you never can tell when it will come to the surface and cause a lot of trouble."

And just in case visions of your poor, overworked husband peeling potatoes weren't enough to cause you to put down that lunchbox once and for all, the experts of the day were only too happy to send you on The Mother of All Guilt Trips by describing the harm you were likely doing to your children. Sheila Stringer Coe did a particularly masterful job of yanking on the maternal heart-strings in an article entitled "I Won't Be a Working Wife" which ran in the July 7, 1957, issue of *Weekend Magazine.* She urged working mothers to "[go] to a kindergarten tea some afternoon and watch the stricken face of a little girl whose mother has not shown up because of an outside job" and to be on the lookout for the poor unfortunate children of working mothers who frequently "[fell] asleep outdoors exhausted by crying and cold" because their heartless, uncaring childcare providers won't allow them indoors.

"Annette, driven by ambition, had to excel in a man's world, to beat men at their own game of business. Being 'just' a woman was not enough. . . . [Women like Annette] have rejected their femaleness. . . . For them, psychiatric treatment is the only help."
– *The Canadian Woman: A Manual of Personal Hygiene* **(1961), describing what was thought to be one of the most common causes of frigidity—wanting to be a man!**

Rosie's Revolving Door

Of course, the national sport of bashing working women didn't manage to maintain this degree of popularity throughout the entire 20th century. The opinion makers were only too happy to change their tune about the evils of working outside the home whenever it was in their best interests to do so.

A shortage of manpower during World War II forced Canadians to encourage rather than discourage women from seeking paid employment. In fact,

Shell cases. National Archives of Canada NAC-PA-112912

massive campaigns were orchestrated to sell Canadian women on the benefits of doing their patriotic duty by stepping into blue-collar jobs in the war industries while their male counterparts fought overseas. Initially, the National Selective Service Agency focused on recruiting single women between the ages of 22 and 24, but, over time, the agency had to cast its net a little wider in order to keep the factories running. Suddenly, being a working girl was in vogue!

World War II Canuck Chicks managed to do themselves and Canada proud by mastering a smorgasbord of blue-collar trades including welding, aircraft assembly, shipbuilding, electronics, drafting, and industrial chemistry. Along the way, they challenged society's ideas about what types of work a woman was and was not capable of doing: "Twelve months ago no thought of woman labour was in the mind of any manufacturer," a representative of the Imperial Munitions Board of Canada admitted toward the end of the war. "Experience has now proved that there is no operation or shellwork that a woman can not do. . . . [Even] the heavy operations which require great physical strength."

They also did their bit at home. In addition to planting victory gardens, knitting and sewing clothes for the troops, and organizing blood banks, they collected fats, paper, glass, metals, rubber, rags, and bones for reuse in war productions. ("From the frying pan to the firing line. Work at munitions production in your own kitchen," one Department of National War Services campaign urged.)

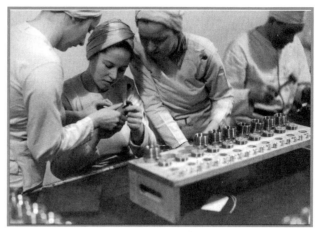

G.E. munitions. Archives of Ontario DIN 10004899

But once the war ended, women employed outside the home were expected to cheerfully relinquish their jobs to returning war veterans and head back home for good. Saskatchewan Cooperative Commonwealth Federation member Dorise Nielsen expressed the prevailing attitude of the day when he attempted to bid the Rosie the Riveters of Canada a rather fond adieu: "Well, girls, you have done a nice job; you looked very cute in your overalls and we appreciate what you have done for us; but just run along; go home; we can get along without you very easily."

Even the federal government did its part to try to kick women back out of the workforce. It passed legislation in 1947 that prohibited married women from holding federal civil service jobs. The restrictions would remain in place for the next eight years.

Roughing It in the Professions

Long before Rosie the Riveter got the chance to strut her stuff and show the guys what a girl can do with an armful of power tools, other gutsy Canuck Chicks were busy making their mark in the various professions. Here's what they managed to accomplish and when.

1867

Emily Howard Stowe becomes Canada's first practising medical doctor. It will be another 13 years, however, before she gains formal recognition from the

Ontario College of Physicians and Surgeons. (Do these guys like to take their time or what?) This isn't Stowe's first noteworthy career breakthrough, of course: back in 1852, she had achieved another Canadian first by making a name for herself as the country's first female school principal.

1875

Grace Annie Lockhart becomes the first woman in Canada and in the British Empire to be awarded a university degree—a bachelor's degree in Science and English Literature from Mount Allison University in New Brunswick.

Jennie Trout becomes the first licensed woman physician in Canada after earning a medical degree south of the border. Women are not yet welcome at Canadian medical schools.

1883

Augusta Stowe Gullen—the daughter of Emily Howard Stowe—becomes the first woman to study medicine and graduate from a Canadian university.

1897

Clara Brett Martin is admitted to the bar and becomes Canada's first female lawyer and the first woman barrister in the Commonwealth.

The Victorian Order of Nurses is established. Early plans to have VON nurses acting as midwives have to be scrapped when there's a huge outcry from members of the medical profession. (Can you say "turf war," boys and girls?)

1898

Emma Casgrain becomes Canada's first woman dentist after graduating from the Quebec College of Dentists.

In Search of Mary Poppins

Domestic service continued to be the number one career opportunity for women during the early decades of the 20th century. Women were hired to cook, clean, sew, do laundry, and care for children in middle- and upper-class households. Working conditions were poor—there was very little freedom or privacy—and the wages were even worse, something that goes a long way towards explaining why would-be employers often had to recruit domestic servants overseas.

1912

Carrie Derick becomes the first Canadian woman to be offered a full professorship. McGill University in Montreal offers her a position as a professor of morphological botany—a position she decides to accept.

1913

Alys McKey Bryant becomes the first female to pilot an airplane in Canada.

1916

Emily Murphy becomes the first female magistrate in the British Commonwealth.

1917

Louise McKinney becomes the first woman to be elected to a provincial assembly in Canada after being elected to the Alberta legislative assembly.

Helen MacGill becomes Canada's first female judge when she is appointed to the bench of the juvenile court in Vancouver.

1919

The first university degree program in nursing in the British Empire is established at the University of British Columbia.

1920

E. Marjorie Hill graduates from the University of Toronto and becomes Canada's first female architect.

The Grass Is Always Greener . . .

By the 1920s, women had established themselves as the dominant sex in the teaching profession, at least at the elementary level. In 1920, 83 percent of elementary school teachers and 50 percent of secondary school teachers were female. Women teachers were, however, routinely paid less than their male counterparts, and they had little chance of being promoted to the better paying positions of principal or school superintendent.

Of course, salaries in the profession as a whole were nothing to write home about. The salaries paid by one Ottawa school board as late as the 1950s made it necessary for teachers to moonlight in order to pay their bills. Some teachers found that they were able to make more money mowing lawns for the school board in question than teaching in the classroom! But even if the salaries were less than stellar, teaching positions tended to offer one perk that few other jobs for women could match: a pension plan.

1922

Margaret Newton becomes the first Canadian woman to earn a doctorate in agricultural sciences.

1927

Elsie Gregory MacGill becomes the first woman to graduate from the University of Toronto with an Electrical Engineering Degree. This is just the first in a string of noteworthy achievements for MacGill, who ends up obtaining a Master's degree in aeronautical engineering from Michigan University, earning a doctorate from the Massachusetts Institute of Technology, and watching an airplane she has designed go into production (all firsts for a woman). Of course, Elsie comes from a line of overachievers: her mother, Helen Gregory MacGill, was one of Canada's first female judges.

1928

E. Barrie Carpenter becomes the first woman to graduate from the Ontario Veterinary College in Guelph, Ontario.

Eileen Vollick becomes the first Canadian woman to receive a pilot's licence.

Queen of the Hurricanes. National Archives of Canada C-146540

The Little Engineer That Could

The Canadian engineering profession was slow to accept women. In 1956, there were 31,000 male engineers but just 23 female engineers.

1930

Cecelia Krieger becomes the first Canadian woman to earn a doctorate in mathematics from a Canadian university.

1936

Alice Wilson—Canada's first woman geologist—becomes the first Canadian woman to become a fellow of the Geological Society of America. Two years later, she will become the first woman to be elected a fellow of the Royal Society of Canada— a national body of distinguished scientists and scholars.

1941

Women in Quebec are finally allowed to practise law.

1948

Anne Underhill becomes Canada's first female astrophysicist after obtaining a doctorate degree from the University of Chicago.

1961

The Bank of Nova Scotia appoints Gladys Marcellus of Ottawa and Shirley Giles of Toronto to the position of branch manager, thereby becoming the first Canadian bank to appoint female branch managers.

1974

The first group of female RCMP recruits begins basic training in Regina.

1975

Grace Hartman becomes the first woman to serve as president of the Canadian Union of Public Employees.

1978

Air Canada hires its first female pilot, Judy Cameron.

1979

Female students are finally allowed to enroll in Canadian military colleges.

1986

The Canadian Labor Congress elects its first woman president, Shirley Carr.

1989

Heather Erxleben becomes Canada's first combat soldier; and Deanna Brasseur and Jane Foster become the first women in the world to fly CF-18 fighter jets.

1992

Roberta Bondar becomes the first Canadian woman to travel in space when she manages to hitch a ride on the Space Shuttle Discovery.

The 77-year-old Canadian Bar Association elects its first woman president, Paule Gauthier.

"The daughters of women who might have picked their occupations by flipping a coin ('Heads, I'll be a nurse; tails, a teacher') could conceivably choose a career today by spinning a roulette wheel."

– Audrey Grescoe, "The New 'Woman's Work,'"
***Homemaker's Magazine*, June 1980**

Teacher reading with students.
Archives of Ontario C 5-1-0-183-1

Modern office, 1907. National Archives of Canada NAC-PA 119420

"The Ideal Canadian Secretary"

One hundred years ago, office work was considered to be a career for men rather than women. After all, in the absence of adding machines and other high-tech bells and whistles, a lot of manual number-crunching was required. And since everyone knew that women were absolutely hopeless when it came to math, it only made sense to have men handling these administrative duties. Or at least that was the theory at the time. . . . Over the course of the next century, a complete flip-flop occurred. While 80 percent of office clerks were male in 1901, within one hundred years, more than 80 percent would be female. The pink-collar ghetto had arrived.

Right from the beginning, female office workers were bombarded with advice on what it took to be the perfect secretary.

In April of 1937, employment expert Mary MacMahon explained to *Chatelaine's* Lotta Dempsey "why secretaries get fired" and what smart secretaries might do to increase their odds of not only keeping their jobs, but possibly even climbing the corporate ladder: "A bright girl is never fooled into thinking the janitor, the office boy, or the scrub woman will look after her employer's desk. . . . Sharpened pencils, a full (but not too full!) inkwell, blotters and pads in place and correspondence properly arranged have meant more money and promotions to many a secretary."

Of course, it wasn't enough to merely keep your boss's desk neat and tidy: you had to feel positively euphoric as you went about sharpening those pencils. Or at least that's what the experts of the day would have you believe. On April 25, 1959, the *Financial Post* introduced its readers to Patricia Fisher, a woman who had been awarded the title of "Ideal Canadian Secretary" in a recent contest by virtue of her, well, virtues! Fisher's employer Gerhard Granek of Granek and Associates consulting engineers described the personal qualities that had made Fisher a shoe-in for this much-coveted title: "She is like a compass to a boat in a storm-swept sea. Attractive, alert and cheerful, she brightens up her surroundings. By telephone, letter, or personal conversation, she is well versed and pleasantly represents the firm. Her efficiency, even disposition and ability to withstand pressure boosts morale." In other words, she was pretty much a candidate for sainthood.

Of course, not all Canuck Chicks were born with the saintlike disposition required to win at the secretarial game. Left to their own devices, some might have muttered under their breath when their bosses bitched about the quality of the coffee or rolled their eyes skyward when the boss insisted that they retype the same stupid boring letter for the umpteen zillionth time. Fortunately, secretarial schools were only too happy to come to the rescue of any Canuck Chick who was born without the gene required to derive tremendous satisfaction from scrubbing the office coffeepot. In 1971, *Chatelaine* reported on the rigorous curriculum at one such institute of higher learning: "Girls are taught speech inflection ('How to sound happy when you don't feel it'), the art of camouflage ('Heavy girls shouldn't wear horizontal stripes, you know'), hair styling . . . and social etiquette ('Tips on how to behave on dates')." That latter course came in handy when it came to dating the boss, I suppose. . . . As it turns out, some of those Canuck Chicks would have done well to skip hairstyling class. After all, being too beautiful could be a liability in the modern office. "I know one personnel manager, in fact, who automatically weeds out the more spectacular beauties applying for secretarial jobs, on the theory that they are likely to take an executive's mind off his work," noted businessman Arthur Bartlett in "It Ain't All Shorthand"—an article that appeared in the April 1, 1947, issue of *Maclean's Magazine*.

Of course, Bartlett and his cronies were downright progressive as compared to 1930s dinosaur F.E. Baily, who seemed to take perverse delight in provoking the readers of *Chatelaine* at every conceivable opportunity. This time, he was determined to convince the magazine's readers that "Women Bring Too Much Sex Into Business." His key point? Women routinely use their womanly wiles to get their own way at work. "Business girls . . . have elevated sponging on men by means of sex appeal to the level of an exact science and something needs to be done about it," he ranted. "The efficiency of an organization is depreciated when the female staff makes it part of their business routine to tantalize the men." Those poor, long-suffering guys . . .

Records and Files Department, Ottawa.
National Archives of Canada NAC-PA 144872

Top Ten Jobs for Women in 1981
1. Secretary/stenographer
2. Bookkeeper/accounting clerk
3. Sales clerk
4. Teller/cashier
5. Waitress/hostess
6. Nurse
7. Elementary school or kindergarten teacher
8. General office clerk
9. Clerk/typist
10. Janitor/cleaner

Muriel McTire

Here's some news that should send shockwaves down the aisles of Canada's ultimate testosterone zone, Canadian Tire. Canadian Tire money was the brainchild of a Canadian woman rather than a Canadian man. Legend has it that Muriel Billes—wife of Canadian Tire co-founder Alfred (A.J.) Billes—came up with the idea for Canada's most famous "funny money" during World War II. Initially, the coupons could only be earned on and applied to gas purchases, but, over time, the program was extended to retail purchases, too.

And if it weren't for our pal Muriel, the semi-nude goddess Diana would be gracing each Canadian Tire bill rather than Scotsman Sandy McTire. A.J. thought that a semi-nude Diana would have greater appeal for Canadian Tire's largely male clientele, but Muriel quickly vetoed the idea.

Over time, Canadian Tire money would take on a life of its own, becoming, in the words of *Saturday Night* writer Wayne Grady "our unofficial second currency."

Burning Down the House

Whether we're staging Mock Parliaments, transforming ourselves into Raging Grannies, or making it known that we're "nobody's baby," we Canuck Chicks have a proud tradition of making our political voices heard. Here's a quick rundown of some of our more noteworthy successes over the years.

1874

The first Canadian branch of the Woman's Christian Temperance Union is founded in Owen Sound, Ontario, by Letitia Youmans. Founded on the belief that alcohol is at the root of all social evils, the WCTU is very much in favour of prohibition. They support the idea of mother's allowances and rally behind the women's suffrage movement because they fervently believe that women are the moral guardians of society and therefore should have the right to vote. The WCTU becomes a powerful training ground for the first generation of Canadian women in politics, including novelist and rabble rouser extraordinaire Nellie McClung.

1876

The Toronto Women's Literary Club is formed to promote the women's suffrage movement in Canada. So much for bookish thoughts . . .

1883

The Canadian Woman Suffrage Association is formed in Toronto.

1893

The National Council of the Women of Canada is formed by Lady Ishbel Marjoribanks Gordon, Countess of Aberdeen and wife of the Canadian Governor General. The National Council helps to bring together representatives from the various women's groups in Canada.

Bell Telephone switchboard. National Archives of Canada NAC-PA 144837

1897

The Federated Women's Institutes of Canada is founded in Stony Creek, Ontario, by Adelaide Hoodless, who is motivated to work for the betterment of women and children after her infant son dies as a result of drinking impure milk.

1902

The Coloured Women's Club of Montreal is founded by the wives of black railroad workers. Its mandate is to seek effective ways of combatting racial discrimination.

1907

The Fédération Nationale Saint Jean Baptiste is established in Montreal to represent the interests of francophone women. Its key areas of concern are education and working conditions.

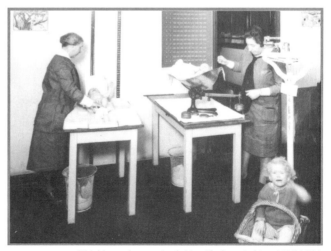

Weighing and measuring babies. Glenbow Archives NA 344516

1916

Women win the right to vote and hold political office in Manitoba, Saskatchewan, and Alberta.

Emily Murphy becomes the first Canadian woman to be named as a judge. It's not just a first for Canada: it's a first for the entire British empire.

1917

The *Military Voters Act* allows a select group of Canadian women—nurses who are serving in World War I—to vote in federal elections. It's the first time any group of Canadian women have been able to exercise the right to vote federally.

The *Wartime Elections Act* extends the vote to the wives, widows, mothers, sisters, and daughters of soldiers.

Conservative Prime Minister Robert Borden is re-elected after promising to extend voting rights to all women over the age of 21.

Women in British Columbia and Ontario win the right to vote in provincial elections.

1918

The *Federal Women's Franchise Act* guarantees female British subjects over the age of 21 the right to vote in federal elections.

The right to vote in provincial elections is extended to women in Nova Scotia.

1919

Women in New Brunswick win the right to vote.

Emily Murphy petitions Conservative Prime Minister Robert Borden to appoint a woman to the Senate. He tells her that he's not able to do so because women are not recognized as "persons" under the terms of the *British North America Act*. Within 10 years, she will manage to prove him wrong on this all-important point.

1920

The *Dominion Elections Act* now makes it possible for women to run in federal elections.

1921

Agnes Macphail—a schoolteacher from the rural Ontario riding of Grey-Bruce—is first off the mark when it comes to getting herself elected to Parliament. For the first time ever, there is a woman sitting in the House of Commons.

1922

Women in Prince Edward Island win the right to vote.

1925

Women in Newfoundland win the right to vote.

1927

Emily Murphy discovers that it's possible to petition the Supreme Court of Canada for an interpretation of any point of law in the *British North America Act*. All you have to do is pull together a group of five people who would also like to see the point clarified. Murphy rallies four other leaders in the women's rights movement to her cause—Nellie McClung, Louise McKinney, Irene Parlby, and Henrietta Muir Edwards—and "the Famous Five" petition Ottawa for an answer to the following question: "Does the word persons in Section 24 of the *British North America Act, 1867*, include female persons?"

1928

The Supreme Court of Canada rules unanimously that women should *not* to be considered "persons" under the terms of the *British North America Act*. This ruling makes it impossible for any woman to be appointed to the Canadian Senate. The Famous Five may be down but they're definitely not out. They simply decide to take their request for clarification to a higher power—the British Privy Council.

1929

The British Privy Council gets it right. It overrules the Supreme Court of Canada decision of the previous year by declaring that women are to be treated as persons under the terms of the *British North America Act*. Finally, Canadian women are "persons."

Women as Persons. Millennium Collection. © Canada Post Corporation. Reprinted with permission

1930

Cairine Wilson, a long-time Liberal Party organizer, becomes Canada's first woman Senator.

1940

Women in Quebec win the right to vote.

1949

Cairine Wilson becomes the first Canadian woman delegate to the United Nations General Assembly. First Canada, now the World!

1951

Marie Thérèse Casgrain becomes the first woman to head a political party in

Quebec when she is chosen to lead the Quebec wing of the Cooperative Commonwealth Federation (later known in that province as Le Parti social démocratique du Québec).

Charlotte Whitton becomes the first woman to be elected major of a major Canadian city—in this case, Ottawa. During her 13 years in power, she earns a reputation for being a political maverick, someone who will say or do pretty much anything. At one point, she reportedly threatens Ottawa's board of control with a cap pistol. And, on another occasion she quips, "Man cannot live by incompetence alone." But she is best remembered for a quote that appeared on coffee mugs and bumper stickers throughout the 1970s: "Whatever women do they must do twice as well as men to be thought half as good. Luckily, this is not difficult."

1962
Blanche Margaret Meagher is appointed Canada's envoy to Austria. She becomes the first Canadian woman to serve as an ambassador.

1967
After intense lobbying from women's groups across the country as well as *Chatelaine* magazine (which, under Doris Anderson, has adopted a gutsy new feminist agenda), the Liberal government of Lester B. Pearson agrees to establish a Royal Commission to report to the federal government on "what steps might be taken by the Federal Government to ensure for women equal opportunities with men in all aspects of Canadian society." Secretary of State Judy LaMarsh—one of the most colourful and controversial politicians of her day—is asked to head up the commission.

1970
The Canadian Royal Commission on the Status of Women issues its much-anticipated report. *Toronto Star* reporter Anthony Westell describes the report as "a bomb already primed and ticking ... packed with more explosive potential than any device manufactured by terrorists . . . a call to revolution." The Commission was calling for reforms in education, employment, immigration, criminal and family law, and childcare.

1971
Journalist Barbara Frum offers *Chatelaine* readers some insider tips on how to get women elected to Parliament. She concludes her article—which runs in the October issue—by commenting on the number of women politicians who end up "inheriting" their husband's parliamentary seats: "A third of all the women who've ever been in Parliament got there on the sympathy vote, as

widows. One hard-eyed pro who dismisses the ability of women to get into politics on their own and has been cynically successful running widows on the black crepe tickets, says, 'The only way you'll ever see a hundred women in the House is to provide a hundred rifles to the wives of sitting members, and then teach them how to shoot.'"

The federal government introduces legislation that makes it possible for women on maternity leave to collect 15 weeks of employment insurance benefits.

1972
The federal government modifies the *Income Tax Act* to make childcare expenses tax deductible.

The National Action Committee on the Status of Women is established. Its mandate? To ensure that the key recommendations of the Royal Commission on the Status of Women are implemented.

1974
Ontario's Pauline McGibbon becomes the first female Lieutenant-Governor in the British Empire.

1977
Parliament passes the *Canadian Human Rights Act*.

1978
The federal labour code is amended to make it illegal to fire or lay a woman off just because she is pregnant.

Hilda Watson—leader of the Yukon Progress Conservative party—becomes the first woman to head up a Canadian political party.

Hazel McCallion wins the mayoralty race in Mississauga, Ontario, an election victory that will eventually earn her the distinction of being Canada's longest-serving female mayor. (Twenty-four years later, she's still going strong!)

1980
Jeanne Sauvé becomes the first woman to serve as Speaker of the House of Commons.

1982
Madame Justice Bertha Wilson becomes the first woman to be appointed to the Supreme Court of Canada.

1984
Jeanne Sauvé becomes the first female Governor General of Canada.

The Slap Flap

On March 19, 1986, Sondra Gotlieb (the wife of Allan Gotlieb, Canada's ambassador to Washington) slapped her social secretary just prior to an important state dinner. The incident—which became known as "the slap flap"—made headlines around the world.

Gotlieb later blamed the incident on a too-tight red dress that she was determined to squeeze into. She apparently spent the day fasting so that she could wear the infamous red dress. The result? She ended up being so "edgy, testy, nervy, and famished" by the time dinnertime rolled around that she slapped her social secretary, Connie Connor, when a last-minute problem with the seating arrangements was brought to her attention. Guess this makes Gotlieb's little red dress the second most famous dress in Washington . . .

The Raging Grannies from *Faces of Feminism* (Pamela Harris). Reprinted with the permission of Pamela Harris

1987

A group of eight peace activists in Victoria, BC, start wearing outrageous-looking hats and singing satirical political protest songs. They call themselves the Raging Grannies. Soon other Raging Grannies groups pop up in other cities including Toronto, Ottawa, Montreal, Kamloops, and Halifax.

1989

Audrey McLaughlin is elected leader of the federal New Democratic Party. She's the first woman to head up a federal political party.

1991

Rita Johnston becomes the first Canadian woman to head up a provincial government. She comes to power after taking over the political reins from British Columbia premier William Vander Zalm, who was forced to resign after a series of scandals rocked public confidence in his Social Credit government.

1993

Kim Campbell becomes the country's first female prime minister.

Sheila Copps becomes the first woman to be appointed deputy prime minister.

1995

United Nations Secretary Boutros Boutros Ghali invites Louise Arbour to serve as the Chief Prosecutor for the UN's International War Crimes Tribunals in Yugoslavia and Rwanda. In May of 1999, she indicts Slobodan Milosevic, president of Yugoslavia, for crimes against humanity—the first time a ruling head of state has been charged with war crimes by an international court. Later that year, she accepts an appointment to the Supreme Court of Canada.

2000

Beverley McLachlin is sworn in as chief justice of the Supreme Court of Canada—the first woman to hold the office.

The Broad Squad

We may not have any Mothers of Confederation to honour (mainly because they were too busy making dinner for the Fathers of Confederation, it would seem!), but we've certainly had our fair share of gutsy broads leave their mark on the Canadian political scene since that time. Here's the scoop on seven women who truly rocked the House during their political careers.

Kim Campbell

While Kim Campbell is best known for being Canada's first female prime minister, she has also managed to achieve a number of other noteworthy firsts over the course of her political career. She became the first female minister of justice and attorney general in 1990 and the first female minister of national defence in 1993. (At that point, she found herself heading into a party leadership race: "Who needs a leadership race?" she quipped, exhibiting the classically irreverent Kim Campbell sense of humour. "I'll just stage a military coup. Don't mess with me. I have tanks.") She also managed to attract a fair bit of attention from beyond our borders, thanks to a racy (by Canadian standards) photo of her that was published in the fall of 1992. The bare-shouldered photo showed her holding her judicial robes in front of her, something that couldn't help but make you wonder if she had actually agreed to pose in the buff. The youthful image that the portrait conveyed was the best pre-election PR that money could buy: she appealed to the same types of voters who had elected Bill Clinton south of the border: "The Clinton envy factor was important," political commentator Richard Gwyn later told *Maclean's*. "Kim was our baby boomer." That wasn't the juiciest compliment that she managed to attract as a result of the now-famous photo: a British tabloid reporter described her as "a sexy, dewy-eyed Madonna." She also received solid backing from

Chatelaine magazine, which named her as its Woman of the Year for 1993 in January 1994.

Sheila Copps

Sheila Copps made a name for herself during the 1980s when she and a group of other young Liberals (John Nunziata, Don Boudria, and Sergio Marchi) and one second-term MP (a baby-faced Brian Tobin) formed the Rat Pack—a political posse whose job was to mercilessly harass key members of the Mulroney government during question period. The Rat Pack attracted quite a following. They printed and sold T-shirts emblazoned with their name and—in 1985—Sheila posed for the cover of *Saturday Night* magazine clad in black leather and straddling a Harley-Davidson. Of course, not everyone was a huge fan of Sheila Copps. At one point, Tory justice minister and resident dinosaur John Crosbie interrupted her when she was speaking in the House of Commons and told her to "quiet down, baby." Her reply? A scathing, *"I am nobody's baby."* Reform Leader Preston Manning was next to hop on the Sheila-bashing bandwagon, warning anyone who was thinking of voting

Sheila Copps (Jim Allen/Spectrum Stock)

Liberal in the 1993 election that they might very well end up with Sheila Copps as deputy PM. (She later confessed to *Maclean's* that she felt almost gleeful when she caught a glimpse of the Reform Leader during her first day back in the House of Commons following the Liberal victory. "I wanted to jump up in the House the first day, and say, 'See, Preston, your worst nightmares have been realized,'" she recalled.) She may have had her rough moments as politician—the infamous GST fiasco comes to mind—but she's proven time and time again that she's a smart and savvy Canuck Chick with staying power. And that's pure political gold.

Deborah Grey

You may not always agree with Deborah Grey's political stands, but you've got to love the woman's style. She's feisty and fearless and has a wicked sense of humour—and she rides a motorcycle, to boot. She's willing to stand up to anyone when there's a principle at stake, something that makes her either a brave and gutsy politician or a bit of a loose cannon, depending on what you think of her. She even had the political smarts to be born on Canada Day—something that represents a fabulous PR opportunity each and every July 1. ("I'm the original Canuck Chick!" she insists.)

Deborah Grey (on the right).
Courtesy of Deborah Grey

Agnes Macphail

Agnes Macphail managed to pull off not one but two political firsts. Not only did she manage to become the first woman elected to the Canadian House of Commons: she also succeeded in becoming one of the first two women to win a seat in the Ontario Legislative Assembly. It kind of makes you wonder what she might have shot for next if she'd decided to go for a hat trick . . .

Judy LaMarsh

Judy LaMarsh's real name was Julia Verlyn LaMarsh, but it's a name she decided to ditch long before entering politics: "My name sounds like something that should be up in lights over a striptease theatre," she once said. One of the most outspoken and flamboyant politicians of the 1960s, LaMarsh managed to wrack

Judy LaMarsh (Ron Roels). National Archives of Canada
PA-126968. Reprinted with the permission of Ron Roels

up some pretty significant achievements during her five years in the House of Commons. While serving as the minister of health and welfare, she implemented the Canada Pension Plan and played a key role in designing the country's Medicare system; and while she was secretary of state, she established the Royal Commission on the Status of Women and presided over the country's Centennial celebrations. She followed up her political career with equally successful careers in print and broadcast journalism and in teaching (she taught law at Osgoode Hall). Despite all her noteworthy successes, however, Canadians sometimes didn't know what to make of the fireball that was Judy LaMarsh. Here's how journalist Heather Robertson described her in 1975: "She is sun and moon, Great White Mother, Virgin Queen, and bitch goddess all in one, dangerous and unpredictable, yet at the same time strong and wise." But above all, she was Judy.

Nellie McClung

Novelist, teacher, and political activist Nellie McClung was, without a doubt, the best-known Canadian feminist during the early 20th century. She was also a gifted writer who knew how to put the power of the pen to work against her political foes. Her play—*How the Vote Was Not Won*—proved to be particularly popular with audiences, who flocked to the Regina Walker Theatre in Winnipeg to watch Nellie McClung argue her case of why *men* should not get the vote. Pretending to be Manitoba Conservative Sir Rodmond Roblin—a staunch opponent of women's suffrage—McClung managed to prove just how ridiculous the arguments against women's suffrage sounded if you turned the tables: "In this agricultural province, the man's place is the farm. Shall I call man away from the useful plow and harrow to talk loud on street corners about things which do not concern him? Politics unsettle men. . . . When you ask for the vote, you are asking me to break up peaceful, happy homes—to wreck innocent lives. . . . It may be that I am old-fashioned. I may be wrong. After all, men may be human. Perhaps the time may come when men may vote with women." The play was credited with helping to defeat the Roblin government—something that helped to pave the way for Manitoba women obtaining the right to vote and hold political office in Manitoba in 1916. Thirteen years later, McClung was ready for an even bigger fight: along with Emily Murphy and three other women—the so-called "Famous Five"—she petitioned the British Privy Council for the definitive decision that allowed Canadian women to be considered "persons" for the very first time in the eyes of the law.

"I wish you could see the proportion of my mail that tells me to go home and darn my husband's socks. I never would have believed that one man's hosiery could excite the amount of interest those socks do—and yet, do you know, they are always darned!"
– Nellie McClung, quoted in *Maclean's Magazine* in 1915

Emily Murphy

You have to wonder if the obnoxious barrister who decided to taunt City of Edmonton magistrate Emily Murphy during her first day on the job lived long

Nellie McClung. National Archives of Canada NAC-PA 30212

enough to see the ramifications of his little jibe—not just for Murphy, but for the country as a whole. "You have no right to be holding court," he insisted. "You're not even a person." Murphy wasn't about to waste her breath arguing the language of the *British North America Act* with a loud mouth such as this: instead, she took her argument to higher authorities, including the British Privy Council. In the end, justice prevailed and women were formally recognized as "persons." Seeing women designated as "persons" under the terms of the *BNA Act* wasn't Murphy's only achievement by any means: not only did she write a best-selling book prior to entering politics—*The Impressions of Janey Canuck Abroad* (1902): she also published *The Black Candle* in 1922: a book on the drug trade that became the standard Canadian reference book for an entire generation.

CHAPTER 7

Hollywood North

Hollywood loves nothing more than to brag about the workings of its star system, but what the studio bigwigs tend to lose sight of from time to time is the fact that many of the stars that they take such pride in claiming as their own are actually 100 percent Canadian-made.

This "what's-yours-is-ours" cultural sleight-of-hand has been going on since practically the beginning of time: it's what's allowed movie industry executives to repackage *our* Mary Pickford as "America's Sweetheart" and to "borrow" *our* Mounties whenever the urge strikes. I suppose we should be flattered by this American fixation with all things Canadian, but sometimes it gets rather a little tiresome. One of these days they're going to try to convince us that Anne of Green Gables was a freckle-faced, red-haired girl from Vermont. You just mark my words . . .

In this chapter, we're going to zero in on some of the many grand dames of the entertainment industry who just happen to hail from our side of the border—everyone from Mary Pickford to Fay Wray to Kate Reid. So grab that bag of popcorn and get ready to be dazzled by some Canuck Chicks with true star power. Ladies and gentlemen, it's showtime . . .

Celluloid Chicks and Theatrical Types

Canada has long been a breeding ground for the entertainment industry's biggest and brightest stars. Here's a quick snapshot of some of our more noteworthy contributions to stage and screen over the past one hundred years.

1886

A star is born (literally). Hamilton-born Florence Lawrence becomes the first actor or actress to be identified by name on the screen or on a playbill—something that earns her the distinction of being the world's first movie star.

1911

The tender sensibilities of movie-going Canuck Chicks are being carefully safeguarded by Big Brother. While Ontario The Good is the first jurisdiction in North America to establish a censor board, Quebec and Manitoba quickly follow suit. (Despite what the rest of the country might think, Ontario no longer has a monopoly on good behaviour.)

1913
Canada's first feature film, *Evangeline,* premieres in Halifax, Nova Scotia.

1929
Mary Pickford kicks off what will ultimately become a three-year Oscar hat trick for Canadian actresses by picking up the Best Actress Award for her role in *Coquette* (1929). Fellow Canuck Chicks Norma Shearer and Marie Dressler will do their part over the next two years, with Shearer winning the Best Actress Oscar for her role in *The Divorcee* (1930) and Dressler winning the Best Actress Oscar for her role in *Min and Bill* (1931).

Mary Pickford. National Archives of Canada NAC-C 52029

More Than Just a Pretty Face

They may have nicknamed her "America's Sweetheart," but she was really one of our own. And by 1920, Toronto-born Gladys Smith (now known as Mary Pickford) was earning over $1 million a year—more than 10 times as much as the president of the United States.

Mary Pickford made her first movie in 1909, at the age of 15. By the time she died in 1979, she had appeared in 245 films, produced or written 35 more films, and walked away with numerous awards. Two of the most noteworthy pieces of hardware she managed to accumulate over the years were the Best Actress Award that she received for her 1929 movie *Coquette* (her first "talkie") and the special Lifetime Achievement Academy Award that she received from the Academy of Performing Arts in 1975.

One of the few silent movie actresses to successfully make the transition to talkies, Pickford was known for playing beautiful, self-confident characters who weren't afraid to fend for themselves: in one of her films, she slapped an overeager suitor in the mouth with a rotting fish. She quickly won the hearts of the filmgoing public with these feisty, good-girl roles: in 1917, she earned the title of "America's sweetheart" after attracting 1,147,500 votes in a magazine popularity contest.

What most people didn't realize at the time was that Mary Pickford was also a shrewd businesswoman. In 1919, she co-founded United Artists along with D.W. Griffith, Charlie Chaplin, and Douglas Fairbanks Jr. (her real-life leading man). She went on to produce movies and to serve as vice-president of United Artists until she sold her shares in the company in 1951.

1933

Alberta-born Fay Wray makes a name for herself as the Scream Queen in *King Kong.* Her scream also gets a workout in future flicks, including *The Mystery of the Wax Museum, Dr. X,* and *The Vampire Bat*—proof that a good pair of lungs can really take you places in Hollywood.

The Main Attraction

One of the biggest roadside attractions in Depression-era Ontario had nothing to do with the entertainment industry at all—well, at least not directly. The attraction in question was the birthplace of the world's first surviving quintuplets, Marie, Annette, Cecile, Yvonne, and Emilie Dionne, who were born on May 28, 1934. Approximately three million curious onlookers made the trek to Corbeil, Ontario, hungry for a chance to see the internationally famous Dionne quintuplets for themselves. The traffic flow to Corbeil was so heavy, in fact, that the Ontario government found it necessary to build a highway to accommodate all the added traffic.

Dionne quintuplets. National Archives of Canada NAC-PA 122615

Of course, it was in the government's best interest to ensure that the tourists arrived at their destination safely. Because the girls had been declared wards of the Crown shortly after their birth, any money they earned landed squarely in government coffers. Olva and Elzire Dionne had lost control of their daughters after Olva—desperate for a way to feed his 10 children—had signed a contract with an American firm that would seen the quints being toured as a sideshow act. The morally outraged government of Ontario Premier Mitch Hepburn stepped in to "save" the five babies from what it saw as shameless exploitation—and then itself went about the business of making money off the quintuplets. Thanks to some lucrative contracts endorsed by Ontario Labour Minister David Croll, the girls ended up flogging everything from soap to syrup and inspiring a smorgasbord of spin-off products, including calendars and dolls. They even made an appearance in the 1936 film *Reunion*, a controversial film that was banned by Chicago's Board of Censors for featuring both an adulteress and a pickpocket. (Two mortal sins in one flick? We couldn't have that!)

It wasn't until 1998 that the Ontario government apologized for its shameless exploitation of the Dionne quintuplets and awarded them $4 million in compensation. Up until that time, the three remaining sisters had been living on a combined pension of just $734 per month. Two of the other sisters had died much earlier on in life: Emilie died at age 20 at a convent following an epileptic seizure and Marie died at age 35 as a result of a blood clot to the brain. Recently, a third Dionne quintuplet passed away: Yvonne died of cancer at age 67.

Dionne quintuplets. National Archives of Canada NAC-PA 122616

"Bringing up a baby is a business—the most important business in the world. . . . Forests, coals, oil—how much would these matter in the national economy if anything went seriously wrong with the year's baby crop which, twenty years from now, will be the national crop of new citizens."

– Alan Roy Dafoe, MD, the doctor responsible for delivering the Dionne quintuplets, in his best-selling baby book, *Dr. Dafoe's Guidebook for Mothers* (1936)

Mountie Barbie

In 1988, Mattel introduced Canadian Barbie, a Barbie doll dressed in a Mountie uniform. The most curvaceous Mountie in history, Canadian Barbie (a.k.a. "Mountie Barbie") came in a box that was designed to eradicate some of the American long-standing ignorance about our country. It featured a map of Canada.

Mickey Mountie

In 1995, the RCMP signed a five-year marketing deal with the Disney corporation that gave the mega-corporation an exclusive licence to market products that incorporated the Mountie image. When the contract came up for renewal, the RCMP decided to assign licensing rights to a non-profit corporation instead, thereby bringing to a close a rather hellish five years of really bad "Mickey Mountie" jokes.

1936

Hollywood catches Mountie-mania. The 1936 version of *Rose Marie*—which stars Nelson Eddy and Jeanette MacDonald—makes the song "When I'm Calling You" famous (or infamous, depending on your feelings about this particular ditty). The film proves successful enough to cause the geniuses at MGM to decide to order a remake in 1954. (Less well received than the first, the remake includes a song with the rather memorable title, "I'm the Mountie Who Never Got His Man.") In between, Twentieth Century-Fox brings out its own Mountie flick, *Susannah of the Mounties*, a 1939 film starring Shirley Temple—a long-suffering moppet who (poor little tot!) is raised in the god-forsaken wilderness of Canada. Two subsequent Mountie movies— *Saskatchewan* (a 1954 film that is filmed in Alberta) and *The Far Country* (a 1954 film featuring Jimmy Stewart) prove to be much less memorable—in fact, actually quite forgettable.

1937

Canadian-born silent film star Marie Prevost is found dead and partially eaten by her dachshund. Four decades later, she'll become the inspiration for the ghoulish Nick Lowe song, "Marie Prevost," which includes the all-too-memorable line, "She was a winner/Who became the doggie's dinner."

1938

Winnipeg-born Deanna Durbin shares a special Academy Award with American actor Mickey Rooney for "bringing to the screen the spirit and personification of youth."

"It was drummed into me that I must never have sex with a man before I was married, and then the next day I was off to the studio where a very different set of rules prevailed. I must admit that it was lovely to be asked and even lovelier to say no . . . or yes."
– Deanna Durbin, quoted in *Glamorous Musicals: Fifty Years of Hollywood's Ultimate Fantasy* by Ronald Bergan (1984)

1939
Studio D—the only all-women English film studio in the world—is created by the National Film Board.

1941
The National Film Board documentary *Churchill's Island*—a documentary about the Battle of Britain—becomes the first Canadian film to win an Oscar.

1942
Canadian actresses Ann Rutherford and Cecelia Parker are awarded special achievement awards for representing "the American way of life" in the Andy Hardy movies. No one seems to be the least bit bothered by the fact that they're, well, um, *Canadian*.

1946
Canada's first drive-in movie theatre opens just outside of Hamilton, Ontario.

1948
Spring Thaw opens in the basement of the Royal Ontario Museum with a memorable ditty entitled "We All Hate Toronto." The show—which becomes an annual rite of passage for Canadians until 1971—will go on to spotlight the talents of such Canuck Chicks as Jane Mallett, Dinah Christie, Salome Bey, Barbara Hamilton, and Joni Mitchell over the years.

1949
Hollywood isn't the only part of the entertainment industry to be hit with a "red scare." Allegations about the existence of Communist cells within the National Film Board results in the Department of National Defence decreeing that no NFB employee will be allowed to work on any defence film.

1956
Vancouver-born Yvonne DeCarlo stars alongside Charlton Heston and Anne Baxter in the Hollywood blockbuster *The Ten Commandments*. She'll go on to make an even bigger name for herself as the supremely creepy Lily Munster in the sixties cult classic TV show, *The Munsters* (1964–1966).

1965
The Charlottetown Festival is launched. Included in the first-year lineup is the show that will become its trademark: *Anne of Green Gables*.

1969
Quebec filmmaker Denis Heroux releases *Valerie*—the first sexploitation film of many to come out of the province during the so-called "Maple Syrup Porn" boom.

1974

Micheline Lanctot stars opposite Richard Dreyfuss in the critically acclaimed film version of Mordecai Richler's equally critically acclaimed novel, *The Apprenticeship of Duddy Kravitz*.

1978

Yellowknife-born actress Margot Kidder plays Lois Lane in *Superman*—a role she'll reprise in sequels in 1980, 1983, and 1987. In 1981, she dates Canada's own superman—or at least super PM—Pierre Elliott Trudeau.

1979

Linda Griffiths wows theatre audiences by playing both passion and reason in the hit stage production *Maggie and Pierre*.

Get in Touch with Your Inner Bitch

One of the few actresses who can claim to have had Tennessee Williams, Arthur Miller, and Edward Albee all write roles specifically for her, Canadian stage actress Kate Reid had this to say about the secrets of her success in a 1979 interview with the *Toronto Star*'s Gina Mallet: "I seem to be known for feisty roles but I love comedy as well. I guess I'm always looking for something else in a person. If you're playing someone nice, you've got to find the bitch."

1981

National Film Board director Bonnie Klein's anti-pornography film *Not a Love Story* has Canadians hot and bothered. After the film is made, the stripper who is featured in the film—Lindalee Tracey—decides to leave the adult entertainment business and pursue a career in broadcast journalism.

1983

Director Terre Nash's film *If You Love This Planet* wins an Academy Award—this despite the fact that it was labelled "political propaganda" by the US Justice Department.

1985

Megan Follows—soon-to-become known around the world as the red-pigtailed Anne of Green Gables—makes her feature film debut in Stephen King's horror flick *Silver Bullet*.

Cynthia Dale
(*Toronto Sun*/Norm Betts). Canadian Press

"It's not really Canadian unless it stars one of the following: Eric Peterson, R.H. Thomson, Saul Rubinek, Booth Savage, a Dale sister, Janet Laine-Green, Fiona Reid, Megan Follows, Gordon Pinsent, and Barbara Hamilton."

– Jim Slotek, "The Canadian Showbiz Century," *Toronto Sun*, January 2, 2000

1987

Patricia Rozema launches her directing career with the critically acclaimed film *I've Heard the Mermaids Singing,* which stars Toronto actress Sheila McCarthy.

Acclaimed actress Jackie Burroughs establishes herself as a writer and director in *A Winter Tan.* She wins a Best Actress Genie for her starring role in the film, which describes a middle-aged feminist's sexual adventures in Mexico. She later tells *Toronto Life* magazine: "They just don't cast me in the goody-goody-roles, the loving grandmother sort of thing."

1988

Actress Jill Hennessy makes her film debut in *Dead Ringers.* She and her real-life twin sister Jacqueline (a.k.a. Jacqui) play twin sisters who are prostitutes.

1991

London, Ontario–born actress Kate Nelligan is nominated for a best supporting actress Oscar for her role in *The Prince of Tides.*

Documentary filmmaker Gail Singer makes *Wisecracks*—a film about female comediennes that spotlights Phyllis Diller, Ellen DeGeneres, Whoopi Goldberg, and fellow Canuck Chick Jenny Jones. *Variety* describes the flick as "refreshingly vulgar and witty"—high praise indeed!

1993

Winnipeg-born (but Australia-raised) actress Anna Paquin, 11, wins the Best Supporting Actor Oscar for her role in *The Piano.*

1994

Jackie Burroughs picks up the first of two consecutive Gemini Awards for best actress for her role as Aunt Hetty in CBC's highly popular *The Road to Avonlea.*

1996

Molly Parker creeps out Canadian filmgoers by playing a necrophiliac in Lynne Stopkewich's controversial movie *Kissed.* It's Parker's first feature film.

1997

Sarah Polley's performance in *The Sweet Hereafter* proves she has what it takes to make the transition from child star to a mature actress—this despite the fact that she grew up in front of the camera on *The Road to Avonlea.*

1999

Critically acclaimed filmmaker Annie Wheeler achieves commercial success with her film *Better Than Chocolate*—a show about two attractive young women who fall in love with one another. (Just in case you were wondering, the chocolate bit comes into play when the two women paint each other with chocolate and roll around on a blank canvas—a rather sinful waste of chocolate, in my humble opinion.)

2000

Filmmaker Mary Harron causes a stir when word gets out that she's directing the screen version of Bret Easton Ellis' notorious book, *American Psycho* (a book made all the more notorious by the fact that it was reportedly the preferred bedtime reading of card-carrying Canadian psycho Paul Bernardo). Controversy is, of course, nothing new for Mary Harron, the daughter of comic actor Don Harron of Charlie Farquharson fame. Her first flick—*I Shot Andy Warhol* (1996)—was an account of a 1968 assassination attempt on the pop culture icon by homicidal lesbian revolutionary Valerie Solanas.

2001

Tonya Lee Williams—best known for her role as Olivia on long-running daytime series *The Young and The Restless*—founds ReelWorld—a film festival that seeks to celebrate multiculturalism on the big screen.

2002

Scientists at the University of Toronto discover that people who win Oscars can expect to live four years longer than other performers appearing in the film for which they won the Oscar. And, to rub even more salt into the wounds, two-time Oscar winners live six years longer, on average. Fame, fortune, *and* a longer life? It just doesn't seem fair . . .

Funny Girls

You could be forgiven for assuming that any Canadian with a sense of humour has to be male. After all, it's our funny guys rather than our funny gals who tend to attract the lion's share of media attention. But, contrary to what your average guy or gal on the street might believe, the Great White North has managed to produce its fair share of funny girls over the years. Here's a quick snapshot of some of the powerful weapons we've got tucked into our Canuck Chick comic arsenal. Ready, aim, fire . . .

Beatrice Lillie

A Toronto-born comic actor who was widely billed as "the funniest woman in the world," Beatrice Lillie enjoyed a comic career that spanned more than a half century. Although she spent the majority of her career on the stage, frequently appearing in the plays of Noel Coward, she managed to make a few films over the course of her career, including *Exit Smiling* in 1926 (her first film) and *Thoroughly Modern Millie* in 1967 (her last).

Lucille Kallen

Los Angeles–born but Toronto-raised Lucille Kallen was hired by TV legend Sid Caesar as one of the original writers for *Your Show of Shows*. One of her key responsibilities was to try to keep the show's rowdy male writers on track (she was the only female). Legend has it that she was the inspiration for the Rose Marie character on the 1960s sitcom *The Dick Van Dyke Show*.

Sandra Shamas

Rather than worrying about airing her dirty laundry in public, Sandra Shamas has made an entire career out of it. Once described by pop culture critic Andrew Clark as "a ferocious, funny estrogen superhero," Shamas is the hysterically funny and razor-witted genius behind the critically acclaimed one-woman shows *My Boyfriend's Back and There's Going to be Laundry* (1987), *My Boyfriend's Back and There's Going to Be Laundry II: The Cycle Continues* (1989), *Wedding Bell Hell* (1993), and—following her searingly painful divorce—*Wit's End* (1999). ("You know when people tell you, 'One day you're going to laugh at this?'" she said of her *Wit's End* show. "Well this is that day.") We can sleep well at night knowing we're unlikely to lose our gal pal Sandra to the infamous American brain drain anytime soon. Because Sandra's business acumen is every bit as sharp as her wit, she's managed to sock away a hefty nest egg that allows her the luxury of deciding where and when she wants to perform. And, for now at least, the comic genius who once admitted to being "rabidly Canadian" is staying on our side of the border. Final score? Canada: 1; The United States: 0.

Mary Walsh

Mary Walsh is best known for playing the role of *This Hour Has 22 Minutes'* Marg Delahunty, a woman *Maclean's* writer Brian D. Johnson once described as "a Zellers nightmare: violet eyeshadow, orange lipstick, big glasses, gold-plated jewelry and a bathing cap barnacled with flowers." What most Canadians don't realize is that she's also an accomplished writer, director, and dramatic actor and the brains behind *This Hour Has 22 Minutes*. I guess the bathing cap tends to throw people off . . .

The Welfare Starlets

The Welfare Starlets were a Winnipeg band that came to the attention of the national media in 1992 as a result of such highly unconventional folksongs as

"Roadkill," "Granny's Hooked on Halcion," and the song that could very well become an anthem for Canuck Chicks everywhere, "The Menstrual Blues." Who would have thought we'd live long enough to hear the Welfare Starlets belting out these classic lines from "The Menstrual Blues" for *Morningside's* Peter Gzowski: "I'm hurtin', I'm achin', I'm menstruatin', Don't touch me, just leave me alone, I don't want to make love and I sure won't make supper, 'til these cramps are gone gone gone gone."

Nancy White. Photo credit: Normunds Verzins. Reprinted with permission

Nancy White

Toronto-based singer/songwriter Nancy White was a fixture on the CBC Radio show *Sunday Morning* until some misguided bean-counter underestimated the value of this national treasure and gave White her walking papers. A Canuck Chick through and through, White got her start as one of four folk singers hired to entertain the crowds who were waiting to get in to see the Centennial Year Confederation exhibits in PEI. She's best known, however, for penning a song about that awful moment in every new mother's life when she realizes it's time to deep-six the romantic fantasies of her (apparently) wasted youth. The song in question? "Leonard Cohen's Never Going to Bring My Groceries In" from White's utterly hilarious *Momnipotent: Songs for Weary Parents* CD.

Canuck TV

Talk Show Queens

While we've yet to produce our own Oprah—a talk show queen who is influential enough to cause bookstore stampedes by merely indicating what book she happens to be reading at the time—we've certainly managed to produce our fair share of memorable female talk show hosts over the years. Here's a quick who's who.

Joyce Davidson

One of Canada's first and most controversial talk show hosts, Joyce Davidson got her start working as a chef's assistant for a Hamilton cooking show and as a model and demonstrator for television commercials. It wasn't until she was brought on board to co-host *Tabloid*—a high-profile news magazine show that ran on CBC-TV from 1953 to 1963—that she became one of the most famous (or infamous) women in Canada. She earned herself a two-day suspension from the show by dissing royalty. (She told the host of the NBC-TV morning news show, *Today,* that "like the average Canadian" she was "pretty indifferent" to the Queen's upcoming visit.) And she ended up being given her walking papers for good when she told journalist Pierre Berton that any woman who was still a virgin at age 30 was "unlucky." After becoming involved in a high-profile love triangle with television producer and talk show host David Susskind, who was—at the time—still married, she decided to take a bit of a timeout from the Canadian broadcasting scene. She crossed the border to co-host a syndicated American TV talk show—*P.M. East - P.M. West*—with rising US TV star Mike Wallace. She later returned to Canada in the 1970s to host a thoroughly unmemorable TV talk show, but by then she had already used up her 15 minutes of fame.

> **TV or Not TV . . .**
>
> Joan Miller of Nelson, BC, became the world's first female TV star when she appeared on the world's first TV show—a show that aired on the BBC in 1936.

Dinah Christie

Dinah Christie is best remembered for being one of the on-air hosts of the hit 1960s CBC-TV show *This Hour Has Seven Days.* It was her job to serve as the show's "talking doll" (the industry's term for female co-hosts who were expected to serve as eye-candy and add a bit of fun and frivolity to the show). While her male colleagues were busy reporting on the most important issues of the day—Quebec nationalism, the sexual revolution, the treatment of the criminally insane, and so on—she was given the opportunity to sing the week's news headlines to the tune of folksinger Woody Guthrie's "Worried Man Blues." So many worries, so little time. . . .

Juliette

Although her birth name was Juliette Augustina Sysak and her married name was Juliette Sysak Cavazzi, by the time she was 13, Juliette preferred to be known simply as "Juliette." Even as a young girl, she clearly had stars in her eyes. While *Juliette* (the musical variety show that she hosted from the mid-1950s to the mid-1960s and that aired right after the Saturday night hockey game), was a hit with Canadian audiences, her 1970s daytime talk show, *Juliette and Friends,* didn't fare nearly so well. According to *Maclean's* Heather Robertson, Juliette seemed to lose sight of the fact that the new show was supposed to be about the "friends"—not just about her: "Juliette is overwhelming. Her evening gowns sparkle with sequins and jewels while her friends, dressed in plain clothes, fade into insignificance. . . . She is not interested in what her guests have to say; she brushes them aside to sing a song or turn the conversation quickly to herself." *Chatelaine* writer Michele Landsberg was equally underwhelmed by the show, describing *Juliette and Friends* as a show that "burbles on mindlessly about make-up and interior decorating and showbiz pals of the host."

Adrienne Clarkson (*Toronto Star*). Canadian Press

Adrienne Clarkson

Long before she stepped into the role of Governor General, Adrienne Clarkson enjoyed a distinguished career as a television producer and interviewer, pioneering such programs as *Take 30, The Fifth Estate, Adrienne Clarkson at Large,* and *Adrienne Clarkson Presents. Take 30*—which Clarkson hosted from 1965 to 1975—was described in 1973 by *Maclean's* as a show with a seemingly tireless appetite for social justice issues: "If there is a social problem anywhere in the world, *Take 30* will be there, full of concern. It's a guilt-ridden old show which is sloppily produced and suicidally depressing." Madame Clarkson has certainly come a long way since her *Take 30* days. She recently took some heat for orchestrating a $2.6 million reno at Rideau Hall, even though her press secretary, Stewart Wheeler, made a point of stressing to the media that his boss only had the nation's best interests at heart: "Her only concern is to preserve the heritage of the building as much as possible."

Jenny Jones

Born Janina Stronski in London, Ontario, Jenny Jones worked as a strip-club hostess before landing gigs as a backup singer for Wayne Newton and an opening act for comedian Jerry Seinfeld. Along the way, she appeared as a game show contestant on shows such as *The Price Is Right* in order to make ends meet. She got her big break in 1986—and a cheque for $100,000—when she was named best comic in the high-profile *Star Search* contest. She was able to leverage her newfound fame into a talk show deal and, in 1991, *The Jenny Jones Show* made its television debut. Although the show was known for catering to the lowest possible common denominator, it truly hit rock bottom when it aired an episode entitled "Same-Sex Secret Crushes" that led one guest, Jonathan Schmitz, to shoot another guest to death three days after the show aired on live TV. Schmitz— a heterosexual—claimed that the show's producers had led him to believe that it would be a woman revealing her secret crush for him, and stated that he had been humiliated when he found out that the person who had the crush on him was, in fact, a man— Scott Amedure. In the end, Jones, the show, the show's distributor, and the show's parent company, Time Warner, were ordered to pay Amedure's family $25 million in damages. (The jury found that by staging the ambush, Jones and her producers had done "everything but pull the trigger"—a rather sobering message for trash TV executives everywhere.)

The Really Big Show

Adrienne Clarkson isn't the only Canuck Chick to enter political life following a career in broadcast journalism. Jeanne Sauvé–Canada's first Governor General–had her own TV show on CBC back in 1956. The show–*Under Twenty-One*–featured interviews with young people on such hot issues of the day as bilingualism and biculturalism. How she managed to find teens who were more interested in talking about federal language laws and immigration (as opposed to, say, Elvis Presley and the rock 'n roll revolution) remains one of the greatest mysteries of our time.

"I am truly one of my guests. I come from dysfunctional. I could be one of the teens on 'Out-of-Control Teens.' My parents could be on 'I Survived an Affair.' I could also be on 'I Survived My Attacker' or 'Sibling Rivalry' because my sister and I did go our separate ways. I can relate to most people's problems. I was where they are."
– Jenny Jones, quoted in *People*, November 10, 1997

Dini Petty

Veteran talk show queen Dini Petty got her start in broadcasting by flying a pink helicopter and broadcasting live traffic reports for radio station CKEY—a job she held from 1967 through 1973. After that, she moved to Citytv, where she hosted or co-hosted such shows as *Sweet City Woman, CityPulse News*, and *CityLine*. In 1989, she switched networks to launch a high-profile daytime talk show, *The Dini Petty Show*, which aired nationally on CTV until 1999, when Petty decided to move on to a career as a motivational speaker and author instead.

Dini Petty (*Maclean's*/Peter Bregg). Canadian Press

Shirley Solomon

Shirley Solomon made Canadian talk show history when her show became the first Canadian daytime TV talk show to be sold into the US market. *Shirley* made its US television debut in 1993. Solomon managed to tolerate the increasingly sleazy US talk show environment for two years before she decided to pull the plug on the show, stating that she didn't like where the industry was headed. While she hadn't managed to steer entirely clear of sleaze—she had, after all, already done shows on men who like to wear diapers, couples who enjoy sadomasochistic sex, and the much-talked-about "naked show" which featured a clothing optional dress code—unlike many of her competitors, she'd at least made an effort to tackle serious issues like gun control and the death penalty at the same time.

Camilla Scott

The Camilla Scott Show was often compared to *The Ricki Lake Show*—a US TV talk show that was big on confession and audience participation. The host of the Canadian show—Camilla Scott—even looked a bit like her US counterpart, thanks to her dark hair, and big, soulful eyes. That's where the similarities ended, however, according to Scott. "[*The Camilla Scott Show*] was geared toward helping people, rather than ruining their lives," she told a newspaper reporter shortly after the show was cancelled in 1998 after a three-year run. But well intentioned or not, the producers at CTV found it difficult to sell Canadians on the idea of airing their dirty laundry in public—a key ingredient in the recipe for success on 1990s television. Consequently, they had to import guests from the United States initially in order to meet the show's angst quota. Fortunately, Scott had a well-established career as a stage and television actress to return to when the show ended, having already made a name for herself by appearing in the Toronto version of the hit musical *Crazy for You* and as Inspector Margaret Thatcher on TV's *Due South*.

Vicki Gabereau

The latest—and some would say the greatest—talk show queen to make a name for herself on Canadian daytime TV is CBC Radio alumnus Vicki Gabereau, a woman who was seemingly born with the gift of gab. ("My father used to say that I was vaccinated by a phonograph needle," she once admitted to a newspaper reporter, "I could go on talking forever.") Known for her chatty demeanour and wacky sense of humour, Gabereau has a knack for putting her guests at ease and getting them to chat up a storm on practically anything under the sun. She's got a shelfful of hardware to attest to her interviewing skills. She walked away with the Best Radio Host-Interviewer ACTRA Award on three separate occasions during her time at CBC Radio. And her TV talk show—*Gabereau Live!*, which hit the airwaves in 1997—has already received its first Gemini Award nomination in the Best Host in a Lifestyle or Performing Arts category. There's only one documented example of a time when the gift of the gab let her down: when she made an unsuccessful run for the position of Mayor of Toronto in 1974. (Hey, you can't win 'em all.)

Vicki Gabereau. Courtesy of Vicki Gabereau

"And now the number one reason why you should appear on a Canadian cooking show . . . "

Described by *Mondo Canuck* authors Geoff Pevere and Greg Dymond as "the Julia Child of Canada, only more loveable and folksy," Madame Jehane Benoit was a fixture on Canadian television for a number of years. She provided a more sophisticated alternative to the mega-dreadful *Celebrity Cooks* show hosted by *The Beachcombers'* Bruno Gerussi. While most of the stars and starlets who schlepped into her kitchen were the usual CanCon suspects—the Pierre Bertons, Dinah Christies, and Farley Mowats of the world—she did manage to attract one rather noteworthy celebrity (albeit long before he became famous): American late-night talk show host David Letterman.

Lady Anchors

Of course, we Canuck Chicks haven't just settled for making a name for ourselves on the talk shows of the nation; we've also staked our claim in the nation's newsrooms, too. Here's the scoop on six of Canada's best-known lady anchors.

She Who Laughs Hardest . . .

Shelagh Rogers (*Ottawa Citizen*/Bruno Schlumberger).
Canadian Press

Love it or hate it, Shelagh Rogers' laugh is one of Canada's national treasures—something that's uniquely us. You don't hear the wind-up Barbies behind the anchor desks on CNN engaging in something so spontaneous and unscripted—so wild and Canadian. We can only hope that the CBC bigwigs have seen fit to insure it or—at the very least—to trademark it. After all, what if Disney was to come and poach Sheila's trademark laugh the same way it did the Mountie's image?

Rogers' present position as the host of CBC Radio's flagship current affairs program *This Morning* is simply the latest achievement in a career that started at a country and western radio station in Kingston during her university days. That, in turn, opened the door for her to become, in 1980, the youngest female staff announcer ever hired by CBC Radio in Ottawa. In 1984, she was invited to host the afternoon current affairs program in Toronto—a job that ended up being a stepping-stone for subsequent positions as the co-host of *Metro Morning* and as Peter Gzowski's sidekick on the highly popular CBC Radio morning show *Morningside*. She also hosted CBC Radio's weekly national arts forum, *State of the Arts*, and became the founding host of *The Arts Tonight*. Along the way, she somehow found time to serve as one-third of the highly popular Humline Trio on *Basic Black*, to make guest appearances on other CBC Radio shows, and to host Chicks With Sticks—an annual pool tournament for literacy featuring women in the media. (Hey, we media chicks know how to pay attention to cues! Get it?) When *Morningside* ended, Rogers made the move to Radio 2, where she hosted *Take Five*. Then, in June 2000, she landed what she describes as her "dream job" as host of CBC Radio's *This Morning*. In the opinion of her many diehard fans, it was about time she inherited the keys to the shop.

Barbara Frum

After making a name on CBC Radio's flagship current affairs show *As It Happens*, Barbara Frum was asked to co-host a high-profile national affairs documentary show called *The Journal* that hit the air in 1981. Her sidekick? Veteran

CBC broadcaster Mary Lou Finlay. Overnight, the two became the First Ladies of Canadian Broadcasting. This wasn't Frum's first time working in front of the TV cameras, however: in late 1974 and early 1975, she'd had her own late-night TV talk show, appropriately entitled *Barbara Frum*.

Mary Lou Finlay

Mary Lou Finlay came to the attention of national audiences when she began hosting *Take 30*—a show that had already made the careers of Adrienne Clarkson, Moses Znaimer, and others. After a brief stint at *Live It Up*—a popular CBC lifestyle show—she began co-hosting *The Journal* with Barbara Frum. The rest, as they say, is history.

Valerie Pringle

Hired straight out of Ryerson after catching the eye of a CFRB recruiter, Valerie Pringle spent 10 years in radio before making the leap to TV. She spent 8 years at CBC-TV's *Midday* and a few years after that doing special projects for the CBC before landing the plum morning job in Canada: co-host of *Canada AM*. From 1993 until 2001, Pringle ruled the airwaves with her trademark perkiness—although she hated it when people described her that way. "I never understood that 'perky,'" she told the *Globe and Mail's* Jan Wong over lunch. "You never hear it about a man. For morning television—hello? Do you want someone glowering at you? Perhaps it's a slight job requirement." Now she's off on a new adventure—quite literally. She's hosting the rather curiously named travel show *Valerie Pringle Has Left the Building* for CTV.

Pamela Wallin

Folks in Wadena, Saskatchewan, had a lot to brag about earlier this year when hometown girl Pamela Wallin managed to land a nice, juicy government appointment—one lucrative enough to encourage her to put her broadcasting career on hold indefinitely. Wallin's new role as the Canadian consul-general in New York City is simply the latest achievement in what has been a rather remarkable career. Most recently the host of *Pamela Wallin's Talk TV* and, before that, *Pamela Wallin Live,* Wallin has had the opportunity to interview most of the key

Pamela Wallin. From *Speaking of Success* published by Key Porter Books

Canadian movers and shakers—everyone from Joni Mitchell to Elvis Stojko to Pierre Elliott Trudeau. She even managed to grasp the brass ring of Canadian broadcasting by co-anchoring CBC's *Prime Time News* with Peter Mansbridge for a short time before being unceremoniously dumped by the CBC brass—a scandal that they still talk about from time to time in Wadena.

Lunch With Jan Wong. Copyright © 2000. Cover photo by Denise Grant Photography. Reproduced by permission of Doubleday Canada, a division of Random House of Canada Limited

Playing with Knives

Never one to be afraid to speak her mind, Pamela Wallin once referred to the *Globe and Mail*'s Jan Wong as "the Hannibal Lecter of the lunch set"—a rather pointed reference to Wong's (in)famous column "Lunch With Jan Wong." Wong herself admitted that the column had attracted its fair share of controversy—and two lawsuits—over its five-and-a-half year run. In fact, one *Globe* reader had written in to suggest that the column be renamed "Lynch With Jan Wong."

Jan Wong. Photo credit: Ted Yao

Wendy Mesley

You have to pity poor Wendy Mesley. She's smart, sexy, and a top-notch journalist and broadcaster, but rather than focusing on her many career achievements, Canadians seem to like to get hung up on the fact that she's Peter Mansbridge's ex. In fact, one of the jokes that keeps making its round of the Internet suggests that you know you're too Canadian if "you spend sleepless nights wondering if Peter Mansbridge and Wendy Mesley will ever find again the blissful love they once knew." So, everyone, could we please give this particular Canuck Chick a break and focus on her résumé for a change? Not only has she been a national affairs correspondent, a parliamentary correspondent, a backup anchor for the CBC *National News* and a regular *Sunday Report* anchor: she's played a key role in bringing two truly innovative TV shows to air: *UNDERCURRENTS* (a show that put media and marketing under the microscope during its six-year run from 1994 to 2000) and *Disclosure* (CBC's newest investigative TV show). Besides, if, for whatever reason, you're inclined to fixate on Peter Mansbridge's love life, it's time to move on: he's been married to actress Cynthia Dale since 1998!

Wendy Mesley (*Maclean's*/Peter Bregg). Canadian Press

Ashleigh Banfield

No one had really heard of MSNBC's Ashleigh Banfield until after the September 11th World Trade Center attacks. But, from that point onward, the Winnipeg-born broadcaster found herself becoming headline news. She reported on the terrorist attacks live from Ground Zero as the tragedy was unfolding, and then served as the overseas war correspondent in Islamabad. Subsequently described as one of the sexiest news anchors in America, she was featured in *People, Vogue, USA Today,* and on *The Tonight Show* and other high-profile US TV shows. And, predictably, fake nude photos of her have shown up on the Internet—the ultimate measure of success in this day and age, it would seem.

The Naked Truth

In 1998, two Toronto entrepreneurs (surprise, surprise, they were guys) hit upon the rather bizarre idea of launching NakedNews.com—an Internet web site that features newscasters who strip while they deliver the news. Initially, the site featured only female newscasters, but, in 2001, the site decided to add male newscasters as well.

While the site routinely attracts 10 times as much traffic as the CBC.ca web site, the CBC is determined to stick to its longstanding "no nudity in newscasts" policy. It simply isn't certain that the Canadian public is eager to know everything there is to know about network anchor Peter Mansbridge.

Voluptuous VJs

Of course, you don't have to run off to the Middle East or hop out of bed at 3 a.m. to host a high-profile morning TV show in order to get yourself noticed on Canuck TV. Three of the most recognizable faces of the 1980s belonged to the mega-cool Canuck Chicks who served as VJs on Moses Znaimer's Brave New TV channel, MuchMusic.

Laurie Brown

Znaimer wasn't kidding when he described her back in 1988 as "quite an intellect" and "serious." While Brown had no problem playing the role of the almost impossibly hip VJ during her MuchMusic days, she was brainy enough to be able to make the leap to CBC-style arts journalism with barely even a hiccup. Since joining the CBC, she's covered arts and culture for *The Journal,* contributed to *The National Magazine,* hosted the CBC's flagship arts show, *On The Arts,* and established herself as one of the country's premiere arts journalists.

Erica Ehm.
Reprinted with the permission of Erica Ehm

Erica Ehm

Erica Ehm wasn't even out of high school when she first made inroads into the wild and wacky rock radio industry. What opened doors for her were her blind ambition and her willingness to ask for what she wanted. Over time, she managed to land not one cool TV job, but two: a job answering telephones at Citytv in Toronto and a job hosting her own TV show on the Maclean-Hunter cable network. (Ehm had perfected the art of career multitasking from a very tender age, holding down part-time jobs at McDonald's and Wendy's simultaneously during her high school years. Unfortunately, her career at McDonald's was rather short-lived: she was fired for chatting too much with the customers.) McDonald's fiasco aside, that gift of the gab has paid off for her time and time again—like when she convinced station owner Moses Znaimer to allow her to become the first female VJ ever to appear on MuchMusic. It's also allowed her to achieve success in a smorgasbord of other entertainment-industry related fields, including acting, songwriting, radio broadcasting, and publishing. Never one to rest on her laurels, Ehm currently has eight separate TV projects in development. So you might want to get ready for what could be Canada's most innovative TV network today, The All-Erica Channel.

Ziggy Lorenc

Variously described by Citytv boss Moses Znaimer as "the essence of empathy" and "a ditz savant," Ziggy Lorenc (born Isabella Anna Lorenc) got her start at the station by working for three years as a "Switchette"— a front lobby receptionist. After a brief stopover in the publicity department, she established herself as a TV personality, working as a VJ on MuchMusic and then pioneering the two romantically themed shows for which she would become famous: *Mushmusic* and *Life on Venus Avenue*. Legend has it that Lorenc was a natural for the show, having experienced heartbreak in her own life: she turned on the radio one day only to discover that her showbiz boyfriend Jim Carrey had dumped her and was dating Linda Ronstadt instead: "It wasn't just that he was dating someone else, but Linda Ronstadt happened to be my favourite singer," she later lamented.

Chart Topper

Denise Donlon is another Citytv/ MuchMusic grad who has made a name for herself in the music industry. Donlon worked as a roadie, an on-air host, a producer, and a journalist before pole-vaulting up the corporate ladder to attain the positions of director of music programming, vice-president, and general manager for the station. Arguably the most powerful woman on the production side of the Canadian music industry, Donlon is currently employed as the president of Sony Music Canada.

What Do Women Want?

It's a question that has caused CBC programmers no small amount of grief over the years: what do Canadian women want to watch when they flip on the tube? Nine times out of 10, they've gotten the answer wrong, forcing generation upon generation of Canadian women to serve as unwilling guinea pigs. Here's the scoop on the five worst TV shows ever to be inflicted upon unsuspecting Canuck Chicks by the CBC:

1. *Some of My Best Friends Are Men* (1975)

If there's a Murphy's Law at work in the world of broadcasting, I suspect it goes something like this: "The likelihood that a particular show will make it to air is inversely proportional to its quality." Don't believe me? That's because you never had to tune into an episode of *Some of My Best Friends Are Men*—CBC's answer to the feminist revolution. A magazine-style television show that somehow made itself into the homes of unsuspecting CBC viewers, the show awarded a "Shiny Golden Porker" award to the most sexist newsmaker of the week. The show also featured weekly sketches from a distinctly unfunny Dave Broadfoot who—as the show's token male chauvinist pig—ended up getting a pie in the face during each episode. Fortunately, the show only lasted for two weeks before someone got wise and pulled the plug, sparing Canadian viewers (and Broadfoot's face) any further misery.

2. *Lady Is a Four-Letter Word* (1975)

Yep, 1975 was a banner year for CBC programmers, particularly when it came to shows aimed at the feminist demographic. In addition to bringing *Some of My Best Friends Are Men* to air, the CBC also saw fit to give us *Lady Is a Four-Letter Word*—a talk show that paired up journalist and broadcaster Elizabeth Gray and "token male" Bob Carl. Based on the same male-bashing philosophy as its evil twin *Some of My Best Friends Are Men*, *Lady Is a Four-Letter Word* was infamous for inscribing the name of the male chauvinist du jour on a roll of toilet paper.

That Seventies Show

The 1970s weren't just the era of really bad clothing. (Think platform shoes, discowear and leisure suits.) They were also the era of really bad television. This was, after all, the decade that gave us two of the most ridiculous and sexist game shows ever to hit the Canadian airwaves—*Anything You Can Do* (which asked teams of male and female contestants to diaper a kewpie doll or roll a massive blob of bread dough across the stage in the hope of winning such prizes as a sewing machine or a deep fryer) and *The Party Game* (a late-night show starring Dinah Christie that offered truckloads of sexual innuendo but little else). It's enough to make you grateful for the eighties, now isn't it?

---

3. *The Marion Clarke Show* (1954)

The Marion Clarke Show was hosted by ordinary Canadian housewife Marion Clarke, a woman whose only claim to fame was the fact that she had made a guest appearance on the much-watched TV show *Tabloid* after winning *Chatelaine*'s "Spring Beauty Week" contest. That single appearance led some desperate producer at the CBC to offer Clarke her own TV show—a decision that he clearly regretted almost immediately. The show—which was set to air on Monday, Tuesday, and Wednesday nights in the late evening—only lasted for one week, thereby leaving Clarke with little more than her proverbial 15 minutes of fame.

4. *The Superior Sex* (1961)

This rather feeble attempt at a game show pitted teams of four women and four men against one another in an attempt to determine which sex was—you guessed it!—"the superior sex." Hosted by a dictatorial Elwy Yost and plagued by electrical malfunctions that allowed contestants to cheat at some of the games of skill, the show earned this high praise from the *Toronto Star:* "Not since the very early days of CBC-TV . . . has there been anything on the screen so comprehensively clumsy and coy and cluttered." Guess that particular reviewer liked alliteration a whole lot more than the show . . .

5. *Make a Match* (1954 and 1955)

Yet another one of those low-budget game shows that has given the CBC a bad name over the years, *Make a Match* asked the show's four panelists to try to figure out which of the show's seven guests (three married couples and one single man or woman) were married to one another. You can imagine how exciting this must have been to watch in an era when risqué questions were out of the question, that being the only thing that made subsequent "couples shows" like ABC's truly awful *The Newlywed Game* even remotely tolerable.

All About Sex

In 1972, the CBC made the rather unusual decision to cancel a TV show before it even hit the airwaves—this despite the fact that it was already much publicized. The show—*All About Women*—had been planned as a 13-week series of half-hour shows covering issues of interest to Canadian women, but news and public affairs chief Knowlton Nash decided to pull the plug on the series because he felt that the show overemphasized sex. The show's co-producers had seen fit to include segments on lesbians, transsexuals, bisexuals, and porno stars. Nash sent the producers back to the drawing board and encouraged them to design another series about women's issues that gave less emphasis to sex. That show, *Ms!*, dealt less with sex and more with such issues as cosmetic surgery and runaway housewives—something that helped to reassure worried network executives that Canadian women had something other than sex on the brain!

Reno Babes and Design Divas

Think home fix-it shows are a relatively new invention? Think again. Reno babes and design divas have been swinging hammers and slapping up wallpaper for at least a quarter century. Back in 1975, CBC-TV aired a home reno show called *Any Woman Can* that was designed to teach Canadian women how to hang wallpaper, repair vacuum cleaners, and tackle other kinds of projects around the home. The show may have been lacking in some of the glitz we've come to expect today, but it was based on the same simple philosophy: you don't have to own a penis to wield a drill.

Without any more ado, please allow me to introduce today's generation of DIY dames.

Mag Ruffman (Korby Banner).
Courtesy of Mag Ruffman

Reno Babe

Mag Ruffman

Dubbed "TV's sexiest home contractor" by the *National Post*, Mag Ruffman isn't afraid to come across as smart, sexy, and capable when the cameras are rolling. (And, of course, even when they aren't!) A licensed contractor and the host of two hit reno shows—*A Repair to Remember* and *Anything I Can Do*—Ruffman has made a name for herself because of her quick wit and clever one-liners. (A classic? "There are so many caulks in the world, it's difficult for a girl to choose the right one.")

Despite the fact that she's Canada's tool queen, Ruffman's acting credits are almost as diverse as the projects she tackles on her shows: she's hosted *Men on Women*, a relationship show for "women who don't understand men" (that's all of us, right?) and played the role of Olivia on *Road to Avonlea*—and that's just for starters. These days, she's hard at work developing a line of tools that will fit properly in a woman's hand, as well as a series of how-to books.

Design Divas

Kimberley Seldon

A Los Angeles–born actress and producer who didn't actually manage to hit the big-time until she came to Canada, Seldon is the host and executive producer of *Design for Living with Kimberley Seldon* and the decorating editor of *Style at Home* magazine. Despite her love of design and her willingness to travel around the world to source new decorating ideas, she is quick to stress that she has no desire to follow in the footsteps of domestic diva Martha Stewart: "Design is supposed to be a backdrop to your life, not your entire life," she insists.

Lynda Reeves

In many ways, Lynda Reeves and Kimberley Seldon are leading parallel lives. They both have their own TV design shows and they both contribute to leading home decorating magazines. Reeves is the host of *House and Home TV*—a home decorating show that also places a strong emphasis on home entertaining—and the publisher of the print magazine *Canadian House and Home.*

Jennifer Corson

Jennifer Corson is the host of *The Resourceful Renovator*—a low-budget but supremely funny show that teaches viewers how to find new uses for old throwaways like broken hockey sticks. What could be more Canadian than that?

Sue Warden

Canada's Queen of Arts and Crafts, Sue Warden is the host of *Sue Warden Craftscapes*—a show that provides step-by-step instructions for a variety of different arts and crafts projects. Her show continues to be the number one homegrown hit for the Life Network.

Sue Warden. Courtesy of Sue Warden

Karen von Hahn

Karen von Hahn is a freelance style writer and host of *The Goods*—a TV show that covers fashion, home furnishings, appliances, collectibles, art, vehicles—basically "anything you can buy." The show has fast become required watching for those Canuck Chicks who consider shopping to be a near-religious experience.

Lynette Jennings

She isn't really ours anymore, nor was she ours to start with, but because it was right here in the Great White North that American-born Lynette Jennings made a name for herself, at least she warrants a quick mention. (After all, if it weren't for all those years she spent dishing up design ideas for magazines like *Canadian Living,* she never would have been able to hang up her shingle at the Atlanta-based Discovery Channel, right?) This is one of *their* stars we can happily take credit for in our classically understated Canadian way. (See, we can borrow their stars, too!)

CHAPTER 8

Snowbirds and Songbirds

Forget about getting signed by the hottest record label or hooking up with the right publicist: the key to making it big in the Canadian music industry is to ensure that your last name starts with the letter "M."

Although there have been a few noteworthy exceptions to this highly scientific "Rule of M"—Shania Twain and Celine Dion immediately come to mind—it's worth pointing out that a disproportionate number of our Canuck Chick superstars have last names that begin with this magic letter. (Think Joni Mitchell, Sarah McLachlan, and Loreena McKennitt.) And, of course, if you team up that "M" with the first initial "A"—as in "Anne Murray" or "Alanis Morissette" or even "Alannah Myles"—you practically end up with a licence to print money.

The Divine Ms. "M"s

I don't know about you, but I think this has the makings of a truly fabulous Canada Council grant application. Unfortunately, I'm already tied up with a few more pressing Canada Council grant applications, so I can't run with this idea myself. (I'm pinning my hopes on what I see as a far more saleable project: a groundbreaking creative non-fiction work on the impact of the Timbit on Canadian culture.) But just in case you're in between gigs right now and you're looking to make a quick buck, I'm happy to share my research notes with you. Here are a few quick facts about each of our Divine Ms. "M"s that should go a long way toward impressing the Canada Council bigwigs. (Or at least that's the theory.)

Anne Murray

Unless you've been stranded on a desert island for the past 30-odd years, you should have a pretty darned good idea who Anne Murray is: the Canuck Chick from Springfield, Nova Scotia, who made Canadian music history in 1969 by becoming the first female Canadian solo artist ever to be awarded an American gold record. The album in question, *This Is My Way,* contained the hit single "Snowbird," which would subsequently become Anne Murray's trademark song.

Anne Murray in 1974. Canadian Press

Murray soon managed to establish herself as a music industry icon—due in no small part, it would seem, to the efforts of the PR firm that she hired to help her to achieve this end. Her name was soon splashed across magazine and newspaper headlines and she made the requisite appearances on TV talk shows. But the pièce de résistance of this particular campaign was the Thanksgiving party that she hosted at the Troubador club in Hollywood—an event that saw her climbing out of a wooden turkey in front of a crowd that included everyone from John Lennon to Alice Cooper to ex-Monkee Mickey Dolenz. (I know: the image simply boggles the mind.)

The investment clearly paid off. By the late-1970s, she had firmly established herself as Canada's best-known musical export. In November of 1974, *Maclean's* magazine described her as "our permanent high-school sweetheart" and, in March of 1978, *Chatelaine* noted that she had become "no less a symbol for things Canuck than the head of state." *Chatelaine* continued: "She is our 'official' pop star the way Pierre Berton is our 'official' author . . . [Imagine] what panic would ensue if an Anne Murray record didn't sound like the Speech From The Throne?"

Of course, not all of Anne Murray's admirers happened to hail from our side of the border. She once found herself on the receiving end of a rather bizarre tribute from US music critic Lester Bangs. What started out as a review for her album *Danny's Song* quickly degenerated into something that seemed to be one part satire and one part erotica. "Anne Murray is God's gift to the male race," Bangs declared, before telling us just what he wanted to do to our Anne. "I want to coo sweet nuttins in her well-formed Canadian ear. Then, while I'm reducing her to a quivering mass of erogenized helpessness, I'll check out the rest of her to see if this soirée is worth pursuing further. I know she's gonna be great because all Canadian babes are tops, it's in their bloodlines and the way they raise them up thar."

Of course, not everyone in the music industry has been quite as passionate about Murray as Bangs. She's also taken her fair share of lumps over the years, with some critics daring to ask whether it is her music or her citizenship that Canadians find so irresistible. In an article that ran in the November 1974 issue of *Maclean's,* Larry LeBlanc implied that Canadians were blindly adoring of Anne Murray simply because she was one of us: "Just as many Canadians are against foreign investment on principle, without any clear idea of what resources are being taken over by whom, many Canadians love Anne Murray on principle, without knowing or even caring much about her music."

Critical barbs aside, Anne Murray has enjoyed a career that has lasted for more than three decades and that isn't showing any signs of slowing down any time soon. She's produced more than 30 albums and has four Grammy Awards and numerous RPM and Juno awards to her credit, and she can always be counted upon to brighten up the holiday season with some sort of Christmas special. If nothing else, the gal's got staying power and, of course, those truly golden initials, "A.M."

Alanis Morissette

Alanis Morissette (Reed Saxon). Canadian Press

Alanis Morissette made her entertainment industry debut on the rather forgettable kids' TV show, *You Can't Do That on Television.* She then used the proceeds from her TV work to bankroll her first recording.

Morissette's first album—*Alanis*—featured a bubble-gum rock ditty—"Too Hot"—that found its way into the top 10 of the contemporary charts in July of 1991, a time when teen queens like Debbie Gibson and Tiffany ruled the airwaves. Her next album—*Jagged Little Pill*—was, however, something completely different (no big surprise there, given that the album was released on Madonna's edgy Maverick Records label). The album went through the roof when an influential LA radio station gave her angry young woman ballad "You Outta Know" a huge amount of airplay.

That, in turn, led to a predictable furor over the use of the f-word in one of the song's verses. (Of course, that wasn't even the raciest part of the song.)

Thanks to both the controversy and the intrinsic quality of the album, *Jagged Little Pill* won four Grammys and became the first album by a Canadian artist ever to sell more than two million copies in Canada.

While her two most recent albums haven't been able to rival her earlier success, she continues to be Canada's ruling rock/alternative queen and one of the county's best-selling artists. And if you visit her web site, you'll initially be greeted with a screen containing little more than the initials "A.M."—perhaps her way of acknowledging the magic of the Canadian "power initials."

Alannah Myles

While the power initials haven't worked quite the same magic on Alannah Myles' career as they have for the two other Divine Ms. A.M.s, she's still had plenty to write home about. Her 1990 self-titled album sold one million copies in Canada and six million copies around the world—the best showing ever for a debut album. And one of the songs from that album—"Black Velvet"—shot to number one on both the Canadian and *Billboard* charts. Add to this the fact that she managed to scoop up three Junos as well as a Grammy for Best Female Rock Vocals and you can see that "the initials" didn't exactly hurt Ms. Myles either.

Joni Mitchell

Once described as the consummate "hippy chick" of her generation, Joni Mitchell (a.k.a. Roberta Joan Anderson) wrote her first song—the classic sixties anthem "Day by Day"—while en route to a folk festival in Toronto from her home in Saskatoon. The following year, she moved to Toronto permanently to pursue a career in music. It didn't take her long to get noticed for both her singing and songwriting talents: her song "Both Sides Now" shot to number eight in the *Billboard* charts after being recorded by American singer Judy Collins.

In 1999, Joni Mitchell was inducted into the Grammy Hall of Fame in recognition of her many recording industry achievements. Over the course of her 30-year career, she has managed to put out 21 albums, win five Grammy Awards, and make the cover of *Time*

Joni Mitchell (*Toronto Star*). Canadian Press

magazine. She's also had the satisfaction of seeing her songs recorded by such highly respected folk artists as Ian and Sylvia and Buffy Sainte-Marie.

Over the years, she has been linked to some of the most fascinating men in the entertainment industry, including David Crosby, Graham Nash, Stephen Stills, James Taylor, Jack Nicholson, and Warren Beatty—something that's provided plenty of fodder for the tabloids.

Sarah McLachlan

Sarah McLachlan (Kevin Frayer). Canadian Press

Sarah McLachlan isn't merely a talented singer and songwriter: she's also a very smart businesswoman who came up with the totally brilliant idea of showcasing the talents of female artists in a concert extravaganza known as Lilith Fair. Not only did Lilith Fair end up being one of the top grossing concert series of 1997 (the first year for Lilith Fair): it also helped to sell truckloads of albums for McLachlan and the other performers—five million albums for McLachlan alone. And, to put the icing on the cake, McLachlan found herself loading up on Junos—four to be exact—at the 1998 Juno Awards in Vancouver. Lilith Fair continued for two more years before McLachlan decided to call it a day, but has since become the inspiration for Amy Sky's popular all-female Phenomenal Woman tour.

Rita MacNeil

Rita MacNeil got her big break when she landed a six-week gig at the Canadian Pavilion during Expo 86. That led to her major label debut the following year, when Virgin Records released *Flying on Her Own*. Over the years, Rita has attracted a strong fan following and has won numerous industry awards, including Junos for Most Promising New Artist (1987), Best Female Vocalist (1990), and Best Female Country Vocalist (1991). She hosted a TV show on CBC from 1994 to 1996, but has turned her attention more recently to operating a tearoom in her hometown of Big Pond, Cape Breton.

Loreena McKennitt

Manitoba-born "eclectic Celtic" singer Loreena McKennitt has managed to sell nearly 10 million records worldwide—no small feat for an artist that is self-managed, self-produced, and the head of her own record label. She's been honoured with a Juno as well as *Billboard's* International Achievement Award and has received gold, platinum, and multiplatinum record status in 10 countries, including both Canada and the United States.

The Winner's Circle

Only a handful of Canadian women have been inducted into the Canadian Music Industry Hall of Fame to date: Joni Mitchell (1981), Maureen Forrester (1990), Sylvia Tyson (and Ian Tyson) (1992), Anne Murray (1993), and Buffy Sainte-Marie (1995). But, in recognition of the unprecedented global success that three Canadian divas were enjoying by the late 1990s, a special International Achievement Award was presented to Celine Dion, Alanis Morissette, and Shania Twain at the 1997 Juno Awards.

Northern Girl Makes Good

Everyone loves a rags to riches success story and Shania Twain's story is just that. The young woman who had little choice but to get a job and support her younger siblings when her mother and stepfather were killed in a car accident in 1987 is now one of the wealthiest Canuck Chicks on the planet. In 2001, *National Post Business* Magazine pegged her net worth at $69.5 million.

Twain's career took off in 1996, thanks to the success of her breakthrough album, *The Woman in Me*. The album sold 12 million copies worldwide (2 million in Canada alone) and earned Twain numerous awards. In addition to being named *Billboard's* Top Country Album Artist for 1996, she managed to pick up a Grammy for Best Country Album and to scoop up countless other awards at the Junos and the American Music Awards. History repeated itself the following year when her third album—*Come on Over*—proved to be a hot seller, garnering six Grammy nominations and selling more than 35 million copies worldwide, something that earned it the distinction of being the best-selling record in country music history.

A health-conscious vegetarian who leads an alcohol-free lifestyle, Twain was named the "sexiest vegetar-

Shania Twain
(Charlie Neibergall). Canadian Press

ian alive" by People for the Ethical Treatment of Animals (PETA) in 2000. She's also been described as "a pop femme fatale in country" by *Billboard* magazine—an acknowledgment of her sizzling sexy "girl next door" good looks.

Not everyone is a huge Shania Twain fan, however. Old country guitarist Steve Earle once described her as "the world's highest paid lap dancer." Of course, he has had equally unflattering things to say about fellow Canuck Chick k.d. lang—proof positive that he's more than a little threatened by the success of our homegrown country music queens. Get over it will ya, Steve?

Quebec's Diva

Celine Dion and René-Charles
(Ryan Remiorz). Canadian Press

When René Angelil first heard Celine Dion sing at the age of 12, he decided to stake his fortune on her career, mortgaging his house so that he could raise the necessary funds to produce her first album. The gamble paid off for both of them, personally and professionally. Not only did Dion end up becoming the top-grossing Canadian singer of the 1990s: she also ended up becoming his wife.

Shortly after Angelil divorced his second wife in 1985, Dion set her sights on him. The two began a romantic relationship when she was 19, but, in her 2000 memoir, *Celine Dion, My Story, My Dream,* she admits to having had her eye on him since she was 17. "He was the one I wanted to impress. I'd have a provocative way of looking at him, a bewitching smile, an air of mystery, a lot of strength, charm, and sex appeal. . . . I was going to train myself in the art of seduction, like a top athlete, and snag René Angelil once and for all."

The two became engaged in 1991 and were married in 1994 in a lavish event at Montreal's Notre Dame Basilica. They weathered a crisis in 1999, when Angelil had to be treated for skin cancer, and then underwent high-tech fertility treatments when their efforts to conceive on their own failed. Happily, their dreams of parenthood came true in 2001 when Dion gave birth to the couple's son, René-Charles.

Clearly, married life and parenthood haven't been enough to douse the flames of passion between Quebec's diva and her man. In April 2002, Dion assured *Redbook* magazine that her marriage was still as hot as ever: "René and I share all our fantasies with each other. I can't share them with you—I can't! But even the things we're too shy to say, we try. It's so-o-o-o exciting."

Celine Dion's Believe It or Not

Looking for a fun way to entertain your guests at your next cocktail party? Why not challenge them to a round of Celine Dion's Believe It or Not? Here are 10 strange-but-true facts about Canada's most successful musical export, Celine Dion.

1. Celine Dion is the only Canadian singer to be featured in a wax museum. You can find her at the San Francisco Wax Museum. (If you're eager to track down other wax Canuck Chicks, you can find Anne of Green Gables at the Cavendish Wax Museum in Cavendish, PEI, and Mary Pickford at the Movieland Wax Museum in Beuna Park, California.)

2. Celine Dion's song "My Heart Will Go On" is a highly popular choice for funerals (except, one would think, in situations where the deceased has succumbed to a heart attack). A British funeral chain conducted a survey of music played at funerals in 1998 and found that Dion's song was the number one pick for music to grieve by.

3. Celine Dion's 1994 "royal wedding" at Montreal's Notre Dame Basilica featured a 12-foot-tall wedding cake and a bridal tiara that weighed 15 pounds. Her brother, Jacques, later shared his own memories of the 500-guest lavish event in an interview with *People* magazine: "We each had our own limousine, and each was escorted by the police. It was as if we were the Mafia."

4. Celine Dion and her husband René Angelil renewed their wedding vows in Las Vegas in January of 2000 in a ceremony that featured exotic birds, belly dancers, and camels.

5. Celine Dion is the only Canadian performer to be invited to appear on US cable network VH1's Divas Las Vegas fundraising gala more than once. While Shania Twain and Nelly Furtado earned a single invite each—Shania in 1998

and Nelly in 2000—Celine managed to get herself invited to the party twice: in both 1998 and 2001.

6. Celine Dion was the top-ranked Canadian entertainer on the *National Post Business* Magazine's "Richest 40 Under 40" list. Ranked ninth overall in the list of filthy-rich young Canadians, Dion was credited as having generated $164,502,000 in earnings over the course of her career. That puts her miles ahead of her two closest competitors, Shania Twain (with career earnings of $69,508,000) and Alanis Morissette (with career earnings of $33,209,000). Dion also showed up on the *Canadian Business* Rich 100, ranked as the 99th richest person in Canada. (That magazine assessed her net worth at an even heftier $240,000,000.)

7. Celine Dion has sold 130 million records over the course of her career—more than twice as many as country superstar Shania Twain, who has sold 50 million records to date.

8. Celine Dion is the only singer in history to have two albums in a row sell more than 30 million copies each.

9. Celine Dion has collaborated with a variety of performers over the years, including Barbra Streisand, Luciano Pavarotti, the Bee Gees, and Bryan Adams.

10. Celine Dion will earn $100 million when her three-year run in Las Vegas begins in 2003. Her showbiz gala will feature no fewer than 70 acrobats and performers.

More Northern Lights

Of course, there's more to the Canadian music industry than just Celine, Alanis, and Shania. Here's the scoop on some of the other music industry superstars we've produced over the years.

Susan Aglukark

The unique musical sound of Manitoba-born but Northwest Territory–raised Susan Aglukark brought her to the attention of music-industry movers and shakers in the mid-1990s. In addition to picking up Junos in 1994 for being the best New Solo Artist and for producing the best aboriginal recording (for her album *Arctic Rose*), she walked away with both the Canadian Country

Music Association's Vista Rising Star Award and the first-ever Aboriginal Achievement Award for arts and entertainment.

Emma Albani

Born more than a century before the current generation of superstars, opera singer Emma Albani was the first Canadian performer to achieve international fame. She even became a personal friend of Queen Victoria's. (Who knew dour old Queen Vicki even had any friends?) Our gal pal Emma attracted such a following in Italy that she decided to "Italianize" her name, dropping her birth name of "Emma Lajeunesse" in favour of the more Italian-sounding "Emma Albani."

Jann Arden

The year 1996 was a banner year for singer/songwriter Jann Arden: not only did she walk away with Juno Awards for Female Vocalist of the Year, Songwriter of the Year, and Single of the Year ("Could I Be Your Girl?"): she made major appearances on such big US TV shows as *David Letterman* and *Dick Clark's New Year's Rockin' Eve*. Known both for her brutal honesty and her fabulous sense of humour, Arden has a loyal fan base in both Canada and around the world. In 1992, her breakthrough song "Insensitive" became the number 10 song on the global music charts and ended up topping the charts in Australia. It's since become the theme song for a jeans commercial in Italy.

Jann Arden (*Toronto Sun*/Mark O'Neill). Canadian Press

Liona Boyd

One of the most glamorous women on the Canadian music scene, classical guitarist Liona Boyd confessed in her memoirs to having carried on an eight-year affair with Pierre Elliott Trudeau. She claimed that Trudeau's driver would drop her off at 24 Sussex Drive for a little after-hours entertainment after she had performed in Ottawa for such important state guests as US President Ronald Reagan, British Prime Minister Margaret Thatcher, and Queen Elizabeth II. Canada's first lady of the guitar recently made headline news again when she was asked to confirm or deny rumours that she was the noisy neighbour who was preventing bad-boy metal rocker Ozzy Osbourne from getting his beauty sleep. She reassured the media that it was another neighbour who was torturing the Osbourne family by playing the guitar and singing at all hours of the day or night: "I don't even sing, and I certainly don't harass the neighbours," she insisted.

Deborah Cox

Three-time Juno Award winner Deborah Cox holds the record for having the longest-running number one song on *Billboard* magazine's R&B charts. The song in question? "Nobody's Supposed to be Here." Rumour has it that she got her career break when she was invited to perform as a backup vocalist for Celine Dion at US President Bill Clinton's 1992 Inaugural Ball.

Ennis Sisters

Maureen, Teresa, and Karen Ennis (a.k.a. "the Ennis sisters") first came to national attention when their 1997 debut album *Red Is the Rose* was named Folk Album of the Year at the Newfoundland and Labrador Music Industry Awards. The following year, they walked away with the Group of the Year

and Female Artists of the Year Awards. Then, two years later, their brand new album— *3*—scooped up Album of the Year honours. Listed by *Maclean's* magazine as among the top 100 Canadians to watch and picked as one of five finalists for the YTV Young Achiever Awards, the Ennis Sisters are definitely rising stars on the Canadian music scene.

The Ennis Sisters (Andrew Bourgeois). Reprinted with permission

Sister Act Times Two

The Ennis Sisters aren't the only East Coast "sister act" to show up on the media radar screen lately. The gals of Black's Mountain managed to get some nice juicy coverage in the *Globe and Mail* after being invited to perform on this year's East Coast Music Awards. With 10 kids and a grandchild between them and ages that average out around 40, the two sets of sisters are quick to stress that they are anything but clones of Britney Spears: "Image has so much to do with [success in the music industry]," group member Donna Bennett told the *Globe and Mail*. "However, we are not poster girls. Except maybe for the big Harley women." The group, which has performed old-time country, gospel, and bluegrass together for 13 years, is made up of sisters Joyce Miller and Dawn Ellis and Donna and Lisa Bennett.

Black's Mountain (Danny Miller). Reprinted with permission

Maureen Forrester

Internationally famous Canadian contralto Maureen Forrester made her professional debut in 1953 at Montreal's YWCA. Three years later, she was performing at New York's Town Hall. Known for her stamina as well as her consistency, she managed to give 120 performances a year while raising five children—something that has clearly earned her the title of Mother of All Contraltos.

Nelly Furtado

The second most famous Nelly in Canadian history (we have to give Person's Case crusader Nellie McClung dibs here since she helped to get us the vote!), pop star Nelly Furtado managed to walk away with four of the five awards she was nominated for at the 2001 Juno Awards—a pretty major coup for someone few people had even heard of two years earlier. Fortunately for Nelly, *Rolling Stone* magazine got wind of her early on, including her on its "Next Big Thing" list in January 2001 and crowning her "this season's spanking-cool pop singer."

The magazine—like the rest of the pop world, it would seem—was quite taken with Our Nelly's debut album *Whoa, Nelly!* and her hit single "I'm Like a Bird."

Patsy Gallant

A bilingual singer who is best remembered for her disco hit "From New York to L.A." (originally *"Mon Pays C'est L'Hiver" en français*), Patsy went on to host her own disco-variety on CTV, *The Patsy Gallant Show*. She likely holds the distinction of being the only Canadian singer to be complimented on her "very sexy shoulders" by an uncharacteristically forthright Prince Charles. He made this comment after dancing with her at a ball held at Rideau Hall in Ottawa in April of 1976. Patsy can thank her lucky stars that she managed to squeeze in her dance with the Prince in his pre-Camilla days. (You can't have any Future Kings talking dirty to Canadian TV stars, now can you?)

Gale Garnett

New Zealand–born singer and actress Gale Garnett moved to Canada at the age of 11. Four years later, she managed to sell an astounding 3.5 million copies of her hit single "We'll Sing in the Sunshine." She went on to star in the Toronto production of *Hair,* to do a one-woman show at Toronto Free Theatre in 1979, and to make numerous TV appearances. And she recently wrote a critically acclaimed first novel, *A Visible Amazement.*

Sarah Harmer (Natasha Nicholson).
Supplied by Sarah Harmer

Sarah Harmer

A radio programmer in Philadelphia helped to catapult folksinger Sarah Harmer to stardom by giving her album *You Were Here* a huge amount of airtime. Her star has continued to rise, thanks to a rave review in *Rolling Stone* and a mention from *Time* magazine, which (wisely) saw fit to include *You Were Here* on its list of the Top Ten albums for 2000. She recently wrote the theme song for the soundtrack of the movie *Men With Brooms*—likely the world's first feature film about curling.

Ofra Harnoy

Canada's best-known cellist, Ofra Harnoy was born in Israel but emigrated to Canada at age six. In 1982, she became the youngest musician ever to win the Concert Artists Guild Award—an achievement that opened the doors for her subsequent Carnegie Hall debut.

Heart

Heart was the name taken by Vancouver singers Ann and Nancy Wilson, a dynamic duo who tore up the record charts in the summer of 1976 with their highly popular album *Dreamboat Annie*. The two managed to get themselves in hot water with the flag-wagging types, however, when they were quoted in the American media as saying that they had never really been a Canadian act. (Ouch!)

Diana Krall

Diana Krall didn't just pick up a Best Jazz Vocal Performance Grammy Award in 1999 for her work on her album *When I Look in Your Eyes:* she also earned the distinction of being the first jazz artist in 25 years to be nominated in the Album of the Year category. Her latest album—*The Look of Love*—debuted on the Canadian record industry charts at number one and managed to sell 30,000 copies in its first week.

Chantal Kreviazuk

A talented songwriter whose introspective lyrics are reminiscent of those of Alanis Morissette, Chantal Kreviazuk managed to arm-wrestle record industry giant Sony Music into offering her one of the most lucrative recording contracts ever signed by a Canadian artist—a $1 million two-album deal. (You go, girl!)

k.d. lang

Never one to shy away from controversy, k.d. lang landed herself in hot water with cattle producers in her home province of Alberta when she became involved with the People for the Ethical Treatment of Animals Meat Stinks campaign and she made headlines around the world when she appeared on the cover of *Vanity Fair* in August of 1993 along with a semi-clad Cindy Crawford. What sometimes gets buried in all the media hype is the fact that lang is one of Canada's most creative and talented artists—a country-punk turned torch singer who boasts a rich, velvety voice. She may not get the same airplay as the Celine Dions and Alanis Morissettes of the world, but she definitely ranks right up there when it comes to being a national treasure.

Ruth Lowe

In 1939, Toronto-born musician Ruth Lowe sat down to write the song of her career, "I'll Never Smile Again." The song—which was inspired by the death of her husband, music publicist Harold Cohen—became the unofficial anthem of couples separated during the war years. Percy Faith introduced the song to

CBC listeners by playing it on his show, and it was subsequently recorded by big band giants Glenn Miller and Tommy Dorsey (a recording that featured Frank Sinatra crooning along with singer Jo Stafford). The song has been recorded more than 100 times to date and Ruth Lowe's life story was once featured in an episode of the hit US TV show, *This Is Your Life.*

Giselle MacKenzie

Winnipeg-born Giselle MacKenzie was the biggest Canadian pop star during the 1940s and 1950s. Her popularity extended across the border, landing her starring roles on US TV for the better part of a decade and her own TV show for a season.

Carole Pope

Known for her provocative lyrics and gender-bending body language, Carole Pope of rock group Rough Trade had Canadians feeling hot and bothered in the fall of 1976. In the November issue of *Chatelaine,* music writer Jack Batten described Pope as "a singer who may top even Mick Jagger for vitality and for riveting androgynous fascination."

Alys Robi

The Celine Dion of her day, Alys Robi was a working-class girl from Quebec City who achieved international stardom during the 1940s. Unfortunately, she missed out on the Celine Dion picture-perfect happy ending: she ended up having a nervous breakdown after falling in love with well-known conductor and arranger Lucio Agostini, who happened to be a married man at the time. Personal difficulties aside, she managed to make a comeback of sorts in the 1970s, gradually acquiring a cult following in Montreal's gay nightclubs, thanks to her Diva-like moves. Over time, she managed to regain her popularity with straight audiences, too—the ultimate Canuck Chicks comeback story.

Buffy Sainte-Marie

Born on a reservation near Regina and raised in Maine, Buffy Sainte-Marie won a 1982 Academy Award for co-writing the song "Up Where We Belong" from the hit movie *An Officer and a Gentleman.* In the 1970s, she made regular appearances with her young son Dakota on the children's TV show *Sesame Street* to educate Big Bird and the show's preschool audience about North America's native peoples. Unfortunately, the producers of the *Tonight Show* were a little less progressive than the folks at *Sesame Street:* she was warned prior to a *Tonight Show* appearance not to sing anything controversial!

Jane Siberry

Best known for her hit single "Mimi on the Beach" (the most popular cut from her 1984 album *No Borders Here*), Jane Siberry is widely recognized as a highly creative singer/songwriter. An independent artist in every sense of the word, Jane Siberry parted ways with record industry giant Warner/Reprise in 1996 to establish her own record label, Sheeba Records.

Teresa Stratas

Teresa Stratas made her radio debut at age 13, singing Greek pop songs. Then—after hitting the stage as Mimi in *La Bohème* at the Toronto Opera Festival—she went on to establish a career as one of the country's biggest opera stars. Over the years, she has won three Grammy Awards, an Emmy Award, a Gemini Award, and an Academy Award citation for her critically acclaimed film *StrataSphere*—a pretty impressive haul for any Chick, Canuck or otherwise!

Michelle Wright

Although her career has been somewhat overshadowed in recent years by the extraordinary success of fellow country star Shania Twain, Michelle Wright was one of the brightest stars in the Canadian country music industry in the early 1990s. She picked up album of the year honours from The Canadian Country Music Association in 1993 for *Now and Then* (this after being named the year's top vocalist for three years running) and was named the top new female country vocalist by the Academy of Country Music in 1993. She also managed to pick up a number of other noteworthy awards over the course of her career and continues to demonstrate that she's a force to be reckoned with on the Canadian country music scene. Clearly, this country queen has got the "wright" stuff.

Music Box Dancers

Canada has produced its fair share of world-class ballerinas over the years, the two best-known being Veronica Tennant (who danced with such ballet-world luminaries as Rudolf Nureyev, Erik Bruhn, Anthony Dowell, and Mikhail Baryshnikov before moving on to a career as a writer, producer, and performer in 1989) and Karen Kain (who danced with Rudolf Nurevey and Frank

Karen Kain. National Archives of Canada
NAC-PA-195686

Augustyn before retiring from the ballet in 1997). Kain also has a few other noteworthy claims to fame: not only did she date Lee Majors (the Six Million Dollar Man) right after his break up with seventies pin-up queen Farrah Fawcett, she also had her portrait painted by Andy Warhol. (And, no, the portrait painting session didn't use up her entire 15 minutes of fame.)

CHAPTER 9

Good Sports

"Stick with those sports in which you compete with a minimum of strain, a maximum of grace, beauty, and rhythm; the sports in which you can compete with pleasure and success and still retain essential femininity, which includes no grime on your face. I mean, speed and figure skating, tennis, golf, swimming, and a few more in which neither grace nor dignity is sacrificed to face-straining and belabored effort."
– Elmer W. Ferguson, "I Don't Like Amazon Athletes," *Maclean's Magazine*, August 1, 1938

Elmer W. Ferguson wasn't the first fellow to get his shorts in a knot at the thought of women sporting a grimace or breaking into a sweat on the sports fields. In fact, he was merely expressing a long-standing dislike of so-called "Amazon athletes"—women who chose to participate in those "violent, face-straining, face-dirtying, body-bouncing, sweaty, graceless, stumbling, struggling, wrenching, racking, jarring and floundering events" that gentlemen found so disturbing.

For decades, the experts had been trying to warn women of the evils of vigorous exercise. They cautioned them that engaging in too much physical activity could zap a woman of her "vital energy" and "nervous force" and rob her of her femininity. Then, when that didn't work, they tried the vanity tact instead, warning

Ladies Curling Team. Glenbow Archives ND-2-208

turn-of-the-century Canuck Chicks that too much exertion could lead to a dreaded condition called "bicycle face." (Supposedly, the grimace that found its way on to your face when you were pedalling up a particularly steep hill or otherwise exerting yourself while riding a bicycle could, over time, lead to an irreversible masculinization of your facial features.)

Of course, what a woman wore while she was exercising was also problematic for the Mr. Busybodies of the world. In the late 19th century, women were warned that bicycling around in skimpy clothing such as bloomers could bring forth "the unholy desires" of boys and men. (One such spoilsport in turn-of-the-century Toronto was only too happy to state his opinion that "One girl in a bloomer costume will create far greater and more widespread corruption among boys than a city full of show bills." For Pete's sake, buddy. Get a life!)

Nineteenth-century health experts were also quick to point out that there was actually no need for women to hop on bicycles in order to give their bodies a workout—not when there was a far superior workout available to them right in their own homes. As John Kellogg so helpfully pointed out in his 1898 book *Plain Facts for Young and Old,* "Housework is admirably adapted to bring into play all the different muscles of the body, while affording such a variety of different exercises and such frequent change that no part need be very greatly fatigued." (Kind of makes you want to make a dash for the old dust mop, now doesn't it?)

Exercise only started to meet with the approval of turn-of-the-century health experts when they clued into the fact that vigorous physical activity could be just what was needed to divert feminine energy that might otherwise find expression through—gasp!—masturbation. As Kellogg noted, "Physical exercise is a most powerful aid to pure thoughts. When unchaste ideas intrude, engage at once in something that will demand energetic muscular exercise. Pursue the effort until fatigued, if necessary, making all the while a powerful mental effort to control the mind. Of course, evil thoughts will not be expelled by thinking of them, but by displacing them by pure thoughts. Exercise aids this greatly."

From Curling Dirvishes to Ice Queens

Fortunately for today's generation of female athletes, some of our great-grandmothers chose to forgo the dust mop workout in favour of something a little more athletically challenging, thereby laying the groundwork for future generations of female athletes. Here's a quick rundown of some of the more noteworthy achievements of Canuck Chicks over the past one hundred years.

1902

Canuck Chicks manage to rock the world of The Reverend John Kerr of Scotland's Royal Caledonian Curling Club, who is shocked to find himself competing against Canadian women after crossing the ocean to bring his all-male curling team to a Canadian bonspiel. And, to add insult to injury, the women manage to beat his team three times. It must have been a rather large pill for Kerr to swallow, given that he had once haughtily proclaimed, "Ladies do not curl." (We Canuck Chicks certainly know how to serve up humble pie when the situation warrants it, now don't we?)

1919

Golfer Ada Mackenzie captures the first of the four Canadian Open Amateur Championship titles she'll win over the course of her career. By the time she decides to put away her golf clubs for good in 1969, she will have managed to rack up six wins at the Canadian Closed Amateur Championships and to fill her trophy shelves with countless other awards. She will also have guaranteed herself a place in the history books by being named Canada's Female Athlete of the Year for 1933.

1923

Three women from Montreal invent the sport of "ornamental or scientific swimming" and organize the sport's first competition at the Montreal YMCA. The rules for the sport—which is later renamed "synchronized swimming"—are drawn up the following year by the Canadian Amateur Swimming Association. Peg Seller—one of the sport's three inventors—lobbies hard to have the sport recognized as an Olympic event. It is first admitted as a demonstration event at the 1952 Olympics Games in Helsinki, but it isn't until the 1984 Olympic Games in Los Angeles that synchronized swimming becomes a full-fledged Olympic event.

1928

Female track and field athletes are allowed to participate in the Olympic Games for the first time ever. The women's track team that represents Canada in Amsterdam is dubbed "the Matchless Six" by the Canadian Press as a result of their truly stellar performance at the games. Team members bring home medals in high jump, the 400-metre relay, and the 100-metre dash. The Matchless Six manage to attract 200,000 people to Toronto's Union Station and another 100,000 to the adjacent parade route when they make their triumphant return to Canada—a very proud day for Canuck Chicks and Canadians as a whole.

Saskatoon Lily

High jumper Ethel Catherwood may have done us proud at the Amsterdam Olympic Games by bringing home Canada's first-ever Olympic gold medal, but the media seemed to be more impressed with her beauty than with her sporting ability: "From the instant this tall, graceful girl from the Prairies tossed aside her long, flowing cloak of purple and made her first leap, the fans fell for her," one sports reporter wrote. "A flower-like face of rare beauty above a long, slim body clad in pure white ... she looked like a tall, strange lily—and was immediately christened by the crowd "The Saskatoon Lily."

Phyllis Dewar
(Canada's Sports Hall of Fame)

1934

Phyllis Dewar wins four medals at the Commonwealth Games in London, setting two individual swimming records in the 100-yard and 400-yard freestyle events and swimming on the winning teams in the 300-yard medley and 400-yard relay events. Chosen to be Canada's Female Athlete of the Year for 1934, she goes on to set new records for the 100-yard, 400-yard, 1,000-yard, 1,500-yard, and one-mile events the following year.

1948

It's a banner year for Canadian figure skater Barbara Ann Scott. Not only does she earn Canada's first (and only) Olympic gold medal at the senior women's figure skating level at the Winter Olympics in St. Moritz, Switzerland: she also wins the Canadian, European, and World senior women's figure skating titles that year—the first North American to stage this particular coup. Known as "Canada's Sweetheart," Barbara Ann Scott goes on to star in TV commercials, operate a beauty salon, author two books, direct a summer theatre, win equestrian medals for the horses she shows and trains, and to serve as a judge at skating competitions around the world.

Barbara Ann Scott. Canadian Press

Figure skater Frances Dafoe becomes the 1948 Canadian junior ladies champion. In 1956, she wins a second medal—the silver—while competing in the pairs competition with skating partner Norris Bowden. The two end up reigning as Canadian Senior Pairs champions from 1952–1955 and as World Champions in 1954 and 1955.

Frances Dafoe (Canada's Sports Hall of Fame)

1950

Fanny "Bobbie" Rosenfeld is voted the Female Athlete of the Half-Century by the Canadian Press. She first came to public attention in 1925 at the Ontario Ladies Track and Field Championships when, in a single day, she placed first in the 220-yard, 120-yard low hurdles, the long jump, the discus, and shot put events, and second in the 100-yard and javelin events. Then, during the Olympic Trials for the 1928 Amsterdam Summer Olympic Games, she managed to set records in running broad jump, standing broad jump, and discus. She caps off her winning streak by coming through with a silver medal performance in the 100-metre dash event.

1951

Winnie Roach Leuszler becomes the first Canadian to swim the English Channel.

1954

On September 9, 16-year-old Marilyn Bell becomes the first person ever to swim across Lake Ontario. She manages to finish the swim even though the choppy lake conditions force her to cover a distance of 45 miles (65 kilometres) in order to get across the 32-mile (51.5-kilometre)-wide lake. Her efforts are well rewarded. Bell is greeted by a huge crowd as she steps out of the water and again when she appears before a crowd of 100,000 at the Canadian National Exhibition to collect $10,000 in prize money. (The money had originally been intended for an American swimmer, Florence Chadwick, who had been forced to abandon her own swim.) The money is the least of her haul, however: enthusiastic Canadians step forward to serve up all kinds of goodies: a pale-blue Austin convertible, seven watches, a garage, a radio for her car, car insurance, gasoline, several fur coats, a $3,000 diamond ring, two television sets, a year's supply of bottled water, a year's supply of Wheaties, $100 worth of vitamin pills, a wedding cake (to be supplied at the appropriate time!), furniture,

Marilyn Bell. Canadian Press

Anne Heggtveit. National Archives of Canada
NAC-PA 209759

dancing lessons, and much more. There is even a rumour of a film offer (apparently she is to co-star with Marilyn Monroe in a film that is to be entitled *The Two Marilyns*), but that doesn't pan out in the end. Good thing, too, because Marilyn isn't ready to hang up her bathing suit quite yet: she goes on to swim the English Channel in 1955 and the Strait of Juan de Fuca (between Vancouver Island in Canada and the Olympic Peninsula of the State of Washington) in 1956, earning her the distinction of being the youngest person to accomplish the latter feat. She also becomes an inspiration for future generations of Canadian marathon swimmers, including Cindy Nicholas and Vicki Keith. Talk about making a splash!

1956
Lucille Wheeler wins Canada's first-ever downhill skiing medal.

Future track-and-field superstar Abby Hoffman successfully infiltrates a boy's hockey team by cutting her hair boyishly short and calling herself "Ab." It's only when her team makes it into the playoffs and she's ordered to produce a birth certificate that the awful truth is revealed: she's actually a girl, not a boy!

1960
Barbara Wagner and skating partner Robert Paul capture Canada's first gold medal in pairs figure skating—this after reigning as the Canadian champions for the previous four years and as World champions for the previous three years.

Anne Heggtveit Hamilton becomes the first Canadian skier to win an Olympic gold medal.

1968
Swimmer Elaine "Mighty Mouse" Tanner—who earned

her memorable nickname because of her small stature and powerful strokes—cleans up at the Olympic Games in Mexico City, taking home two silvers and a bronze. Her medal hauls at the 1967 Pan Am Games and the 1966 Commonwealth Games were equally impressive, netting her a total of 11 medals, including 6 gold. Her achievements are unprecedented for a Canadian swimmer of her era and earn her the 1966 Lou Marsh Trophy for Canada's outstanding athlete of the year—a pretty significant achievement for a girl of 15.

Golfer Sandra Post becomes the youngest player ever to win a major golfing championship, in her case the 1968 Ladies Professional Golf Assocation (LPGA) championship. She's just a few weeks past her 20th birthday.

1976
Track and field athlete Abby Hoffman is chosen to be the flag bearer for the Canadian team at the Montreal Summer Olympic Games. It's her fourth consecutive Olympic Games.

Cross-country skier and kayaker Sue Holloway earns the distinction of being the first woman ever to compete at the Winter Olympic Games and Summer Olympic Games in the same year. Although she doesn't pick up any medals at either Innsbruck or Montreal, she'll get her chance to step up on the medal podium eight years later when she wins silver and bronze kayaking medals at the Los Angeles Olympic Games.

1977
Cindy Nicholas becomes the first woman to make a non-stop double crossing of the English Channel. She also manages to beat the time record held by American marathon swimmer Jon Erickson by an astounding 10 hours and five minutes.

1979
Sandra Post has the kind of year of which golfing dreams are made, winning three tournaments and finishing second on the LPGA money list—achievements that earn her the Lou Marsh Trophy for Canada's outstanding athlete of the year.

1986
Downhill skier Laurie Graham is named Canadian Female Athlete of the Year. Over the course of her 11-year skiing career, she'll represent Canada at three consecutive Winter Olympic Games (in 1980, 1984, and 1988) and win six World Cup skiing competitions.

1984
Anne Ottenbrite leaves the Los Angeles Summer Olympic Games with a full

Sylvie Bernier (Athlete Information Bureau/Canada's Sports Hall of Fame)

set of medals: a gold in the 200-metre breast stroke (a win that makes her the first Canadian woman swimmer to ever come away with Olympic gold), a silver in the 100-metre breast stroke, and a bronze in the 4 x 100-metre medley relay).

Sylvie Bernier wins an Olympic gold medal in diving at the Los Angeles Olympics.

Linda Thom wins a gold medal in the short pistol competition—proving once and for all that you don't have to be a guy to pack a pistol.

1985

Carling Bassett becomes the eighth-ranked women's tennis player in the world—the best showing ever for a Canadian women's tennis player. She ends up being the top-ranked Canadian women's tennis player from 1982 to 1986.

1986

Sharon Wood of Canmore, Alberta, becomes the first North American woman to reach the summit of Mount Everest.

The Canadian Curling Association finds itself in the hot seat after organizing a male-female curling match that it promotes as the "Battle of the Sexes." Describing the event as a "leering sexist circus," Laura Robinson, advocacy chairperson for the Canadian Association for the Advancement of Women and Sport, objects to the exchange of goodies that took place at the outset of the match: the women's team brought a cake while the men's team brought flowers.

1987

Fourteen-year-old hockey player Justine Blainey wins the right to play hockey in a boys' hockey league in her hometown of Toronto—the culmina-

Darling Carling

Her name was Carling Bassett, but the media called her "Darling Carling" because of her stunning, girl-next-door good looks. A highly gifted athlete who had managed to establish herself as Canada's top female athlete by the age of 13, Bassett made her movie debut playing a budding tennis star in the 1982 feature film *Spring Fever*. It wasn't her first time in front of the camera, however: three years earlier, she had made a guest appearance on TV's *The Littlest Hobo*.

tion of a four-year court battle that went all the way to the Supreme Court of Canada. The Supreme Court ruled that a clause in the Ontario Human Rights Code that had allowed for sex discrimination in sports was in violation of the country's *Charter of Rights and Freedoms*.

1988

Carling Bassett places fifth in the doubles competition at the Seoul Olympics alongside fellow Canuck Chick Jill Hetherington. They will hold the record for Canada's best Olympic showing in tennis until two male players manage to win gold in 2002.

Speed skater Sylvie Daigle goes home with five medals from the Winter Olympic Games in Calgary: a gold in the 1,500-metre, silver in the 1,000-metre and the 300-metre, and bronze in the 500-metre and 3,000-metre relay events. Four years later, she'll share another gold medal with the other members of her relay team at the Albertville Winter Olympic Games.

Figure skater Elizabeth Manley has to settle for a silver medal, but she wins the hearts of Canadians with her performance on the ice at Calgary's Saddledome—an achievement that earns her accolades as *Chatelaine*'s "Woman of the Year." Over the course of her career, the Belleville, Ontario, native will accumulate 51 national and international medals while serving as the inspiration for the highly popular Elizabeth Manley doll.

Carolyn Waldo wins two gold medals for synchronized swimming at the Summer Olympic Games in Seoul. She had previously won a silver medal at the 1984 Olympic Games in Los Angeles.

1989

Vicki Keith swims her way into the sports record books by becoming the first person to swim across the English Channel using the butterfly stroke. Two years earlier, she'd managed to complete a two-way crossing of Lake Ontario.

Isabelle Brasseur is awarded the first of five Canadian pairs titles she will win with skating partner Lloyd Eisler. By the

Carling Bassett-Seguso
(Canada's Sports Hall of Fame)

Elizabeth Manley (*Edmonton Journal/* Chris Schwarz). Canadian Press

Carolyn Waldo (Athlete Information Bureau/Canada's Sports Hall of Fame)

Isabelle Brasseur (Athlete Information Bureau/Canada's Sports Hall of Fame)

time they decide to wind up their amateur skating careers, they will also have managed to accumulate 2 Olympic medals, 5 World medals, and 20 medals from international competitions.

1992

Silken Laumann wins a bronze medal in the rowing singles just six weeks after sustaining a serious injury to her right leg in a rowing accident. Her doctors had earlier warned her that she would be unable to compete in the Barcelona Summer Olympic Games and that the injury could, in fact, prove to be career-ending. The Canadian Club chooses her as its Canadian of the Year as a result of her gutsy comeback and subsequent world-class showing.

Mrs. Great One

Movie actress Janet Jones found herself in hot water with Canadian hockey fans when her fiancé, Wayne Gretzky, made the decision to leave the Edmonton Oilers in order to marry her and move to LA. It didn't take Canadians long to shift the blame, however, placing it smack-dab on the shoulders of Edmonton Oilers owner Peter Pocklington.

The Gretzkys were married on July 16, 1988, in St. Joseph's Basilica in Edmonton. The wedding—which was broadcast live across Canada—reportedly cost The Great One $1 million dollars, including $40,000 for his bride's wedding dress.

Gretzky Family (Stuart Ramson). Canadian Press

Synchronized swimmer Sylvie Frechette experiences heartbreak both in and out of the pool at the Barcelona Summer Olympic Games. Not only does her fiancé commit suicide a week before the Games, but a judging error also costs her the gold medal. The judge reports her mistake immediately—she inadvertently keyed in a score of 8.7 rather than the 9.7 she had intended to award Frechette—but the referee refuses to alter the score. It's not until 16 months later that Frechette is finally awarded the medal she so richly deserved.

Twenty-year-old Manon Rheaume makes hockey history by becoming the first woman to play in the National Hockey League. Stepping into the Tampa Bay Lightning net for a period in a pre-season game, she manages to stop seven of nine shots on goal.

Skier Karen Lee-Gartner wins Canada's first-ever downhill gold medal at the Winter Olympic Games in Albertville, France.

Sylvie Frechette (Athlete Information Bureau/ Canada's Sports Hall of Fame)

1994

Biathlete Myriam Bédard makes Olympic history not once but twice. Not only does she become the first Canadian woman ever to win two Olympic gold medals (she racks up her wins in the 7.5-kilometre and 15-kilometre events at Lillehammer), she also becomes the first North American athlete ever to win gold in an Olympic biathalon event (a feat she accomplishes twice over, to boot). This isn't Bédard's first trip up to the medal podium, however: two years earlier, she had won a bronze medal at the Winter Olympic Games in Albertville, France.

Myriam Bédard (Athlete Information Bureau/ Canadian Sports Hall of Fame)

1996

Rowers Marnie McBean and Kathleen Heddle become Canada's first triple-gold Olympic medallists. After sharing in gold medals in pairs rowing and as part of the eights crew in Barcelona in 1992, the two athletes take first-place honours in the double sculls at the Summer Olympic Games in Atlanta.

Sandra Schmirler (Fred Chartrand). Canadian Press

1998

Biggar, Saskatchewan's Sandra Schmirler makes Olympic history by skipping the first women's curling team ever to compete at the Olympics. The team—made up of third Jane Betker, second Joan McCusker, and lead Marcia Gudereitto, ends up winning the Olympic gold medal. Recently described by fellow curling record holder Colleen Jones as "the greatest team in the world, of all time," the Schmirler rink also manages to win three Canadian and world curling championships (in 1993, 1994, and 1997). The team are inducted into the Canadian Curling Hall of Fame in 1999, a year before Sandra Schmirler tragically loses her battle with cancer.

1999

Chantal Petitclerc is honoured by the International Amateur Athletic Federation for her contribution to the advancement of women in track and field after winning two medals in wheelchair racing at the Paralympic Games in Barcelona and five medals at the Paralympic Games in Atlanta.

Alpine skier Nancy Greene is chosen as the Canadian female athlete of the century by Canadian Press–Broadcast News.

2000

Golfer Lorie Kane is named Female Athlete of the Year for 2000 by Canadian Press–Broadcast News. It's the second time she's earned the title: she was a winner in 1997 and a runner-up to speed skater Catriona Le May Doan in 1998. (The speed skater also ended up earning the title a second time, too—in her case, in 2001.)

The Canadian women's cross-country ski team produces a *Nordic Nudes* fundraising calendar.

2001

York University kinesiology-and-biology-student-turned-wrestling-star Trish Stratus generates even more controversy than usual when she strips down to her underwear in the ring, gets down on all fours, and barks like a dog on the World Wrestling Federation show *Raw.* Even some diehard fans give the latest plot twist a firm thumbs down: "Sponsors don't want to be associated with a middle-aged man browbeating a twentysomething girl and forcing her to strip in front of 15,000 teenage boys," says wrestling journalist Jeff Marek in an interview with *Saturday Night*'s James Cowan. The controversy only seems to add to Stratus's popularity, however: in addition to appearing on her usual assortment of wrestling and body building magazine covers, she manages to make it on to the covers of *Saturday Night* and *TV Guide* (albeit with a few more pieces of clothing on than usual!).

Colleen Jones (Andrew Vaughan). Canadian Press

2002

Colleen Jones becomes the first skip ever to capture four Canadian women's curling titles. Her first and fourth wins span two decades.

February 2002

Speed skater Catriona LeMay Doan becomes the first Canadian to successfully defend a gold medal at any Olympic games. She now has two gold medals (from the 500-metre events at Nagano and Salt Lake City) and one bronze medal (from the 1,000-metre event at Nagano) to her name.

Clara Hughes becomes the first Canadian athlete in history to win medals at both the Summer and Winter Olympic Games. Her bronze medal win in the 5,000-metre long-track speed-skating event at Salt Lake City in 2002 comes on the heels of her two bronze medals in cycling at the 1995 Summer Olympic Games in Atlanta.

Jamie Salé and her pairs figure skating partner David Pelletier have the satisfaction of seeing their silver medal upgraded to gold after a particularly messy judging scandal. Rather than yanking the medals from the Russians who had initially been declared the event's winners, the International Olympic

Committee decides to award gold medals to both the Canadian and the Russian athletes.

The Canadian Women's Hockey Team wins gold at the Olympics in Salt Lake City 2002 after narrowly missing out on the gold medal four years earlier in Nagano. The victory is made all the sweeter when the men's team pulls off its first Olympic hockey victory in 50 years—to the day. It's his-and-hers gold medals all around. What a way to end the games. . . .

CHAPTER 10

Chick Lit

It's no wonder we Canuck Chicks have been making our presence felt in the world of publishing since practically the beginning of time. (Or at least the beginning of Canadian time.) Writing is one of the few pleasures in life that is totally compatible with the extremes of our climate—a pastime that can be enjoyed equally well in the midst of a summer heat wave or winter gale.

Just don't assume that our love of all things book-related means that we're a nation of Marian the Librarian types. After all, the very first book ever penned by a Canuck Chick was a rather steamy romance! And as you'll discover while you make your way through this chapter, there's been a whole lot of sex going on between the covers ever since, with the possible exception of the "Bush Whackers"—that all-too-famous group of early Canadian scribes who made it their mission to bitch and complain about Canada.

Bush Whackers

There's no point beating around the bush about it: Catharine Parr Traill was a woman on a mission. She felt it was her moral and/or patriotic duty to let would-be emigrants in Britain know just what they would be getting themselves in for if they decided to relocate their families to the wilds of Canada. She felt that earlier writers had tended to either white-wash the facts or—in the case of male guidebook writers—to leave out the key details about wilderness life: after all, you could hardly trust a man who had never so much as cleaned a privy in his entire life to give you an accurate account of what was involved in running a pioneer household, now could you?

Traill set out to right that wrong by writing a guidebook of her own—a "girl's guide to Canada," so to speak—that would tell prospective settlers (and prospective female settlers, in particular) the plain, unvarnished truth about life in the Canadian wilderness. That book—*The Backwoods of Canada*—was published in London in 1836.

Traill's message to upper-class women who thought it might be fun to play house in the great outdoors was direct and to the point: prima donnas need not apply for the position of pioneer woman. According to Traill, "young ladies who have been brought up at fashionable boarding-schools, with a contempt of every thing useful or economical" were unlikely to find happiness by coming to Canada. "For persons of this description . . . Canada is the worst country in the world. And I would urge any one, so unfitted by habit and inclination, under no consideration to cross the Atlantic; for miserable, and poor, and wretched they will become."

"Young men soon become reconciled to this country, which offers to them that chief attraction to youth—great personal liberty. Their employments are of a cheerful and healthy nature; and their amusements, such as hunting, shooting, fishing, and boating, are peculiarly fascinating. But in none of these can their sisters share. The hardships and difficulties of the settler's life, therefore, are felt peculiarly by the female part of the family."
- Catharine Parr Traill, *The Backwoods of Canada*, 1836

Although Traill was the one who got the Canadian truth-in-advertising campaign really rolling, her younger sister, Susannah Moodie, also got in on the act. She did her best to dish the dirt on life in Canada, concluding her 1852 book *Roughing It in the Bush* with this rather self-satisfied statement: "If these sketches should prove the means of deterring one family from sinking their property, and shipwrecking all their hopes, by going to reside in the backwoods of Canada, I shall consider myself amply repaid for revealing the secrets of the prison-house, and feel that I have not toiled and suffered in the wilderness in vain."

Funnily enough, Moodie used to get really miffed when people accused her of trashing Canada in her book. (Sorry, Susanna, but terms like "prison-house" don't generally find their way into puff piece travelogues!)

"I know that it would be easier for me to gain the approbation of the Canadian public, by exaggerating the advantages to be derived from a settlement in the colony, by praising all the good qualities of her people, and by throwing a flattering veil over their defects; but this is not my object, and such servile adulation would do them no good, and degrade me in my own eyes. I have written what I consider to be the truth, and as such I hope it may do good, by preparing the minds of emigrants for what they will *really find*, rather than by holding out fallacious hopes that can never be realized."
- Susanna Moodie, *Life in the Clearings versus the Bush*, 1853

Of course, Catharine Parr Traill and Susanna Moodie weren't the only women to take it upon themselves to write detailed guidebooks for would-be settlers. Anna Brownell Jameson did her bit by penning *Winter Studies and Summer Rambles in Canada* in 1838. Her key message to poor, unsuspecting British Babes whose husbands were considering a move to the colonies: you ain't gonna like it here, sister: "I have not often in my life met with contented and cheerful-minded women, but I never met with so many repining and discontented women as in Canada," she noted. "I never met with one woman recently settled here, who considered herself happy in her new home and country. I heard of one, and doubtless there are others, but they are exceptions to the general rule."

Another pioneering lass, Anne Langton, who moved to Upper Canada to help keep house for her politician brother, noted in her journal around that time that Canada had become a too-easy target for discontented British-Babes-turned-Canuck-Chicks. "Poor country!" she wrote on July 4, 1839. "It bears the blame of all the various sins of the motley herd that inhabit it, besides the sins inherent in itself that it has to answer for." However, she then went on to engage in a little bit of kvetching of her own: "I have sometimes thought, and I may as well say it, now that it is grumbling day—woman is a bit of a slave in this country."

That's not to say that every single British Babe who ever stepped foot on Canadian soil considered the Canadian wilderness to be a total drag. One such transplant—Frances Brooke—was so inspired by her surroundings, in fact, that she sat down and wrote North America's first romance novel in 1769. Set in the frozen wilderness of Quebec, *The History of Emily Montague* told the story of the passionate courtship between Colonel Rivers and the woman of his dreams, Miss Emily Montague. The book was peppered with deliciously purple prose, like Emily's passionate declaration of her love for Old Man Rivers: "When you appeared, my heart beat, I blushed, I turned pale by turns, my eyes assumed a new softness, I trembled, and every pulse confessed the matter of my soul. . . . Be assured your Emily never breathed a sigh but for her Rivers!"

The Art of *Not* Packing Light

Elizabeth Simcoe—wife of Upper Canada's first lieutenant governor, John Graves Simcoe—was reportedly a bit of a maverick, a fun-loving gal who enjoyed riding horses through the forest, setting fields on fire just for fun, and (when the opportunity presented itself) sneaking off for discreet *tête-à-têtes* with the young and handsome Colonel John Talbot. She also knew how to throw a good party, having made a point of bringing a boatload of ball gowns, jewellery, sterling silver, and a French chef with her when she emigrated to Canada. (You know: the bare necessities for roughing it in the bush.)

Between the Covers

It's kind of fitting that Canada's first contribution to the literary scene was a romance novel. After all, romance writing has played a major role in the publishing industry in this country. And nobody's done it better than Harlequin Enterprises Limited, the Toronto-based publishing phenomenon. Blissfully immune to the publishing-industry roller-coaster ride that tends to leave other Canadian publishers grasping at their hearts, Harlequin manages to bring out 80 new titles a month and to sell 153 million books per year into 100 international markets, come rain or come shine.

Founded in Winnipeg in 1949, Harlequin's fortunes really took off in the 1970s when a former Procter and Gamble marketing executive decided to apply laundry detergent merchandising techniques to the book industry. The name of the game? Increase brand awareness, create a hunger for your product amongst your target audience, and ensure that your product is readily available in the pharmacies and grocery stores of the nation. Almost overnight, Harlequin romance novels started showing up in boxes of Kotex and packages of Bio-Ad laundry detergent—a rather clever way of infiltrating Canadian homes!

Of course, not every publishing venture the company experimented with over the years ended up hitting pay dirt: a 1975 venture into science fiction publishing proved to be a total bust. Harlequin executives learned the hard way that the marketing moves that worked so well with a female target market couldn't always be replicated on a primarily male audience. (For one thing, they don't buy Kotex!)

But it's the company's willingness to change with the times that's allowed it to stay at the top of its game. Over the past few years, Harlequin has introduced Blaze romances (books with "a strong sexual edge") and a new Red Dress Ink imprint (to appeal to the *Sex in the City* and *Bridget Jones* demographic) to increase its appeal to women who might otherwise shy away from buying romance novels—just the latest plot twist for this 53-year-old Canadian publishing success story.

Red Hot Writers

When it comes to writing about love and romance, we Canuck Chicks are pretty much second to none. Not only have we produced three of the world's top-selling romance novelists—Virginia Henley (a former Scarborough housewife whose potent combo of historical settings and hot sex earns her an estimated

$1 million a year), Jo Beverley (a BC writer who has won truckloads of awards over the years for her historical and regency romances), and Marsha Canham (the undisputed queen of 17th-century pirate romances)—we've also established ourselves as a breeding ground for some sizzling hot erotica writers.

One of the hottest of the bunch is Tamara Faith Berger, whose novel *Lie With Me* (2000), features first-person narratives about sex spoken by a woman and her various male partners. The cover of the book—which features infantile drawings of naked women that Berger drew at the age of seven after stumbling across a stash of *Playboy* magazines—has managed to attract attention and stir up a bit of controversy at the same time.

Helena Settimana is another noteworthy homegrown erotica writer. She's taught workshops in erotic writing for a Toronto sex store, written for *Penthouse,* and contributed a story to *Best Women's Erotica 2001*. (The story in question, "The Mark," was about women who molest men on the subway during rush hour. She told an interviewer at the time that the story was inspired by her experiences of being on the receiving end of a few unwanted gropes on the subway in Toronto. Sorry, fellas, it's payback time!) She feels that while there's growing acceptance of erotic fiction, people still tend to mix it up with "porn." As she puts it, "Someone with a King James in his hand will be sure that I'm wedded to the Anti-Christ no matter how good the story is."

Of course, if there's one Canadian writer who's managed to get the moral majority all hot and bothered, it's Oni the Haitian Sensation, a Montreal-based erotica writer and performance artist who puts so much sexual energy into her work that she once had what she describes as "a convulsive climax" onstage. One of the few Canadian writers who can claim to have had a drink named after her (the "Me So Oni," just in case you're wondering), Oni thinks it's about time we Canuck Chicks shed some of our Victorian attitudes toward sex. As she likes to put it in her characteristically forthright fashion, "It's too bad that many of us were taught to feel awkward about our Canadian beavers. If our beavers are featured on a Canadian nickel and on Roots clothing, then why is it that they live in shame on our individual brand names?"

Canadian society may have long-since shed its Victorian skin when it comes to attitudes about sex, but women who write erotica still tend to get treated as second-class artists. Ottawa sex writer Katka Moore—who writes "serious fiction" under her real name—is the first to admit that it can sometimes be difficult to get treated as a "literary" writer if word gets out that you also happen to write about sex. Besides, she noted in an interview with *Ottawa Xpress*, a *nom d'eros* can come in handy "if you don't want your priest or your great aunt to know what you do for a living."

Of course, you don't have to go digging through the erotica department of your local bookstore if you're eager to track down a homegrown lusty read. Some of the most respected members of the Canadian literati have given us pretty steamy stories. A quarter century after the fact, Canadians are still talking about Marian Engel's 1976 novel *Bear,* which detailed an erotic love affair between a librarian and a bear. And of course, who can forget the two hot-and-spicy CanLit offerings that were behind the much-talked-about 1993 "Sexual Gothic" reading tour: Susan Swan's novel *The Wives of Bath* (a tale of cross-dressing, lesbianism, transsexualism, and castration set at a private girls' school) and Barbara Gowdy's *We So Seldom Look on Love* (a novel that introduces two truly memorable characters: a woman who works for an undertaker so that she can have sex with the dead and a woman who discovers on her wedding night that her new "husband" is actually a woman). Add to that media critic Lynn Crosbie's critically acclaimed sex/body positive anthology *The Girl Wants To* (1993) and Ottawa fiction writer Nichole McGill's sexually charged short story collection *13 Cautionary Tales* and you can see that we've got a whole lot going on between the covers in this country.

Naomi Klein. Photograph courtesy *The Herald/* Gordon Terris © SMG Newspapers Ltd

More Book Babes

Of course, you don't have to write about sex to get noticed on the bookstore shelves. Some Canuck Chicks have managed to become media sensations by writing on such decidedly un-sexy topics as economics and low-fat cooking!

Brand X

Canuck Chick Naomi Klein—author of the international best-seller *No Logo: Taking Aim at the Brand Bullies*—is the undisputed "it girl" of the anti-corporate movement. Not only did she manage to earn a mention in *Rolling Stone* magazine last year (it awarded her the title of "hot culture critic" on its annual "Hot List"), but *The Times* of London also gave her credit for being "probably the most influential person under the age of 35 in the world." Closer to home, *National Post* editorial editor Jonathan Kay attributed her phenomenal popularity to the fact that she had managed to achieve the (near) impossible: appealing to both the "Joe Six-Packs" and "Johnny Tofus" of the world. Of course, not every media commentator has been quite so kind to Klein: former *National Post* gossip columnist Shinan Govani once referred to her as "the Nelly Furtado of the New Left"—proof once again that even the coolest of Canuck Chicks can't manage to please all of the people all of the time.

Cuisine Queens

If there's a recipe for a Canadian best-seller, the Podleski sisters of *Looneyspoons* and *Crazy Plates* fame must have it tucked away somewhere in their kitchen. After all, the dynamic duo of low-fat cooking has managed to sell more than one million cookbooks over the past seven years. While Janet and Greta Podleski have certainly benefited from the publishing savvy of business partner David Chilton (yes, the same David Chilton of *Wealthy Barber* fame), the two are marketing machines in their own right: they once managed to sell 10,000 copies of their cookbooks during an eight-minute segment on a US shopping channel. These days, they're focusing their efforts on bringing a new line of frozen entrees to market—no easy task, according to Janet: "The food manufacturing industry makes the publishing industry seem like a breeze."

Janet and Greta Podleski, the Looneyspoons sisters
(Tom Hanson). Canadian Press

Chick Lit

Of course, no chapter about women authors would be complete without a mention of the Grande Dames of CanLit. So, without any further ado, it's time for a quick crash course in Chick Lit.

> "Few would seriously argue, anymore, that there is no Canadian literature. . . . Mordecai Richler's well-known jest, 'world-famous in Canada,' ceased to be such a laugh. . . . The erstwhile molehill of CanLit has grown to a mountain."
> – Margaret Atwood, "Essays on the Millennium/2000: Survival, Then and Now," *Maclean's*, July 1, 1999

1893

Meaford, Ontario–born Margaret Marshall Saunders becomes the first author in Canada to sell more than one million copies of a book. The book in question? *Beautiful Joe.* By the 1930s, more than seven million copies of this popular dog tale will have been sold.

1904

Sara Jeannette Duncan writes *The Imperialist,* the only one of her many novels, incidentally, that happens to be set in Canada. Duncan has already achieved another rather noteworthy claim to fame: in 1886, she became the first woman to obtain a full-time editorial position with the *Toronto Globe.*

Lucy Maud Montgomery in 1932.
Archives of Ontario F 1075

1908

Lucy Maud Montgomery's book *Anne of Green Gables* is published in Boston after she is unable to interest any Canadian publishers.

1925

Martha Ostenso writes *Wild Geese*, a novel that wins Dodd Mead and Co.'s Best Novel of the Year Award. The book will be made into a motion picture on two separate occasions—in 1941 and in 2000.

1927

Mazo de la Roche's book *Jalna* wins the *Atlantic Monthly* competition—an achievement that brings de la Roche plenty of fame and $10,000 in fortune.

1945

Elizabeth Smart publishes her autobiographical novel *By Grand Central Station I Sat Down and Wept.*

1946

Gabrielle Roy's book *Bonheur d'occasion* (1945) is released in English under the title *The Tin Flute.* The book paints a decidedly unromantic picture of Quebec life and is widely credited for having laid some of the groundwork for the Quiet Revolution of the 1960s.

1947
Dorothy Livesay wins her second Governor General's Award for poetry, just three years after her 1944 win.

1961
Mohawk poet Pauline Johnson becomes the first aboriginal person, woman, and author to have a postage stamp issued in her honour. The stamp is issued on the 100-year anniversary of her birth.

1964
Margaret Laurence writes *The Stone Angel*—the first in her famed Manawaka series. The book will be followed up with *A Jest of God* (1966), *The Fire-Dwellers* (1969), *A Bird in the House* (1970), and *The Diviners* (1974). While the sex scenes in *The Diviners* are decidedly tame by today's standards, the book leaves some 1970s Canadians feeling hot and bothered and it is banned from some school libraries.

1966
Margaret Atwood wins the first of many Governor General's Awards, officially launching her career as a CanLit Queen. Her first bit of hardware is for her critically acclaimed poetry book *The Circle Game*.

1968
Alice Munro wins a Governor General's Award for her book *Dance of the Happy Shades*. She'll be back at the podium again in 10 years' time to pick up her second award—this time for her 1978 book *Who Do You Think You Are?*

1970
Quebec novelist, poet, and two-time Governor General's Award winner Anne Hébert publishes *Kamouraska*—a book that's as much a hit with English-speaking audiences as it is with French-speaking readers.

1981
Mavis Gallant publishes her critically acclaimed short story collection *Home Truths*. She'd started her career as a reporter at the *Montreal Standard* before exiting journalism—and the country—to write fiction full-time.

1993
Carol Shields' book *The Stone Diaries* wins both the Governor General's Award and the Pulitzer Prize. A subsequent book—*Larry's Party*—will be shortlisted for the Giller and win Britain's Orange Prize.

1995

Marie-Claire Blais wins the Governor General's Award for her novel, *Soifs*. It's the latest achievement in a rather remarkable career that began when she published *La Belle Bête (Mad Shadows)* at age 20.

1997

Jane Urquhart wins the Governor General's Award for 1997 for her book *The Underpainter* and Anne Michael's novel *Fugitive Pieces* wins the Orange Prize for fiction.

Ann-Marie MacDonald (photo by David Hawe/ Courtesy of CanStage)

2002

Novelist and Governor General's Award–winning playwright Ann-Marie MacDonald becomes the first Canadian woman and the second Canadian author to have one of her books selected for the Oprah Book Club. The book in question is *Fall on Your Knees,* a novel that won the Commonwealth Writers Best Book prize in April of 1997. Oprah pronounces the book "the perfect cold weather page-turner" noting that it delivers "the kind of pleasure you get from cuddling up with a dark classic like *Wuthering Heights* and *Jane Eyre*." (Hey, we Canuck Chicks definitely know what we're doing when it comes to keeping warm!)

A Rather Novel Offering

The brainchild of York University cultural studies professor Caitlin Fisher, *These Waves of Girls* is a "hypermedia novel" about coming of age. The online novel—which can be found at www.yorku.ca/caitlin/waves/—was based on a themed collection of print short stories that Fisher had written earlier. The novel won the Electronic Literature Organization's 2001 Award for Fiction.

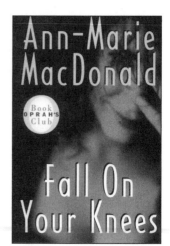

Cover of *Fall on Your Knees* by Ann-Marie MacDonald. Copyright © 1996 by Ann-Marie MacDonald. Cover photograph by Ryder and Walsh/Photonica. Reproduced by permission of Vintage Canada, a division of Random House of Canada Limited

Media Mamas

Canada has certainly managed to produce its fair share of colourful newspaper reporters and columnists over the years—everyone from Rosie DiManno to Christie Blatchford to Rebecca Eckler to Jan Wong. But long before today's generation of media mamas had even stepped foot in a newsroom, three Canuck Chicks were busy establishing themselves as the Grande Dames of Journalism.

Kit Coleman

Nineteenth-century journalist and advice columnist Kit Coleman had a no-nonsense approach to affairs of the heart that could have put even Dr. Laura to shame. Consider her reply to a woman who had written to her to bare her soul about a string of extramarital affairs: "Your nauseating immorality and endless whining appall me. Please find someone else to listen to you. A priest, your mother, a deaf male, anyone but me." Although she was best known for her contributions to "The Woman's Kingdom" page that she wrote for the *Toronto Mail,* she also earned the distinction of being the world's first accredited war correspondent when she headed to Cuba to report on the Spanish-American war—a major achievement for a woman of her day.

Ma Murray

A feisty broad who left her native Kansas in 1912 in the hope of hooking up with a Canadian cowboy, Margaret "Ma" Murray ended up finding the man of her dreams in a Vancouver newsroom. That led to the beginning of a colourful career in journalism, the likes of which hasn't been seen before or since. A true old-school hack, Murray loved peppering her articles with colourful words like *craporini, damshur,* and *snaffoo.* Never one to shy away from a good story, she found herself being named in no fewer than seven divorce actions after publishing the guest registry of a local hotel in her newspaper, the *Bridge River-Lillooett News.* But even though she was notoriously rough around the edges, she—unlike many journalists before and since—understood the basic fact that she was in business to entertain her readers. She even went so far as to offer her readers an iron-clad guarantee: "a chuckle every week or your money back." Good luck finding that kind of warranty on a newspaper these days . . .

Zena Cherry

Globe and Mail society columnist Zena Cherry was one of the most powerful women in Toronto from 1955 to 1987. She was able to make or break careers by indicating which up-and-coming social climbers had been rather unceremoniously shifted from the "A" list to the "B" list. Although her column was generally quite restrained and genteel, she managed to bring the Toronto establishment to its knees in 1967 when she published the names of people who had purchased apartments in the brand new Sutton Place Hotel. Some of these property owners were married gents who had no legitimate reason for acquiring a second residence—unless, of course, they were planning to squeeze in a late-afternoon romp in the hay before heading home to suburbia.

Magazine Mamas

Of course, that's not to say that the newspaper industry has held a monopoly over journalism talent in this country. The two most noteworthy periodical editors this country has ever produced were magazine mamas right from day one.

Chatelaine covers. Courtesy of *Chatelaine*

Doris Anderson

One of the gutsiest magazine editors of her generation, male or female, Doris Anderson found herself at the helm of *Chatelaine* magazine during the key years of the women's movement. Determined to give her readers "something serious to think about, something to shake them up," she extended *Chatelaine*'s editorial reach far beyond the traditional fashion, beauty, and home décor beat.

During Anderson's time at the magazine, *Chatelaine* readers were offered well-researched and thought-provoking articles on such hot topics as contraception, abortion, sexuality, and feminism. She didn't just deliver groundbreaking editorials, however: she was a trailblazer in other ways as well. During the early 1960s, she made Canadian magazine history by becoming the first editor at Maclean-Hunter to remain on the job throughout her pregnancy. (Apparently, she was asked to use the back door so as not to offend the

Chatelaine was the only women's magazine published in Canada between 1957 and 1969. The year 1975 would mark the debut of the magazine's key competitor, *Canadian Living* magazine.

tender sensibilities of Maclean-Hunter executives unaccustomed to encountering pregnant bellies in the workplace.)

Bonnie Fuller

Canadian-born Bonnie Fuller rocked the magazine world in 1996 by taking over the editorial reins at *Cosmopolitan* magazine when Helen Gurley Brown—the original "Cosmo Girl"—decided to call it a day. Fuller came to the attention of industry headhunters after orchestrating two of the most successful magazine launches of the late 1980s and early 1990s: the launches of *YM* and *Marie Claire*. Then, in 1998, Fuller hopped ship again, moving over to *Glamour* when 70-year-old Ruth Whitney—*Glamour's* editor for the previous 31 years—was unceremoniously dumped.

Canadian Living cover. Courtesy of *Canadian Living*/Telemedia

Fuller didn't quite manage to deliver the editorial goods this time around, something that led to her being given her walking papers in 2001. At that point, she was hired to develop a lifestyle magazine called *LivingRoom* for the publishers of *Better Homes and Gardens*. (Some critics questioned whether she was the right gal for the job, given her history of giving her readers sex, sex, sex, and more sex. *The New York Observer* noted rather dryly that Fuller would have to start thinking of "the G spot" as "the place where Granny sits at the Thanksgiving table" rather than as a sexual mecca for women.) But, as it turned out, the *LivingRoom* gig was but a temporary stopover for Fuller, who soon

found herself en route to bigger and better things: the editorship of the entertainment industry *Us* magazine (which immediately began stealing readers from *People* magazine) and a contract to write her first book. (The book—which is scheduled to hit the bookstores next year—may very well have the worst title in self-help book publishing history. Unless some book editor can convince Bonnie Fuller to see the error of her ways, her book will be saddled with the truly awful title *From Geek to Oh My Goddess: How to Have the Big Career, the Big Love Life, and the Big Family—Even if You Have a Big Loser Complex Inside*).

Bonnie Fuller—then editor of *Cosmopolitan* (Adam Nadel). Canadian Press

Surfer Girls

Canuck Chicks have managed to find some totally fabulous ways of harnessing the power of the web to achieve some uniquely girly ends. Here are just a few examples of Great White North womanpower in action.

Happywomanmagazine.com

The tagline for this web site says it all: "We think so you don't have to." The brainchild of Toronto comic Sharon Grehan, Happywomanmagazine.com delights in poking fun at traditional women's magazines (e.g., "How to Be Miserable in Ten Easy Men or Less," "Is Your Grout Killing You?" and—a classic—"The Happy Woman Rules: Track Him, Trick Him, Trap Him"). Lest you be dense enough to mistake Happywomanmagazine.com for the real thing, Grehan offers this all-important disclaimer: "Happy Woman is a parody publication so don't come crying to us if someone accidentally took out your liver or you starved to death on our diet." Consider yourself warned.

Boyfriendsgonebad.com

Hell hath no fury like a Canuck Chick wronged—unless, of course, it's two Canuck Chicks wronged. Tracey Arnold and Kelly Flannigan decided to launch their web site in order to provide support and commiseration to other gals

Evelyn Hannon. Photo courtesy of Evelyn Hannon

who'd managed to hook up with Mr. Wrong. The two have already published a *Boyfriendsgonebad* journal and scrapbook that allows women to keep track of details about their failed love affairs, and they reportedly have plans in the works for a Boyfriendsgonebad Hock Shop that will allow brokenhearted gals to rid themselves of diamond rings and other unwanted souvenirs from love affairs gone wrong.

Journeywoman.com

It's hard to say who's the more famous these days: Erica Ehm or her web-savvy mother, Evelyn Hannon. Thanks to the success of her travel web site for women, Journeywoman.com, Hannon has been featured in *People, Time,* the *New York Times,* the *Guardian* and other world media. The web site—which got its start as a print magazine—

allows women travellers to swap tips that will allow them to travel safely and travel well. It's a site that gives a whole new meaning to the nineties catch-phrase, "You go, girl!"

Comic Genius

Cartoon strip supplied by Lynn Johnston. © Lynn Johnston Productions Inc. Reproduced by permission

There's no denying it: Lynn Johnston is the biggest star Canada has ever produced on the comic book front. Her comic strip *For Better or For Worse* is carried by more than two thousand newspapers in 20 different countries around the world. And in 1986, Johnston made comic strip history by becoming the first woman ever to win a Reuben Award—the comic strip industry's equivalent of an Oscar.

While most comic strips tend to stay on fairly safe turf, Johnston has never been one to shy away from tackling tough issues like child abuse, homosexuality, unplanned pregnancy, and death. (She reportedly ignored the pleas of her mentor, Charles Schulz, who begged her not to kill off *For Better or For Worse*'s dog, Farley: "If you kill Farley, I'm going to have Snoopy hit by a truck," he quipped.)

Art Attack

While the power of the pen is indisputable, Canuck Chicks have also taken great delight in rattling the art establishment's cage over the years. Here's the scoop on four homegrown artists who dared to break the rules.

Lynn Johnston. Photo courtesy of Ed Eng

Frances Anne Hopkins

Late 19th- and early 20th-century painter Frances Anne Hopkins made a career out of painting Canadian landscapes at a time when landscape painting was decidedly out of vogue. Even though she managed to have 13 of her works accepted for exhibit by the highly prestigious Royal Academy in London, England, she continued to be relatively unknown in both Canada and her native Britain. "I have not found Canadians at all anxious hitherto for pictures of their own country," she remarked in 1910. Now—nearly a century later—she is recognized as one of the best landscape artists of her day and her paintings of the Canadian fur trade are widely reproduced in Canadian history textbooks. Go figure.

Joyce Weiland

Joyce Weiland managed to prove to the world that you don't have to be a guy to pull off a major art show in this country. Her 1971 *True Patriot Love* art exhibit at the National Gallery in Ottawa—an exhibit that featured live ducks, taped loon calls, and "Sweet Beaver perfume"—was heralded as the first major show by a living Canadian woman.

Jana Sterbak

Jana Sterbak's National Gallery exhibition of a dress made of raw meat (*Vanitas: Flesh Dress for an Albino Anorectic*) attracted a huge amount of media attention in 1991—most of it negative. Gallery staff received telephone threats and excrement-smeared mail, and critics described the exhibit as wasteful and disgusting, noting that Sterbak used 23 kilograms of raw meat (valued at $300) to construct her exhibit. This wasn't the first time that Sterbak has decided to push the envelope, nor would it be the last: over the years, she's created exhibits featuring human bones made out of chocolate, a metal seduction couch that zaps anyone who touches it, and a wire-mesh dress with a skirt that is encircled with wire coils that heat up whenever viewers approach.

Barbara Woodley

Photographer Barbara Woodley created a small scandal in 1992 when she decided to publish a two-year-old photograph of a semi-clad Justice Minister Kim Campbell. It's hard to tell from looking at the photo, in fact, whether Campbell is wearing anything other than her birthday suit. (She is rather coyly posed holding up her judge's robes for the camera.) Rather than ruining her shot at the leadership of the Progressive Conservative Party, the photo ended up doing good things for her leadership bid, convincing party faithful that she was anything but another Brian Mulroney—the best possible message she could have helped to convey at the time. (Of course, Canuck Chicks weren't finished making mince-meat out of Mulroney quite yet: it would still be another two years before Stevie Cameron's best-selling book *On the Take: Crime, Corruption and Greed in the Mulroney Years* showed up on the bookstore shelves.)

The Group of Nine

While the Group of Seven was officially an all-guy group, it managed to have a major impact on the careers of two of Canada's most famous women painters: Doris McCarthy and Emily Carr. In 1926, McCarthy was awarded a full-time scholarship to the Ontario College of Art by Arthur Lismer, a founding member of the Group of Seven, and, in 1928, Carr received some much-needed encouragement about her art while visiting with Group members. Unlike most of her contemporaries, members of the Group of Seven recognized the calibre of the work Carr was producing and encouraged her to stick with her painting. Carr remained relatively unknown in the art world, however, until after her death. During her lifetime, she was better known for her writing in the Governor General's Award-winning book *Klee Wyck* (1942), which told of her experiences living and painting amongst Canada's native peoples.

Emily Carr. BC Archives H-02813

It's a Bird, It's a Plane, It's... Canuck Chick!

Forget Wonder Woman and Super Girl: we Canuck Chicks can lay claim to three female superheroes of our own: Nelvana of the Northern Lights, Fleur-de-Lys, and Poutinette.

Nelvana of the Northern Lights (a.k.a. "Alana North") was a 1940s comic book superhero who got her name because she drew her magical powers from the Northern Lights. She was loosely based on a figure from Inuit mythology—an old woman named Nelvana—but her creator, Adrian Dingle, decided to make her younger and sexier by giving her long hair and a miniskirt. Her six-year comic book run ended in 1947.

Fleur-de-Lys took up the fight against darkness and evil between 1984 and 1992. The creation of Montreal writer Mark Shainblum and Montreal artist Gabriel Morrissette, Fleur-de-Lys joined forces with fellow superhero Northguard and used her non-lethal fleur-de-lys-shaped light sabre to fight a threatened takeover by right-wing evangelical groups and organized crime. Dressed in a catwomanlike costume, she had one blue-and-white fleurs-de-lys emblazoned on her forehead and two more on her body. In 1995, Fleurs-de-Lys and Nelvana of the North became the first two female superheroes to be featured on Canadian postage stamps.

Poutinette (a.k.a. Thérèse Papineau) is the most recent Canuck Chick superhero. Another brainchild of the Shainblum-Morrissette comic book writing team, she appeared in the cult classic *Angloman* comics during the 1990s. Dedicated to fighting "evil, injustice, and health food" she took to scooting around town on her Tenderflake-powered Poutine Cycle, armed with a deadly poutine blaster that had criminals eagerly surrendering out of sheer terror of the cholesterol.

The Last Word

And so there you have it—the inside scoop on Canuck Chicks and Maple Leaf Mamas from every walk of life: authors and artists, songbirds and snowbirds, babes and bimbos, dancers and divas. And now, as we prepare to bid our fond adieus, I think it's only fitting to give the last word to Anne of Green Gables, the most celebrated Canuck Chick of the past one hundred years. (Okay, the most celebrated Canuck Chick who actually managed to keep her clothes on.) Anne, more than anyone else, would have understood how this book ended up being both overlong and overdue. Like PEI's best-loved redhead, I simply found myself with too much to say. As Anne (a.k.a. actress Megan Follows) stated so emphatically in the 1985 film version of *Anne of Green Gables:* "I know I chatter on far too much . . . but if you only knew how many things I want to say and don't. Give me *some* credit."

Five Fabulous Facts About Anne

1. The Mattel toy company recently saw fit to add an Anne of Green Gables doll to its highly popular "When I Read, I Dream" collector doll series. The other story-book heroines who've been included in the series to date are Jo of *Little Women*, Fern of *Charlotte's Web*, and *Heidi*. (Thank goodness neither *Rebecca of Sunnybrook Farm* nor *Pollyanna* managed to make the cut! The collector dolls would have had to come equipped with a barf bag.)

2. The 1919 film version of *Anne of Green Gables* starred Mary Miles Minter, a Hollywood actress who was once described as "Mary Pickford's closest rival." (Mary Pickford, for her part, had recently been paid $350,000 to play Anne's closest rival, Rebecca of Sunnybrook Farm!) Unlike Mary Pickford, who carried on a Celine Dionesque love affair with Hollywood leading man Douglas Fairbanks Jr., who was many years her senior, Mary Miles Minter saw her career destroyed when she became involved in a messy love triangle.

3. Two CBC employees working on a script for the 1954 musical version of *Anne of Green Gables* inadvertently triggered a cross-border Communist scare. The FBI became alarmed by the number of "red" references in the telexes that were going back and forth from Toronto to New York—the perils of writing about a red-haired heroine, I suppose.

4. The actress who played Anne in the 1934 film version of *Anne of Green Gables* and in the 1940 sequel, *Anne of Windy Poplars* was so taken with her roles in these films that she permanently changed her name to Anne Shirley. Up until then she'd been known as Dawn O'Day (ugh!), although her birth name had been Dawn Paris.

5. Three times as many people visit Green Gables (the country home of L.M. Montgomery's cousins and their parents, Alexander and Lucy MacNeill) as visit Province House in Charlottetown, the birthplace of Confederation. Altogether Green Gables attracts 700,000 tourists each year, including some 10,000 visitors from Japan, where the Anne books are hugely popular.

Required Reading for All Canuck Chicks

Although I spent most of my time poring over old magazine and newspaper articles (mainly prehistoric issues of *Canadian Living, Chatelaine,* the *Financial Post, Homemaker's Magazine, Maclean's Magazine, Saturday Night,* the *Toronto Star,* and the *Globe and Mail*) while I was researching this book, the following books were also very helpful to me.

Many of these books are no longer in print, but if you're lucky and persistent (and—like me—you can't pass a second-hand bookstore without venturing inside to see what treasures you might uncover!), you're bound to track down at least some of these titles. I don't expect you to read all of them— hey, who has the time or the budget for that?—but I highly recommend that you treat yourself to at least a couple of the books on this list. Trust me, you'll thank me for it. . . .

Acton, Janice, Penny Goldsmith and Bonnie Shepherd, eds., *Women at Work 1850–1930.* Toronto: Canadian Women's Educational Press, 1974.

Aitken, Kate. *Canadian Etiquette for Daily Living.* Toronto: Wm. Collins Sons & Co. Ltd., 1953.

   It's Fun Raising a Family. Toronto: Wm. Collins Sons & Co., 1955.

   Kate Aitken's Canadian Cook Book. Toronto: Wm. Collins Sons & Co., 1950.

   Lovely You: A Blueprint for Beauty. Toronto: Wm. Collins and Sons, 1951.

Aldrich, Mary. *Babies Are Human Beings.* New York: Macmillan Company, 1946.

Arnup, Katherine. *Education for Motherhood: Advice for Mothers in Twentieth-Century Canada.* Toronto: University of Toronto Press, 1994.

Backhouse, Frances. *Women of the Klondike.* Vancouver: Whitecap Books, 1995.

Baker, Maureen, ed. *The Family: Changing Trends in Canada.* Toronto: McGraw-Hill Ryerson Limited, 1984.

Bauer, W.W. *Potions, Remedies, & Old Wives' Tales.* New York: Doubleday & Company, Inc., 1969.

Beecher, Catharine E. *Miss Beecher's Housekeeper and Healthkeeper.* New York: Harper and Brothers, 1873.

Beker, Jeanne. *Jeanne Unbottled: Adventures in High Style.* Toronto: Stoddart Publishing Co. Limited, 2000.

Boulton, Marsha. *Just a Minute More: Glimpses of our Great Canadian Heritage.* Toronto: McArthur & Company, 1999.

The Just a Minute Omnibus: Glimpses of our Great Canadian Heritage. Toronto: McArthur & Company, 2000.

Bristow, Peggy, Coordinator. *We're Rooted Here and They Can't Pull Us Up: Essays in African Canadian Women's History.* Toronto: University of Toronto Press, 1994.

Brown, Jeremy and David Ondaatje. *Canadian Book of Lists.* Toronto: Pagurian Press Limited, 1978.

Canadian Broadcasting Corporation. *Women in the CBC: Report of the CBC Task Force on the Status of Women.* Toronto: Canadian Broadcasting Corporation, 1975.

Canadian Women's Educational Press. *Never Done: Three Centuries of Women's Work in Canada.* Toronto: Canadian Women's Educational Press, 1974.

Chavasse, Pye Henry. *Advice to a Wife on the Management of Her Own Health: and on the Treatment of Some of the Complaints Incidental to Pregnancy, Labour, and Suckling, with an Introductory Chapter Especially Addressed to the Young Wife.* Toronto: Hunter, Rose, 1879.

Cinberg, Bernhard. *For Women Only.* New York: Dell Publishing Co., Inc., 1964.

Clark, Andrew. *Stand and Deliver: Inside Canadian Comedy.* Toronto: Doubleday Canada, 1997.

Cochrane, Felicity. *Margaret Trudeau: The Prime Minister's Runaway Wife.* Scarborough, ON: Signet Books, 1978.

Colombo, John Robert. *Colombo's Canadian References.* Toronto: Oxford University Press, 1976.

The Dictionary of Canadian Quotations. Toronto: Stoddart Publishing Co. Limited, 1991.

The 1995 Canadian Global Almanac. Toronto: Macmillan Canada, 1994.

1000 Questions About Canada. Toronto: Dundurn Press, 2001.

Colombo's Concise Canadian Quotations. Edmonton: Hurtig Publishers, 1976.

Cooke, Maud C. *Social Etiquette or Manners and Customs of Polite Society: Containing Rules of Etiquette for All Occasions.* London, ON: McDermid & Logan, 1896.

Conacher, Duff. *More Canada Firsts.* Toronto: McClelland & Stewart, 1999.

Conran, Shirley. *Superwoman: Everything You Need to Know About Running a Home in Canada Today.* Markham, ON: Penguin Books, 1978.

Superwoman in Action. Markham, ON: Penguin Books, 1980.

Cook, Sharon Anne, Lorna McLean and Kate O'Rourke, eds., *Framing Our Past: Canadian Women's History in the Twentieth Century.* Kingston: McGill-Queen's University Press, 2001.

Coomber, Jan, and Rosemary Evans. *Women Changing Canada.* Toronto: Oxford University Press, 1997.

Coontz, Stephanie. *The Way We Never Were: American Families and the Nostalgia Trap.* New York: Basic Books, 1992.

The Way We Really Are: Coming to Terms with America's Changing Families. New York: Basic Books, 1997.

Crean, Susan. *Newsworthy: The Lives of Media Women.* Toronto: Stoddart Publishing, 1985.

Creighton, Luella. *The Elegant Canadians.* Toronto: McClelland & Stewart, 1967.

Dafoe, Allan Roy. *Dr. Dafoe's Guidebook for Mothers.* New York: Julian Messner Inc., 1936.

Davis, Ozora and Emma Drake. *Safe Counsel of Practical Eugenics.* Chicago: J.L. Nichols, 1926.

Department of National Health and Welfare Canada. *The Canadian Mother and Child.* Ottawa: Queen's Printer for Canada, 1970.

Up the Years From One to Six. Ottawa: Information Canada, 1971.

The Dominion Home Cookbook. Toronto: A. Miller, 1868.

Douglas, Ann. *The Complete Idiot's Guide to Canada in the '60s, '70s, and '80s.* Toronto: Prentice-Hall, 1999.

The Complete Idiot's Guide to Canadian History. Toronto: Prentice-Hall, 1997.

The Incredible Shrinking Woman: The Girlfriend's Guide to Losing Weight. Toronto: Prentice-Hall, 1997.

Doyle, Kevin and Ann Johnston, eds. *The 1980s:* Maclean's *Chronicles the Decade.* Toronto: Key Porter Books, 1989.

Dundas, Barbara. *A History of Women in the Canadian Military.* Montreal: Art Global, 2000.

Eaton's of Canada Spring and Summer 1961. Toronto: Eaton's of Canada, 1961.

Ehrenreich, Barbara and Deirdre English. *For Her Own Good: 150 Years of the Experts' Advice to Women.* New York: Anchor Press, 1979.

Finkel, Alvin, Margaret Conrad and Veronica Strong-Boag. *History of the Canadian People: 1867 to the Present.* Toronto: Copp Clark Pitman Ltd., 1993.

Five Roses Cook Book. Montreal: Lake of the Woods Milling Company Limited, 1915.

Fraser, Sylvia, ed. *A Woman's Place: Seventy Years in the Lives of Canadian Women*. Toronto: Key Porter Press, 1997.

Frum, Barbara. *As It Happened*. Toronto: McClelland & Stewart, 1976.

Frum, Linda. *Barbara Frum: A Daughter's Memoir*. Toronto: Ballantine Books, 1996.

Gerber, Mrs. Dan. *Bringing Up Baby*. New York: Pocket Books, 1972.

Gillmor, Don. *Canada: A People's History*. Toronto: McClelland & Stewart, 2001.

Girvan, Susan, ed. *Canadian Global Almanac 2002*. Toronto: Macmillan Canada, 2001.

Goldbloom, Alton. *Care of the Child*. Toronto: Longmans, Green and Co., 1945.

Graham, Virginia and Jean Libman Block. *Don't Blame the Mirror: A Book of Beauty*. New York: Meredith Press, 1967.

Grant, Julia. *Raising Baby by the Book*. New Haven: Yale University Press, 1998.

Green, Harvey. *The Light of Home*. New York: Pantheon Books, 1983.

Gregg, Allan and Michael Posner. *The Big Picture: What Canadians Think About Almost Everything*. Toronto: Macfarlane Walter & Ross, 1990.

Griffith, J.P. Crozer. *The Care of the Baby*. Philadelphia: W.B. Saunders, 1898.

Hacker, Carlotta. *The Indomitable Lady Doctors*. Halifax: Goodread Biographies, 1984.

Hanle, Dorothea Zack. *The Hairdo Handbook: A Complete Guide to Hair Beauty*. New York: Doubleday & Company, Inc., 1964.

Hayden, Leslie. *On the Go: A Beauty Guide for the Active Woman*. Montreal: Alberto-Culver Canada Inc., 1982.

Hilliard, Marion. *A Woman Doctor Looks at Love and Life*. New York: Doubleday & Company, Inc., 1957.

Hope, Jackqueline. *Big, Bold, and Beautiful: Living Large on a Small Planet*. Toronto: Macmillan Canada, 1996.

Innis, Mary Quayle, ed. *The Clear Spirit: Twenty Canadian Women and Their Times*. Toronto: University of Toronto Press, 1966.

Jameson, Anna Brownell. *Winter Studies and Summer Rambles in Canada*. Toronto: McClelland & Stewart, 1990.

Jefferis, B.G. and J.L. Nichols. *Safe Counsel or Practical Eugenics*. Chicago: Nichols, 1893.

Safe Counsel or Practical Eugenics. 38th ed. Chicago: Franklin Association, 1926.

Johnston, Gordon. *It Happened in Canada*. Richmond Hill, ON: Scholastic-TAB Publications Ltd., 1973.

Kealey, Linda, ed. *A Not Unreasonable Claim*. Toronto: Women's Education Press, 1979.

Kearney, Mark and Randy Ray. *The Great Canadian Book of Lists*. Toronto: Dundurn Press, 1999.

Kenter, Peter. *TV North: Everything You Wanted to Know About Canadian Television*. Vancouver: Whitecap Books, 2001.

Kieran, Sheila. *The Non-Deductible Woman: A Handbook for Working Wives and Mothers*. Toronto: The Macmillan Company of Canada Limited, 1970.

Kome, Penney. *Somebody Has to Do It: Whose Work Is Housework?* Toronto: McClelland & Stewart, 1982.

Korinek, Valerie. *Roughing It in the Suburbs: Reading* Chatelaine Magazine *in the Fifties and Sixties*. Toronto: University of Toronto Press Inc., 2000.

Kostash, Myrna. *No Kidding: Inside the World of Teenage Girls*. Toronto: McClelland & Stewart, 1987.

Kostash, Myrna, Melinda McCracken, Valerie Miner, Erna Paris, and Heather Robertson. *Her Own Woman*. Halifax: Goodread Biographies, 1975.

The Ladies Book of Useful Information. London, ON: Publisher unknown, 1896.

LaMarsh, Judy. *Memoirs of a Bird in a Gilded Cage*. Toronto: McClelland & Stewart, 1969.

Langton, H.H., ed. *A Gentlewoman in Upper Canada*. Toronto: Clarke, Irwin & Company Limited, 1950.

Lenskyj, Helen. *Out of Bounds: Women, Sport & Sexuality*. Toronto: The Women's Press, 1986.

Lewis, Dio. *Our Girls*. Toronto: J. Lovell, Adam, Stevenson, 1871.

Light, Beth and Veronica Strong-Boag. *True Daughters of the North*. Toronto: Ontario Institute for Studies in Education, 1980.

Lloyd, Tanya. *Canadian Girls Who Rocked the World*. Vancouver: Whitecap Books, 2001.

Luxton, Meg. *More Than a Labour of Love: Three Generations of Women's Work in the Home*. Toronto: Women's Press, 1980.

Luxton, Meg, Harriet Rosenberg, and Sedef Arat-Koc. *Through the Kitchen Window: The Politics of Home and Family*. Toronto: Garamond Press, 1990.

MacDonald, Ann-Marie. *Fall On Your Knees*. Toronto: Vintage Canada, 1996.

MacEwan, Grant. *And Mighty Women Too.* Saskatoon: Western Producer Prairie Books, 1975.

MacLaren, Sherrill. *Invisible Power: The Women Who Run Canada.* Toronto: Seal Books, 1991.

Maclean's. Canada in the Fifties: Canada's Golden Decade. Toronto: Viking, 1999.

MacLeod, Elizabeth. *Lucy Maud Montgomery: A Writer's Life.* Toronto: Kids Can Press, 2001.

Mason, Diane Baker. *Last Summer at Barebones.* Toronto: McArthur & Company, 2001.

McBryde, Linda. *The Mass Market Woman.* Eagle River: Crowded Hour Press, 1999.

McClung, Nellie. *In Times Like These.* Reprint edition. Toronto: University of Toronto Press, 1972.

McQueen, Rod. *Can't Buy Me Love: How Martha Billes Made Canadian Tire Hers.* Toronto: Stoddart Publishing Co. Ltd., 2001.

The Eatons: The Rise and Fall of Canada's Royal Family. Toronto: Stoddart Publishing Co. Limited, 1999.

Merck & Co. *Merck's 1899 Manual.* New York: Merck & Co., 1899.

Merritt, Susan. *Her Story: Women from Canada's Past.* St. Catharines: Vanwell Publishing Limited, 1994.

Her Story II: Women from Canada's Past. St. Catharines: Vanwell Publishing Limited, 1995.

Her Story III: Women from Canada's Past. St. Catharines: Vanwell Publishing Limited, 1999.

Minister of Education Ontario. *Manners.* Toronto: McClelland Goodchild & Stewart Limited, 1914.

Mitchinson, Wendy. *Giving Birth in Canada: 1900–1950.* Toronto: University of Toronto Press Inc., 2002.

Modern Housekeepers' Guide. Toronto: General Steel Wares Limited, 1929.

Monk, Katherine. *Weird Sex & Snowshoes and Other Canadian Film Phenomena.* Vancouver: Raincoast Books, 2001.

Montgomery, L.M. *Anne of Green Gables.* Toronto: McGraw-Hill Ryerson Limited, 1908.

Moodie, Susanna. *Life in the Clearings Versus the Bush.* Toronto: McClelland & Stewart, 1989.

Roughing It in the Bush. Toronto: McClelland & Stewart, 1962.

Morgan, Lael. *Good Time Girls of the Alaska-Yukon Gold Rush.* Vancouver: Whitecap Books, 1998.

Morgan, Marabel. *The Total Woman.* Old Tappan: Spire Books, 1973.

Moss, John. *A Reader's Guide to the Canadian Novel.* Toronto: McClelland & Stewart, 1987.

Sex and Violence in the Canadian Novel. Toronto: McClelland & Stewart, 1977.

Mulvey, Kate and Melissa Richards. *Decades of Beauty: The Changing Image of Women: 1890s to 1990s.* New York: Octopus Publishing Group, 1998.

Murphy, Claire Rudolf and Jane G. Haigh. *Gold Rush Women.* Portland: Alaska Northwest Books, 1997.

Nader, Ralph, Nadie Milleron and Duff Conacher. *Canada Firsts.* Toronto: McClelland & Stewart Inc., 1992.

Napier, JoAnn, Denise Shortt and Emma Smith. *Technology with Curves: Women Reshaping the Digitial Landscape.* Toronto: HarperCollins Publisher Ltd., 2000.

Neering, Rosemary. *Wild West Women: Travellers, Adventurers and Rebels.* Vancouver: Whitecap Books, 2000.

Nichols, Grandma. *The Great Nineteenth Century Household Guide.* Toronto: Coles Publishing, 1978.

On the Go: A Beauty Guide for the Active Woman. Montreal: L.E.L. Marketing Ltd., 1980.

O'Shea, M.V. *The Child: His Nature and His Needs.* New York: The Children's Foundation, 1924.

Pevere, Geoff and Greig Dymond. *Mondo Canuck: A Canadian Pop Culture Odyssey.* Scarborough, ON: Prentice-Hall Canada Inc., 1996.

Poulton, Terry. *No Fat Chicks: How Women Are Brainwashed to Hate Their Bodies and Spend Their Money.* Toronto: Key Porter, 1996.

Prentice, Alison. *The School Promoters: Education and Social Class in Mid-Nineteenth Century Upper Canada.* Toronto: McClelland & Stewart, 1977.

Prentice, Alison, Paula Bourne, Gail Cuthbert Brandt, Beth Light, Wendy Mitchinson and Naomi Black. *Canadian Women: A History.* Toronto: Harcourt Brace Jovanovich Canada Inc., 1988.

Priest, Lisa. *Women Who Killed: Stories of Canadian Female Murderers.* Toronto: McClelland & Stewart, 1992.

Rawlinson, H. Graham and J.L. Granatstein. *The Canadian 100: The 100 Most Influential Canadians of the 20th Century.* Toronto: McArthur & Company, 1997.

Robertson, Heather. *A Terrible Beauty: The Art of Canada at War.* Toronto: James Lorimer & Company, Limited, 1977.

Romar and Lee. *The Canadian Woman: A Manual of Personal Hygiene.* Vancouver: Modern Films Distributors of Canada, Ltd., 1961.

Russell, Paul and Robert Jeffrey. *The Queen on Moose Handbook.* Toronto: Methuen, 1985.

Savage, Candace. *Our Nell: A Scrapbook Biography of Nellie L. McClung.* Saskatoon: Western Producer Prairie Books, 1979.

Schlesinger, Benjamin, ed. *The Chatelaine Guide to Marriage.* Toronto: The Macmillan Company of Canada Limited, 1975.

Schremp, Gerry. *Kitchen Culture: Fifty Years of Food Fads.* New York: Pharos Books, 1991.

Schwartz, Hillel. *Never Satisfied: A Cultural History of Diets, Fantasies and Fat.* New York: The Free Press, 1986.

Simpsons-Sears Spring and Summer 1961. Toronto: Simpsons-Sears, 1961.

Sinclair, Sonja. *I Presume You Can Type: The Mature Woman's Guide to Second Careers.* Toronto: CBC Publications, 1969.

Slocum, Annette. *For Wife and Mother: A Young Mother's Tokology.* Chicago: Shrewsbury Publishing Co., 1900.

Spock, Benjamin. *Baby and Child Care.* New York: Pocket Books, Inc., 1957.

Dr. Spock Talks With Mothers. Greenwich: Fawcett Publications Inc., 1961.

Spring, Joyce. *Daring Lady Flyers: Canadian Women in the Early Years of Aviation.* Porters Lake: Pottersfield Press, 1994.

Stephenson, Marylee, ed. *Women in Canada.* Toronto: new press, 1973.

Stern, Bonnie. *HeartSmart Cooking for Family and Friends.* Toronto: Random House Canada, 2000.

Stockham, Alice B. *Tokology: A Book for Every Woman.* Toronto: McClelland & Goodchild, 1893.

Tokology: A Book for Every Woman. Toronto: McClelland, Goodchild, and Stewart, 1916.

Strange, Carolyn. *Toronto's Girl Problem: The Perils and Pleasures of the City, 1880–1930.* Toronto: University of Toronto Press, 1995.

Streatfeild, Noel. *The Years of Grace*. London: Evans Brothers Limited, 1950.

Strong-Boag, Veronica and Anita Clair Fellman, eds. *Rethinking Canada*. Toronto: Copp Clark Pitman Ltd., 1991.

Thompson, Lana. *The Wandering Womb: A Cultural History of Outrageous Beliefs About Women*. New York: Prometheus Books, 1999.

Trofimenkoff, Susan Mann and Alison Prentice, eds., *The Neglected Majority: Essays in Canadian Women's History*. Toronto: McClelland & Stewart, 1977.

Van Kirk, Sylvia. *"Many Tender Ties": Women in Fur-Trade Society, 1670–1870*. Winnipeg: Watson & Dwyer Publishing Ltd., 1980.

Wallace, Claire. *Canadian Etiquette Dictionary*. Toronto: Harlequin Books Limited, 1960.

Mind Your Manners. Toronto: Harlequin Books Limited, 1953.

Wallin, Pamela. *Speaking of Success*. Toronto: Key Porter Books, 2001.

Watson, Patrick. *The Canadians: Biographies of a Nation*. Toronto: McArthur & Company, 2000.

Wiggin, Kate Douglas. *Rebecca of Sunnybrook Farm*. New York: Baronet Books, 1995.

Wilson, S.J. *Women, The Family and The Economy*. Toronto: McGraw-Hill Ryerson Limited, 1986.

Wong, Jan. *Lunch with Jan Wong*. Toronto: Doubleday Canada, 2000.

Wyatt, Valerie. *The Kids Book of Canadian Firsts*. Toronto: Kids Can Press Ltd., 2001.

Note:

You can find electronic versions of some of the older child-rearing and health manuals at Early Canadiana Online: www.Canadiana.org. And you can find thousands of early 20th-century newspaper and magazine advertisements (many of them Canadian in origin) by accessing Duke University's Ad★ Access web site: http://scriptorium.lib.duke.edu/adaccess/.

Index